LAND
OF THE
MOON-CHILDREN

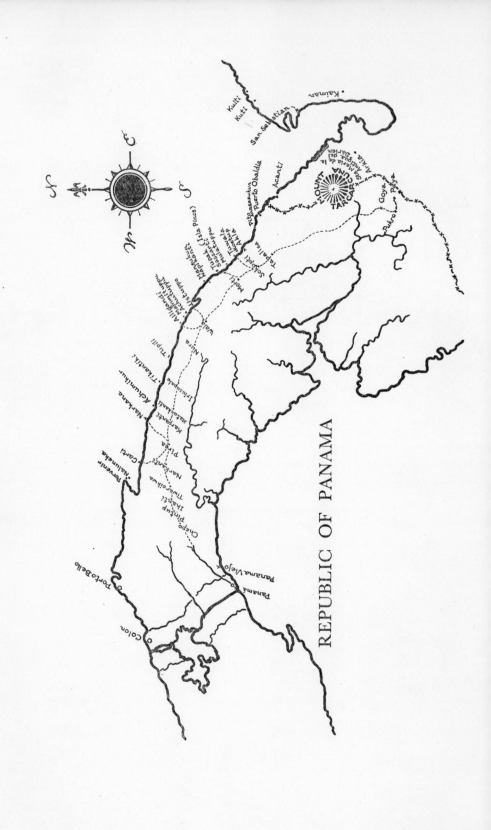

CLYDE E. KEELER

LAND
OF THE
MOON-CHILDREN

The Primitive San Blas
Culture in Flux

University of Georgia Press
Athens

For Jo and Irma

CONTENTS

◊　◊　◊　◊　◊　◊　◊

ILLUSTRATIONS

❖ ❖ ❖ ❖ ❖ ❖ ❖ ❖ ❖

PREFACE

◊ ◊ ◊ ◊ ◊ ◊

THREE currents of interest have caused me to write this book. The first started in a biological laboratory at Harvard University more than a decade ago. When I took in my hands several ferocious looking black mutant creatures born among grey barn rats, they did not try to bite me as the grey ones did. Observations on albino doves and albino paradise fish showed them to be of more gentle disposition than their fellows of normal pigmentation. Ordinary black mink are notoriously savage but some silver-blue platinum ones can be carried about like kittens. These and many controlled observations forced me to conclude that certain hereditary mutations affecting pigmentation must have slight effects also upon form, function, and consequent behavior of some animal species.

It must be true for certain animals, but does it apply to man? That question of interest to biology and medicine could only be answered by the survey of a human population exhibiting a high incidence of some simple pigment sport or mutation. The albinistic moon-children of San Blas, Panama, appeared to represent the best material for this scientific investigation. A grant from the Rockefeller Foundation made my study possible.

The second current of interest developed while I was studying the moon-children in San Blas. I found myself among painted wooden idols, ceremonial chants and procedures for appeasing or exorcising evil spirits, elaborate programs for celebrating puberty and readiness for marriage, and the fertility rites of an ancient Earthmother religion that is in the background of the religious philosophy of all peoples still today. The recording of this primitive animistic culture was most fascinating, especially because much of its meaning is a tightly locked secret that has defied the probing anthropologist.

Nobody can live in San Blas very long without noting that great transformations are now taking place; old tribal customs are rapidly dying out, and the Cuna Indians are swiftly embracing the ways of the Western World. The most potent factor producing this change is the San Blas Mission, a non-Catholic project that struggled along independently for many years but which has received sponsorship recently from the Southern Baptists of the United States. Observing the efforts of the missionaries manning the San Blas Mission formed my third current of interest.

By mixing these three currents of interest I have tried to produce a fair description of the primitive Cuna culture, the changes that are taking place, and the forces which are bringing about those changes.

This account is not meant to be a scientific treatise but rather a description of my personal experiences. Therefore, I have not often referred to the efforts of other scientists who have made studies among the Cuna Indians. To those in whom my stories of San Blas may engender a desire to examine the findings of others I commend the following references:

Holmer, Nils M., "Cuna Crestomathy," *Etnologiska Studier,* Vol. 18. Göteborg, 1951.

McKin, Fred, "San Blas, An Account of the Cuna Indians of Panama." *Etnologiska Studier,* Vol. 15. Göteborg, 1947.

Nordonskiöld, Erland, "An Historical and Ethnographical Survey of the Cuna Indians," *Comparative Ethnographical Studies,* Vol. 10. Göteborg, 1938.

Stout, D. B., "San Blas Acculturation: An Introduction," Viking Fund Publications in Anthropology, Vol. 9. New York, 1947.

Wassen, Henry, "Original Documents from the Cuna Indians of San Blas, Panama, as Recorded by the Indians Guillermo Haya and Ruben Perez Kantule," *Etnologiska Studier,* Vol. 6. Göteborg, 1938.

Wassen, Henry, "Contributions to Cuna Ethnography," *Etnologiska Studier,* Vol. 16. Göteborg, 1949.

For help in the preparation of this book I am particularly grateful to Mrs. Ida Bonner and Dr. Henry King Stanford of Milledgeville, Georgia, for their suggestions and encouragement. Also I am indebted to all the missionaries of Ailigandi, Mulatuppu, and Ustuppo, and to many native informants. Especially do I wish to thank my friend Alcibiades Iglesias, Director of the San Blas Missions.

For permission to reprint material from my articles I wish to express thanks to *Archaeology,* the *Journal of Heredity, Eugenical News,* the *Journal of the Tennessee Academy of Science, The Month in Panama,* and the Milledgeville *Union-Recorder.*

Clyde E. Keeler
Georgia State College for Women
Milledgeville, Georgia

Chapter I

◇ ◇ ◇ ◇ ◇

GETTING ACQUAINTED

IT WAS raining at the small Paitilla Airport as it had been doing for twenty-four hours in the drenched and temporarily dismal City of Panama. It is sometimes like that during the wet season. I stood in the hangar with my baggage. I walked around nervously, pulled up my coat collar, and waited impatiently. I looked at my watch. It showed seven-thirty. The officials said no planes would venture out that day, but I had no other place to go. So I waited on and on.

About 10:30 A. M. there was a rift in the clouds. The sunlight poured through, and the pilot said he would try it with the little red-and-yellow Piper Cub; so we quickly rolled out the tiny plane, raced our small engine, and zoomed up through a few white-fringed, cumulus formations. We sped down the Pacific Coast with its dark pencil line waves chasing each other over the surface of the gray sea, to disappear one after another upon the hazy shore. A plane from a rival company roared off the field and followed us through the bank of small, cottony wisps into which the enormous black rain clouds were rapidly separating.

We climbed 75-100-150-200-250 feet as we flew down the coast. Twenty-five miles from Panama City we pointed the Cub almost due east where the clouds were dense, black, and foreboding. "The other plane has turned back," said the pilot.

The clouds suddenly lost their cumulus formation. They dissolved and we were swallowed up completely in a torrent of blinding rain. The water washed over our windshield as though we were plowing along in the depths of a mighty river. Sudden

1

flashes of lightning split into a thousand pieces the neutral gray,
water medium through which we were boring, and the Cub rocked
and shivered with the crashes of thunder.

"I'm lost," called the pilot, trying to make his voice carry above
the noise of our engine. "I guess we should have turned back!"

"Well, why don't you turn back if the weather is too bad?" I
yelled in reply.

"It's too late now. We're over the jungled Cordillera and there
are no instruments on this plane."

On and on through lightning and water the monotonous engine
roared. We climbed up and up into the gray uncertainty before
us. The moments were tense.

"I hope we are not off our track because there are two peaks
and we must fly between them," said the pilot.

I knew what would happen if we *were* off the track; so I did not
ask. I just hoped and prayed that we were *on* the track. Further
and further we groped blindly through the water and each moment seemed like an hour. We were expecting at any instant to
feel the sudden crash of our Cub in some tall jungle tree. I had
never felt so close to eternity.

The pilot had been straining his eyes to differentiate the neutral
gray avalanche of water before us. He kept peering this way and
that, and at last he said: "I think I see a V over there. I hope I'm
right, because if I am it is the mountain pass between the two
peaks." I fervently hoped that he was right, as we made for the
half-imagined V. As luck would have it, he was correct, and a few
minutes later we swept between the gray, cloud-covered peaks. A
little more time and we burst out of the water into the golden
sunshine of a crystal clear day on the beautiful San Blas coast.

We followed the shoreline with its coconut plantations, skim-
ming gayly over the trim little brown cane-and-thatch Indian
towns of Narkana, Tikantiki, Tupili, and the rest. Dozens of
green, palm-fringed atolls glowed in the sunshine like so many
miniature Paradises.

At Ailigandi we put down on the mainland, dropped myself
and my baggage among a dozen colorfully dressed, exotic-looking
native women and girls, and the aviator was off again. Among
them was a moon-child girl! That was encouraging since I had
come to Panama to study the moon-children.

"Iki pe nuka?" asked a woman through her big, golden nosering.

I had expected to find someone who could speak Spanish, English, French, German, or Latin. But no, for the first time in all my travels words failed me.

"Pia pe neka?"

That didn't register either, nor did the final question: "Ipua?"

Realizing that we were getting nowhere, the woman and her daughter deposited my bags in their dugout and I made an embarrassing demonstration of my ignorance of how to get into a canoe. They paddled me to the Island of Ailigandi, and as we approached I saw an old Indian woman jumping up and down on the shore, brandishing her bony fists and screaming angrily at me.

"Maldita!" said the woman in front of me in Spanish as she turned her head and smiled behind her nosering, while nodding indicatively toward the enraged woman at the water's edge.

When we had passed my welcoming committee of one, and her screams had died down, the woman and her daughter brought the canoe to shore and I stepped out to shake hands with a smiling, brown-skinned Indian in neat American clothes. It was Alcibiades Iglesias, the native Cuna Indian missionary who was educated in New York and Iowa, and whose Christian school is well known to thousands of people in the Canal Zone and in the United States.

INTRODUCTION TO SAN BLAS

Imagine that we are sitting in a cane-and-thatch hut on a palm-fringed, coral atoll of the wild Caribbean coast of Lower Panama. Outside there is only the blackness of night teeming with myriads of evil spirits, both miniature and gigantic. The devil who lives in those nearby coconut trees is a huge fellow with a voice like the shriek of a hurricane, but he may have living with him a dozen lesser devils as small as the blood-sucking bats that roost on his shoulders.

Today "Sinna," the kingfisher, in his striking livery of blue, black, white, and red has flown about the town giving his death call that strikes fear into the hearts of the Indians. Worse than that, at dusk half-a-dozen women saw a wispy, gray devil the size of a child standing on a housetop and they were afraid to go home. Yes, somebody in the town is going to die!

The wind rises until it whistles between the wall canes and rustles the dry palm thatch continuously. Gathering force, it rips loose batches of thatch that fly off in the air. It whips up frothy waves that pound the sharp coral promontory and dash up white

spray. The palm trees bend over and their green fronds flap
frantically as the wind tries to take them with it. Sand and debris
sweep across the island. Everywhere the suffocating fumes of hot
pepper permeate the village, offered up as incense before a hundred habitations to drive away the house-smashing monsters that
ride the impending storm. Legions of night demons have taken
possession of the darkened little farm plots on the mainland, and
even now the horrible, broadwinged, shaggy-bellied Achusimmutupalit, who devours human beings all except their heads, is
sweeping the mountain trails in search of victims.

Within the hut a dim, yellow-flamed "kwallu" outlines flickering forms and shadows. Over there it reveals a sick child lying in
a hammock. Under the hammock is a box of painted wooden
idols, and beside it on a low stool sits the "apsoketi" tending his
smouldering clay pot of incense, while he drones on monotonously
through the endless measures of the Cocoa-bean Chant:

> This is singing to the little child.
> Here you are in your hammock sick.
> Here you are in your hammock sick.
> You have lost your spirit.
> You have lost your spirit.
> You are lying motionless in your hammock.
> Now you are shivering.
> Your hammock strings are vibrating.
> You dream of Uncle [poetic name for disease]
> Do not dream any more of Uncle!
> Neles [wooden idols] beneath the hammock,
> Come close to this child!
> They will seek out your spirit
> In the earth, and bring it back to you.
> Here, little spirit, they come
> Into the earth to find you!
> Ka! [hot pepper incense] give forth
> Smoke through their clothes,
> And make them [the devils] cough!
> The evil spirits cough—
> The evil spirit that has your spirit coughs, too!
> Neles! go into their houses!
> Tear down their houses, look for them!
> Uchu-Ka- [wooden idols] go underground now!

Thus, the chanter sends the good spirits of his wooden idols
down underground to the cities of the evil spirits to snatch the
soul of the sick child from the culprits who stole it.

We see that the child is dying of malaria and we offer guanatol, but the mother says, "No! It is these little, wooden men who will bring back the spirit of my sick child." Several days later the child is dead; and as the plumed and painted spirit-sticks are placed with it in its hammock for burial, and as the death chanter sings his "massar ikar," the sorrowing parents repeat, "Pap uruwe! Pap uruwe!" (God is mad at us!)

Such a situation as this could have been described for any one of at least fifty Caribe-Cuna Indian towns on similar palm-fringed atolls skirting the Panamanian coast from just east of the Canal Zone on down beyond the Colombian border, as well as in the more primitive Cuna towns that nestle among the mountains of the mainland.

When Columbus explored the San Blas coast in 1502, the Caribe-Cunas were spread the width of the Isthmus and numbered about 750,000. At this time the ancestors of the present group were mostly concentrated near Mount Tarcarcuna. But the Conquistadores decided upon their extermination. Because bows and woodtipped arrows were no match for armor, swords, guns, and fierce wardogs, these Indians were eliminated from south of the Cordillera and reduced to 10,000 or less. During later days San Blas was the famous Pirate Coast and Caribe-Cuna men, wearing but a clout and golden earrings, were taken as sailors by the swashbuckling British buccaneers, who hid their vessels among the many San Blas islands to plunder Spanish shipping. Only during the past century, however, have the Indians dared to come down from the mountains in numbers to occupy the off-shore islands.

Mangrove swamps and salt marshes covered with semi-aquatic vegetation characterize much of the shore line, rising to drier regions that support coconut and dozens of other palm, mango, lime, calabash, avacado, balsa, and mahogany trees. Still higher on the hillsides the slash-and-burn fields are planted with maize, plantains, and bananas. Above these foothills rises the blue, jungled Cordillera of San Blas, with its bank of cottony clouds that soften the skyline.

Tarpon and turtles, giant stingrays and sharks, red snapper and alligators swim the coastal waters and the mouths of rivers. Wild pigs, tapirs, agoutis, iguanas, and monkeys live among the rank foliage of the jungles. Brilliantly colored butterflies flit about in the bright sunshine. Leaf-cutter army ants are forever on the march, each displaying its freshly snipped oval banner. Above the pastel green and blue waters glide flocks of silent white

cranes and dirty brown pelicans, while swarms of squawking green-
and-yellow parrots and twittering parakeets fly among the verdant
upland trees.

There is powerful venom in these tropics. It is found in snake,
lizard, centipede, tarantula, scorpion, and dozens of plants. Indeed death from this venom is common.

The natives are short and brown-skinned, often having pleasing
features according to Western standards.

At the time of the Spanish explorers the Caribe-Cunas were
naked, body-painting cannibals, but today they do not eat human
flesh and the adults all wear clothing, at least outside the house.
The man's costume consists of a black felt hat from Panama, loose
trousers, and a curious, bright-colored shirt with long, narrow cuffs
and puckered areas at the shoulders and front. This is said to be
identical in style with the shirts wrested from captured Conquistadores four hundred years ago. The boys, however, go naked save
for a necklace of teeth, and even some of the girls upon occasion
are clad only in shell beads and a nosering. Babies and small children often bear witch marks on the nose and forehead and they
may be painted completely black against the devils that cause
the diseases of childhood.

Cuna women go in for huge, golden noserings, enormous round
earplates, a dozen golden-band fingerrings (often two or three
rings on each finger). When dressed up, they weight down their
chests with heavy strings of half dollars, to which may be added
colorful plastic alligator teeth, made in New York, which may now
be purchased from the coconut boat. The women and girls bind
their arms and legs tightly with long strands of red and yellow
beads that form a wide band of attractive design, because to be
beautiful a woman must have skinny arms and legs.

The greatest glory of the Cuna women and girls is their "mola,"
a short-sleeved blouse of complicated applique and inlay upon
which needlework they may have diligently bestowed as much as
two and a half months of spare time. These molas bear animals,
birds, trees, people, or abstract designs beautifully rendered in red,
yellow, white, orange, green, blue, and black. The mola is worn
with a sarong. Red paint on the cheeks and a black noseline are
added for beauty's sake, and their shortcropped hair is covered
now-a-days by a large, red-and-yellow bandana from England.

The objects of their culture, save for a few things introduced
from civilization recently, are based upon wood, and these primi-

tive people could not progress further alone because of lack of stone and hard metals. Thus, native arrows and spears have sharp, black-palm barbs, and maize for the family diet must be ground on grandmother's hard, molar teeth.

The houses of the people are built as community projects, from a frame of poles to which are tied cane and thatch by means of long and pliant jungle vines pulled down from the tall trees that they entwine. The household organization is a primitive matriarchy, the oldest woman in the house being the final authority. Beneath her control come her husband, her daughters, their husbands and children, often as many as forty relatives living in a single house. Usually the home consists of two huts, one containing a balsa camp fire and the other one strung with hammocks for sleeping.

Because the household rule is a matriarchy and the groom becomes the virtual slave of his mother-in-law, frequently young men can be married off only after being made drunk at the three-day "coming-out orgy" of some debutante. Incidentally, there are no mother-in-law jokes in San Blas, but on the contrary, the poor, hen-pecked father-in-law is always the butt of much mirth.

Cuna government is strictly local and is the man's province. Each town now has First Chief, Second Chief, Secretary, Policemen, and Commissioners of such things as roads, boats, house construction, and so on. In each town there is a large Council House (Sunmakket Neka) where the men meet almost every evening to discuss current problems, bad behavior, the activity of devils in the region, etc. Here visiting chiefs and dignitaries of other islands are entertained. Here traditional chants are sung. Here also devil-exorcising rites for the community are carried out, using powerful word-formulae, enormous rope-like cigars smoked backwards, and hot pepper incense. The Council House is equipped with crude wooden benches for the common folk, arranged about a central hollow square in which are suspended four or more hammocks for the chief and his guests.

Adults are punished by popular vote at the Town Council, and penalties vary from fines and beatings to more serious recompense for infringement of the unwritten code. From time to time, even in more recent years, the death penalty has been imposed and brutally carried out with machetes, while sub-lethal doses of a poisonous plant, *Spigelia anthelma,* have been administered upon occasion.

The women are called into the Sunmakket Neka several times a week during the daytime, to be kept in line by chants on the Cuna way of life, as well as by admonitions from town officials and witch doctors. The town children are forced to appear about once a week for disciplinary talks and the punishment of unfavorable actions by striking their bare bodies with poison-filled, fever-producing nettle stems, called "takke," known to scientists as *Jastropha urens.* The result looks like a severe and painful poison ivy infection.

The unwritten laws are the customs and traditions that have been passed down for centuries by word of mouth from one generation to the next, because the people possessed no method of phonetic writing.

The Cuna religion, as you may have gathered already, is an unorganized and primitive animism, there being evil spirits, devils, dragons, and monsters believed to reside in many of the objects and forces of nature. Huge rocks, gnarled trees, hurricanes, whirlpools, a sudden bend in the river, wild animals, and, in fact, any danger of the environment is the abiding place of evil spirits that must be appeased by means of ceremonial chants. Aside from these are the Creatorgod, a Sungod, and the Earthmother, who are rather passive about the devil situation.

Many persons are considered to be possessed of devils and must be treated for the good of the community by the professional witch doctors, for whose services the "possessed" must pay heavily. All dreams have direct meanings and persons may be found guilty of any crime they are seen to commit in somebody else's dream. Let us examine one of these crime dreams.

DREAM OF MURDER

The town of Ailigandi was in a turmoil one morning early in June. The population was seething. There was much rushing to and fro. An important meeting had been called at the huge Council Hall shortly after dawn to consider the evidence because a serious crime had been committed tantamount to attempted murder, and a murderer could be dispatched at once by several hundred machetes. It was my first morning in San Blas, since I had arrived the afternoon before.

"I guess you'll have to leave the island," said Alcibiades, the native missionary, at breakfast. His tone was grave, and there was a sadness in his voice that appeared to indicate that he felt the goings on at the Town Council were unfair.

"What's the matter?"

"Well, last night a woman in that house which you see over there woke up screaming. She had dreamed that a white man was choking her to death, and the Town Council is investigating the crime. Because you are the only white man within one hundred miles of here, naturally everybody believes that it was your spirit that invaded their house and entered her dreams."

This was my introduction to the fact that the Cunas believe that all dreams have meaning and that the person who appears in your dream may be tried, and if found guilty, may be punished for any crime that he commits in your dream, whether against you, against somebody else, or against somebody's property.

After breakfast, the investigation went on very seriously, and the woman was questioned in greater detail to identify the assailant of her dream. Finally, she admitted that she did not know just how light in color the man was, since very often dreams are presented in shades of gray. Here, at last, was a shadow of doubt, but what really exonerated me was the next point. The woman was so frightened by the nightmare that she could not remember whether or not the criminal wore a moustache. All I could say was: "Thank God for my moustache!"

Then the witch doctors got together with their incense, charms, and clairvoyant faculties. Taking the evidence as a point of departure and by consulting the underworld they finally established the fact that the evil spirit must have been that of a certain demented Indian of fairly light complexion who had lived at Ailigandi some years before, but who had been publicly declared a Sikwikolo and had been ostracized because of several strange acts of behavior, especially that of getting into people's dreams with a calabash of poison in his hands.

Once the crime was solved and the blame placed, nothing could be done about punishing the culprit because he no longer lived in Ailigandi. All that could be decreed was that the affected household must immediately get the villain spirit out of their place of residence and off the island. This required hot pepper in an incense pot, an apsoketi (devil driver) with his long ceremonial cigars and his powerful chant, and a few hours of time. Oh yes, it required one thing more — twenty-five American dollars to pay the chanting devil-driver for his services.

And because nobody else dreamed about a white man all summer, I had a safe and pleasant visit at Ailigandi. But although I
was allowed to stay on the island, Alcibiades guaranteeing my
good behavior, nearly everybody was suspicious and children followed me constantly yelling after me: "Waka! Waka!" which
means: "That horrible foreign face!"

TIMELESSNESS OF SAN BLAS

The primitive Cuna culture is timeless still today and all accounts lose their sequence. There are no calendars and no written
record of dates and events. Of course, there are dawns and noons
and dusks, days, nights, moons, seasons, and years; but because
there is no writing, life becomes fragmented into many undated
happenings, the accounts of which start out like fairy tales with
"once upon a time" or "one morning early."

"Kilupippi comes in mango season," said Upikinya the Medicine Man, "because I remember that I saw him eating mangoes."
But he could not say whether it was last mango season or several
mango seasons before that he had seen me.

"My Suzu was born in Ikwana Season about five or six or maybe
seven years ago," said a mother.

"The town burned down while Supreme Chief Nele Kantule
was alive."

Life for the Cunas is a monotonous round of rising, washing,
eating, working the fields, fishing, and hunting, mellowed by such
activities as basket weaving, attending Town Council and Inna
Feasts, getting married, having babies, appeasing devils, and burying the dead.

Events are placed by the Cunas in the following and other
seasons:

Little Seasons

Ikwana and wild turkey: January-February
Avocado: April 15-June
Mango: May-June
Maize: July
Massart reeds: last of July-first of August
Rayfish: August
Orange: November-December

Big Seasons

Dry Season: December-April
Rainy Season: May-November
Turtle: May-September
Tarpon: May-November

Not being able to carry through precise daily plans, even my research had little sequence. I simply wedged it in wherever opportunity arose in the motley collection of incidents that were taking place. I could not say, "Today I shall go to Tikantiki to collect pedigrees and measure moon-children." On the contrary, I had to wait until somebody with friends or relatives living there could take me to Tikantiki and vouch for my harmlessness before the Chief and the Town Council.

I could not say, "Tomorrow I shall go to Mammitupu," because this island receives no visitors, and Captain Peterson who had sailed the coast on a coconut boat for twenty-five years warned me, "I never go ashore at Mammitupu." Of course, without very special arrangements, no foreigner is allowed on any island after sundown. Thus, my objectives became to make friends with the people, to get to all the islands possible under approved escort, and at each island to learn as much as I could.

For these reasons my experiences in San Blas do not logically follow each other, but are discrete and timeless, like the primitive Cuna culture itself, and dating them does not bring any logical order to the relating of these events. I have tried to collect them under chapter headings, but the reader will recognize that many of the episodes of my narrative could just as well have been placed under other headings.

However, with some of the rising generation going to school, writing and calendars are now coming in, and birthdays are occasionally recorded. A few Indians have watches, but they are usually not running.

KIERMINA

Several times I went by canoe to Achutuppu where Atilio and Alcibiades had kept a Sunday School going for ten years. We set out on Saturday morning so that the afternoon could be devoted to friendly visits, first aid, and athletics for the young men of the town. On Saturday night we held a religious meeting. We commenced by singing songs in the dialect, after which Atilio preached

with a fervor and zeal that would compare favorably with the
performances of American revivalists. Finally, second-hand American Christmas cards with their bright pictures were distributed to
the children because the cost of new Sunday School cards put them
out of the question.

We held our services at the house of the Kantule or Inna Feast
Chanter with a few curious men in the background, more cautious
women peeking through the cane walls of the house, and a swarm
of squirming children who occupied all available stools and pros-
trate tree trunks. Several nature boys watched the proceedings by
lying flat upon the high, horizontal house braces beneath the roof.
While looking up at them I noticed a suspended collection of
fifteen incense pots and twenty-two gourd rattles together with a
number of long, reed flutes used at the Inna Feast.

The girls were variously dressed in bright molas, with many
silver half dollars and strings of beads about the neck, plus the
traditional golden earplates and nosering. The boys with few
exceptions were naked. Two little brown females sat in the front
row quite unconscious of the fact that they were less adorned than
the others. One was attired in her nosering only, and the other
had left her nosering at home.

In the evening after worship at the Kantule's house, Atilio conversed with a circle of men and women while I and several other
men lay in hammocks. Though most of the children were sleepy,
one beautiful, happy, little three-year-old girl was wide awake, and
she took me for a kind friend rather than a dangerous foreigner.
She was naked save for a nosering. With shrill shouts of joy and
the clapping of her hands she danced back and forth between her
mother sitting in the shadows and my hammock near the kwallu.
Upon reaching my hammock she would clamber up onto my
stomach and gleefully and proudly shout to me the name she had
been given, Kiermina.

COMMUNITY WAILING

Supper was over and darkness had just fallen on my second day
in San Blas when I was aroused by the most peculiar wailing that
I had ever heard. It appeared to be a community affair in Ailigandi and because of having been a suspect in the Sikwikolo case
I had become apprehensive.

"Is the chief dead or what has happened that people are wailing
all over town?"

Marvel Iglesias laughed and replied: "No, the chief is not dead and nothing has happened except that my husband has brought movies to the mission school from time to time."

"But what has that to do with this universal wailing?"

"Don't you recognize that sound?"

"No."

"Well, then, just listen again, for that is Tarzan's call."

"So it is, but what is it for?"

"It is bed time for the younger boys, and they are calling to each other to say that they are in their hammocks and wish their friends 'Good night!' "

WHAT IS YOUR NAME?

It was a primitive island upon which my Cuna friend Peter, the native missionary, and I had landed. We looked about for the Saikla and finally we found him sitting in the shade of a coconut palm on the breeze side of the town. He was weaving a fancy basket and he was conversing with an old crony, who was plucking his beard between a thumb and the blade of a huge machete.

I presented him with one of our yellow covered primers by which we had reduced the Cuna spoken language to printed phonetics, and I explained to him what a knowledge of these wilupkana could do by way of recording all the sacred old customs that the conservative Indians feared would become lost forever under the impact of civilization. And in order to impress the chief with my gift, I decided to write his name inside the cover. So I asked him his name.

I was not yet acquainted with the forms of Cuna politeness, modesty, and the old feeling that it is bad luck to speak your own name. For this reason I was quite surprised when the chief smiled, turned to his friend and said with some embarrassment:

"Will you please tell him my name!"

Years ago if a boy grew up and became an important man he could have a name in San Blas, but the Cunas did not bother to name the women. They would simply be called by their husband's name preceded by Ome (woman). The children would be called Dark, Light, Skinny, Fatty, and so on. But now-a-days most men have Spanish or Indian names; so the Indians had to have something to call me.

One day an old man asked Alcibiades what my name was, and the ubiquitous, naked, eavesdropping boys thought that he replied

"Kilu" (uncle). These boys reported all over town that my name
was Nele Kilu, the doctor uncle. So my name became Nele Kilu.

Next year when I returned, a few Indians remembered that my
name was Kilu, and one old woman was very generous. Having
seen how I had tried to be friendly and helpful, she said: "Kilu
is not a nice name. Any man can be plain 'uncle.' We should
call him Kilupippi, the Little Uncle." This name had the emphasis on the diminutive of endearment, pippi, and so I became
Kilupippi. My status was improving.

The third year while I was treating the Medicine Man, Manitikinappi, for a huge carbuncle on his back, some boys near his hut
asked my American name again. They heard the "r" at the end
of it this time and reported that it was really Kilor. But since "or"
in Spanish becomes "olo" in Cuna, they modified it to Kilolo, or
the "Golden Uncle." Once the old Medicine Man, Upikinya, addressed me as T-ipa Nele (brilliant savant seer). That was the
highest honor one could possibly do me, because to call something
"T-ipa" means that it is superb. Those latter names, however,
went a bit too far and I became known as Kilupippi all up and
down the coast.

THE BOYS

According to the treaty of 1925, the Cuna Indians have autono-
mous local government, and since they fear what civilized men
have done to them in the past, ordinarily no foreigner is allowed
to remain on any island after sundown. The first year I was re-
stricted to Ailigandi, although through the assistance of Alcibiades, Peter, and Atilio I got to peep in on Narkana, Achutuppu,
and Mammituppu. In spite of my attempts to be friendly, even
many Indians at Ailigandi were cold to my visit and kept questioning me. "When you leave island?" they asked in a sober, suggestive manner.

For several weeks most of the children had little to do with me,
but I overcame their fear by making folded paper birds that
flapped their wings, and paper snakes that whirled around a stick
when held over the hut fire. I had a manuometer for measuring
strength of hand squeeze and that quickly collected some enthusiastic friends. Crowds of children, leaving their games and their
pets, swarmed about me on all occasions anxious to compete with
each other in handsqueeze.

The clothed schoolboys considered themselves on a social level higher than that of the naked ones not going to school and always pushed the latter to the periphery of the crowd. But since I wanted the friendship of all, from time to time I would stop the clamorous schoolboys and shout: "Solamente mis amigitos sin ropa!" (Only my little friends without clothes.) And then the brown skinned, happy-go-lucky nature boys in their toothy necklaces would dance about me stretching their arms eagerly to get hold of the manuometer and try their strength. Thus, eventually I got most of the children of Ailigandi on my side, whereas their parents remained aloof. How was I to gain the confidence of the adults, especially those conservative heathen adults who feared Christianity and all foreigners?

I felt that my best bet was to be helpful and coöperative wherever possible, and that friendliness would work in the long run. So I started carrying medicine to the sick. This did more to get me acquainted than one can imagine. I helped try to pull the town boat out of the water for repairs. I helped launch and beach the canoes. I planted coconut trees. More than that, I tried to be helpful about the work of the mission, with whose civilizing project I was in complete sympathy.

Sometimes mothers would not allow me to give medicine to their children, and would run away with them when they saw me at the medicine cabinet. Often children with minor wounds would scream and refuse to let me administer first aid, but I stuck to my guns. I treated the sick as I tagged along with Alcibiades wherever he went.

One day I was sitting under the big coconut tree that shades the Iglesias kitchen door. Two nature boys were standing behind me entirely too quiet for comfort. I looked about and caught them up to something, at which they both began to grin. They were catching lice on each other's heads and sympathetically dropping them onto mine, so that I, too, might have a supply like the rest of the tribe. I considered this to be a sign of complete social acceptance among the small fry.

ROSITA

When night classes were held in the auditorium of Escuela Colman to teach the Indians of Ailigandi to read the Cuna Language, an average of about thirty-five persons came to the course.

By attending these classes I made many friends in Ailigandi. The chief and several leaders of the town came, as did Williams, the peglegged sailor who had been around the world and spoke some broken English. But before the end of the course they had nearly all dropped out because they found the Roman symbols entirely too difficult. However, a number of young men and women, boys and girls of the town, persisted valiantly and mastered the subject.

In general, the women and girls sat on the right and the men and boys on the left, as they did in church. Alcibiades stood up front and taught them, making words with large cards upon a flannel board. Upon the cards I had painted capitals and little letters. The Indians were amazed to observe that I was able to read the Cuna phonetics, and they did not suspect that often, although what I read made sense to them, I did not have the slightest idea about what I was reading.

It was inspiring to see the reactions of mature persons who mastered such symbols for the first time, because learning to read opened whole new horizons of understanding to them and the accomplishment gave them a thrill. For example, one girl figured out a sentence from the symbols and in her astonishment and delight she said, "Why, this piece of paper is talking to me!"

There was much interest on the part of some young folks who came early and crowded about me before the class began formally. For them I gave a preview of the evening's lesson. Among this eager group there were two moon-child girls, and although they had to hold the paper close to their eyes and squint to make out the letters on the mimeographed lesson sheets, they did quite well, especially Rosita, a girl about twenty years old. Rosita was proud of her ability, and she loved to bring her lesson to me and read it off after she had figured it out.

One night after the phonetics class, as we were all crowding out of the big double doors of the auditorium and down the wide front steps, the gasoline engine that powered the school dynamo broke down and all Ailigandi was plunged into pitch darkness.

I had begun to descend the steps and when the light went out I started to grope my way with my feet. Suddenly there was a firm grasp on my right hand, and a hand squeezed mine tightly all the way down the steps. As we reached the sand at the bottom of the steps, the hand released and several seconds later the lights all over town came on again. Wondering who had grasped my hand in the darkness, I glanced about to note who it might have been, and I saw Rosita, the moon-child girl, threading her way quickly through the crowd, with a neighbor's little boy whom she had brought along to class. "No wonder her hand found mine," I thought, because being a moon-child, Rosita had little pigment in her retinae and could see like a cat in the dark.

Rosita must have thought that it was leap year, too, because next day she asked Marvel whether I was married, and when she learned that I was and had a daughter she was very sad.

I was much interested in Rosita's psychology, because as a moon-child on Ailigandi, she had seen all her pigmented girl friends get married and enjoy the thrill of motherhood, and she would never be allowed to do so. She realized not only that she was born severely handicapped but also that she was the eternal victim of a powerful taboo, and she wanted so badly to find a husband, experience love, and fulfill the joyous destiny of her sex. She could not marry a brown Indian because she was white, but here was a white man much like herself, and if she could marry him, he would take her away from this prejudiced island on which she was born, and she would go to live among the glowing marvels of Nu Yak (New York), which the returned sailors of Ailigandi said were second only to the delights of Heaven. At least the tenuous possibility of her dreams was worth giving expression to the impulse. In the secrecy of pitch darkness it was worth administering a violent and protracted handsqueeze.

Ei nueti makke (Become good friends)

Although Saikla (Chief) Ikwaniktipippi had spoken to me briefly now and then because of his acquaintance with Alcibiades, he was very reserved, and the time of my first visit to Ailigandi slipped away without any evidence that to him I was more than just another unwanted foreigner. However, about supper time on the day before I was to leave, the Saikla came over and said to Alcibiades: "If Kilupippi is agreeable to it, I shall be willing to conduct a friendship ceremony with him."

Alcibiades said that it would be valuable to me, should I ever want to return to Ailigandi, and so I agreed to it.

The three of us went to Ikwaniktipippi's hut, where Alcibiades interpreted for us. The chief had me sit down on a tree trunk stool, while he stood before me with three white hen eggs in a pan. He approached me and said: "Now I am showing you these three white hen eggs with which we are about to swear a pact of eternal friendship."

Then he retreated about ten steps and approached me again. "I hope that when you return to your family you will find your wife and daughter in good health!"

Another retreat and approach: "And if we both get to Heaven I hope that I shall see you there."

Then it was my turn and I took the pan of eggs while the Saikla sat on the stool. I went through the same procedure of action and speech ending up with: "I wish the Saikla, my *ai nueti,* long life and I desire much prosperity for the island of Ailigandi." Ikwaniktipippi gave the eggs to his wife, and Alcibiades and I went home.

When supper was over, there was Ikwaniktipippi leaning against the cement block house wall near the kitchen door. "Eggs ready now," he said.

We went once more with Ikwaniktipippi. At his hut we sat on stools facing each other with the three shelled boiled eggs together with several pieces of boiled fish in the pan before us on the earth.

In silence Ikwaniktipippi put a piece of egg and a piece of fish in my hand, and I did the same for him. We ate them. We did this three times, and then the Saikla took pieces of egg and fish, bit off half, and placed the other halves in my hand, bidding me with a motion of his finger to eat them. And that was the end of the ceremony.

I suppose that the meaning of this procedure is lost in antiquity. Possibly it indicates that you cannot call a man your friend until you trust him enough to eat of the same food with him. In other words, you believe that he will not poison you!

And the ceremony did mean something to Saikla Ikwanikti-pippi, too, because next morning he came to the boat to see me off, and the following three years he greeted me upon my arrival with a bear hug.

THE CARIBE-CUNA INDIAN MOLA

"Madame, this is a genuine Caribe-Cuna applique mola! It was made by a primitive Indian girl of the San Blas Islands, that lie along the Caribbean Coast a hundred miles east of here."

The speaker may be "Jungle Jim" Price, one of the colorful props who lends a flavor of exotic adventure to the new and swanky Hotel Panama. Or it may be a snappy-eyed, brunette sales-girl in one of the exclusive shops. In either case the next words are also the same: "These blouses sell at fifteen dollars, when we can get them. They are not made for the trade and we can obtain them only when some Indian girl is willing to sell the new dress that she made for herself."

"But why are American women so anxious to buy these colorful, impressionistic blouses, aside from collecting them as curiosities?"

"They do two things with them. They make them into unique sports jackets bearing upon them the primitive tang and ripple of colors characteristic of the Central American jungles. And they trim both front and back applique strips with black satin, turning them into cushion covers with which to liven up the stuffy den or playroom."

If you examine carefully the workmanship of a mola you will see that it is constructed from at least three or four plies of brightly colored cotton cloth appliqued together. Orange, red, and black usually predominate, but often green and lavender may be present in the primary strips. To these are added dozens of tiny pieces inlaid as fancy dictates, and all are put together with a dexterity of stitch that would do credit to any civilized needle artist. Front and back designs are alike, although the details are varied.

"But these primitive, heathen women, still wearing huge golden noserings, who have fought off civilization for four hundred years — how is it possible for them to take such exquisite stitches? When did they learn to sew?"

I agree that this is a most interesting contradiction, but four summers of scientific study among the Caribe-Cuna Indians of the San Blas coast have given me answers to the questions.

"The Indians painted me with red and blue and yellow, all bright and lovely," proudly quilled the famous pirate, Lionel Wafer, across a page of his thrilling manuscript that became a popular book at the close of the sixteen hundreds.

His close friend of buccaneering days, William Dampier, relates: "Mr. Wafer was painted like an Indian and was sometime aboard before I recognized him."

From these statements and others it is certain that the Cunas were once body-painters. The body painting art has almost disappeared and both women and girls today wear brightly decorated applique blouses most of the time. This remarkable change in customs intrigued me into trying to trace the evolution from body painting to complicated mola needle-work, especially because the change seems to have taken place so recently that intermediate steps might be discoverable.

If you are permitted to go ashore at all, you are likely to see on almost any of fifty inhabited San Blas islands black babies or possibly a black girl who is very much embarrassed and rushes into hiding. These are not cases of decorative body painting, but are the result of ceremonials accompanied by special and expensive professional chants intended to make the person unattractive to devils. The paint is junipera juice, often applied to baby girls, girls at the time of their hair-cutting ceremony following the puberty rite, or at the time of their Inna Feast, to assure that they will live until marriage. Mothers may paint their babies of either sex with junipera without benefit of witch doctors because they say that it prevents skin diseases.

Men who have seen snakes in the jungle often cut a gash in their great toe and paint it with "black medicine" so that snakes will not bite them. Nakkruses (heathen cross-symbols that antedate the Spanish Conquest) may be daubed on the bodies of children in black or red to keep away the devils that steal the soul and cause the diseases of childhood. Added to the noseline may be devil-scaring lines of various sorts that I have seen on Cuna children. Women customarily draw a traditional black noseline and some paint a red disc on each cheek. At Ustupo there is a variation of cheek painting in which the red is extended across the nose bridge and about the eyes. To those who chide the few ladies that still wear crimson cheeks, they reply that it is "good medicine" against the sunshine, but this is definitely not the primary reason. Even Indian men look twice at scarlet cheeks!

We have remarked that the noseline and red cheeks may be indulged in even by males at the Inna Feast or "coming out party" of a girl. Indeed, I saw an official of Ailigandi wearing red on his cheeks and upon inquiry he said that it was "skin medicine," but he did not say for what purpose.

Recently I observed on a girl a noseline to which were added two dots, on the nose wings. These dots are the hangover of a nose wing decoration in the form of a box that was popular in times past. The box was quartered and a dot was placed in each quarter. Upon being questioned, middle-aged persons said they remembered that as recently as forty years ago most conservative women from Kaiman and Arkia painted an alligator, lizard, or scorpion, head downward upon their nose.

At Okupseni (Playon Chico) I had been taken to the Council Hall for routine questioning by the chief, and a crowd of curious Indians were looking me over. Remarked one woman in the throng: "I like his nose! His grandmother must have pulled it a great deal when he was a baby."

Since the Indians look at a person's nose first, they say it is the feature most suited for decoration. The decorative marks are put on with medicinal junipera juice mentioned above or with fruit seed powder added to the junipera to produce a red color. About the quality of these junipera marks I learned the hard way.

One day as I was returning home from carrying medicine to a family of Ailigandi I passed a doorway in which sat a woman applying the black, decorative noseline to her daughter. She motioned to me that she wanted to give me a noseline, too. And because I always try to be friendly and sociable, I sat down on a tree-trunk stool while she deftly drew a line down my nose with a small stick dipped in the dye. Then we all laughed.

After thanking her I rushed home to scrub the decoration off, and succeeded in removing all traces. However, when I chanced to look in the mirror half an hour later, much to my embarrassment I found a black line that did not completely disappear for two weeks.

It is known that the Cunas have raised a little cotton for ages. They had spun yarn, and woven some cloth up to two generations ago. This was not fashioned into women's garments but was left in strips for various purposes. The art of cloth weaving is now lost because of the many hued cotton fabrics offered in trade for coconuts by the wind-jamming "tabulus" manned by Negroes from Colombia. In addition, the diesel-motored "Nemi" of the Colon-Import-Export Company makes regular visits to the San Blas coast. All that is left of weaving is the production of hammocks by the grandmothers for their grandchildren, the making of which is considered to be such an accomplishment that there is a special house in "Indian Heaven," says Chief Ikwaniktipippi, for women who know how to weave hammocks.

It appears that in the early contact period at Darien needles were obtained from the Spaniards and the women embroidered clothing. Wafer and others mention ceremonial robes. Subsequently, when the Indians fled to the mountains, clothing seems to have been reduced to a minimum, and body painting was resumed.

I reasoned that a primitive people would not leave body paint-

ing and plunge directly into fine needlework such as is displayed
in the elaborate mola of the Cuna women today. There should
be an intermediate step when clothing was first adopted in which
the painting of cloth would replace the painting of the skin, and
the use of painted clothing having to do with some ritual might
be expected to persist longest. So I inquired.

During my first year in San Blas the only information that I
could get was from Alcibiades Iglesias, who said that when he was
a boy (about 1910) his grandmother in Narkana wore a "picha
makkalet" or painted loin cloth. It had blue designs upon it and
it must have been one of the last on the island. Old people agreed
that once there had been pichas painted with black as well as blue.
During my second summer I learned that such a loin cloth had
been owned by an ancient lady of Ailigandi as recently as three
years before but that she had sold it to a visitor. During my third
summer, however, greatly to my delight, I discovered at Mulatupu
a family in which the old grandmother still makes the traditional
painted pichas for her daughters and granddaughters, one to be
first worn at their puberty ceremony and one at their coming out
party. She proudly showed me a picha makkalet in process. It
was being sketched free hand with indigo which she said was very
difficult to obtain, and the indigo was being applied with a stick
chewed at one end into a fiber brush.

Two other painted pichas were shown me in this family, and
best of all, a daughter was willing to sell me one that had been
in use for many years. I copied the design of one of the others.

Today, Cuna schoolboys on several islands may be seen wearing
shirts bearing large initials, or a name, or even a simple little
design in bright cross-stitch, but these notes of elegance have been
adopted only during the past year or so. I have observed that the
traditional shirt for men is undecorated.

When the women started to produce molas, say the old folks,
they put no designs upon them at all and they were of white
cotton. But the innate Cuna desire for colorful decoration made
them add a narrow strip of bright cloth about the bottom. Later
they sewed little bits of cloth together to vary the colors. When
they had learned the technique of stitching, they widened the
border and began adding simple designs in applique, which, although they might appear abstract to the foreigner, were usually
based on some familiar object of their environment. Cuna women
are very proud of their needlework, and as is the case for the

hammock makers, there is also a very special house in Heaven for women who are accomplished in needlecraft. An elderly American lady in Panama told me that the molas of the gay nineties were very crude affairs and even had pieces of broken mirrors sewed upon them. The old Indians of the coastal islands all remembered a time when the appliqued portion of the mola was merely a narrow band, rather than covering all available space save collar and sleeves as it does today. Furthermore, in the mountains, where women have not yet learned to applique, the mola is white even now.

At the time of the pirates ceremonial robes were worn by the men of the mountains at Inna Feast, and ill fated John Gret and his companions donned robes. Piedrahita reports that the women made beautifully-decorated clothes near Sassarti.

The exquisite modern molas for which the Cunas are famous have many patterns that change periodically, so that those popular two years ago will be generally replaced by new styles this year.

Simple, continuous decorations made with straight lines (often black lines upon orange cloth) are known as "Mukan mola," or the kind of mola that grandmother used to make. Some rather elaborate designs have developed recently in this line of work, which are popular with the old women.

I collected one "Mukan mola" of considerable interest. It consists of a maze of boats and islands. It is said that if you do a thing too perfectly you will be cursed, for perfection is an attribute of the gods only. Accordingly, on one side of this mola the artist appliqued a man lying down upon an island, just to make the copy imperfect.

Of native designs one of the most artistic is the "Sammu mola" or palm tree design, showing a symmetrical tree with enormous fruits cut open to exhibit the seeds. The Sammu mola was popular all along the coast. Another mola shows three palm trees and their reflections in the ocean. Another features an albinistic Moonchild shooting the sky dragon at the time of eclipse to prevent the dragon from swallowing up the moon completely, which event would bring the world to an end.

A most elaborate mola was made by a woman at Mulatuppu depicting men on the scaffolding of the fish wier in the act of spearing tarpon and a giant sting ray. Another mola bears a picture of the Earthmother giving birth to the first snakes; a third shows a skeleton in its grave surrounded by toads. Many molas evidence the effects of civilization. One mola bears a huge cow, complete with such enormous horns and udders that one suspects the model to have been a comic strip cartoon from the United States—especially because the Cunas have never seen cattle. Another mola shows three copies of Escuela Colman, the mission school at Ailigandi, and each building has a flag flying over it. Between these copies of the school may be placed people and animals. Often the name "Iglesias" appears on this mola, since Alcibiades Iglesias is the director of the school.

Three years ago the French telephone design was popular. It was obtained from a Sears, Roebuck catalogue, and because the needle woman had never seen a telephone she took certain liberties with the design. The circle of finger holes in the dial reminded her of spots on the conejo pintado. Accordingly, on the finished product a spotted rabbit crouches where the dial should have been.

An amazing mola has upon it the "coat-of-arms" copied from a can of Holland Snuff. Beneath the escutcheon at the lower edge of the mola is a waving ribbon bearing the motto in large letters: "For ladies and gentlemen."

I obtained an interesting mola that represents a table set with Gorham silverware. An Indian woman copied it from a colorplate in the *Ladies' Home Journal.* Not being familiar with the objects depicted, she saw a jumble of lines that she did not understand but which she tried to incorporate in her design. By studying the result carefully one may distinguish what should have been goblets, knives, forks, and side dishes among other things.

Thus, in summary, we may say that the Cuna women of three hundred years ago painted designs all over their bodies, and those within the memory of persons still living today painted animals upon their faces. The face designs are generally reduced today to a single vertical beauty line. This line is said to make the nose appear longer, and the longer the nose the more beautiful it is to a Cuna. A remnant of the intermediate cloth painting step is present in the all but vanished "picha makkalet" loin cloth. And finally, old people of the coastal islands still remember the white mola with its narrow, colored border, which was the forerunner of the complex modern mola. The white mola still exists in mountain towns where the art of applique needlework has not yet been developed.

Chapter II

⋄ ⋄ ⋄ ⋄ ⋄ ⋄

CARIBE⸱CUNA HISTORY

THE WHITE MAN knows more about Cuna history than does the Indian himself because the white man has written it down, and the white man's paper remembers. On the other hand, as Supreme Chief Yapilikinya once told me while we sailed together past Akla beneath the bellied sails of a wind-jamming coconut boat, "Sometimes the Indian forgets!"

Cuna history starts off, as might be expected, with an Heroic Age, having gods, demi-gods, men, and messengers from Heaven. There were eight great savant seers who came down from the sun on golden discs to teach the Cunas how God wanted them to live. There are ceremonies venerating the umbilical cord and the amniotic veil. There are stories of the Creation of plants, animals, and man. There was a Garden of Eden at Yeye, the ancestral Holy City from which the Cunas (the Golden Ones) came. It was located by an imaginary lake on top of Mount Tarcarcuna (Grass Palm Covered Mountain of Gold) near the Colombian border.

During the ancient days of Chief Tata Akpan people multiplied on the earth and became very wicked. They stole, fought over nothing, became repulsively vulgar in speech and action, killed, and forgot God. Then Tiosaikla sent a great flood that drowned nearly everything. It covered all the earth except the top of the sacred mountain of the Cunas, Tarcarcuna, where a few people, including a savant seer (nele), were saved.

A new stock of men were let down from Heaven. These eventually became evil and were punished by many days of great darkness. From the first great darkness a few people were saved in an

25

especially constructed house. From the second great darkness some were protected in a huge, purposefully designed clay jar buried in the earth.

Then came the most illustrious of all Cuna heroes, Ipeorkun, who became master of Tarcarcuna. He taught his people how to make maize beer, how to heal the sick, how to develop the powers of a savant seer, how to observe the puberty ceremony of girls, how to use uchu idols and nakkruses, and how to cast gold. He taught them about forbidden foods, moral law, and Heaven. He also prophesied concerning the coming from Heaven on golden sun discs a series of savant seers. But more about Ipeorkun later.

The mystical holy ones came as prophesied, usually at the new-born stage of development, although one of them could walk and talk. Some of them brought with them from Heaven incense to-bacco, clay incense pots, and ceremonial rattles. The neles grew up and rounded out the spiritual teachings and ceremonies of the Cuna people.

One day aged Mastapepi showed me a sketch in his medicine notebook. He said it was a picture of the house that Olowaipip-pilele (the Great Spirit) had built. "First he constructed one and was not satisfied with it; so he built a bigger one" — and the way Mastapepi had drawn it he must have had a photograph of the New York skyline as his model.

On another page Mastapepi had represented three trees with a snake twined about each of them. A bird sat on a bare branch of each tree. Between the trees were two devils (niakana). "The pic-ture tells this story," said Mastapepi. "Once there was a manzana sapi [apple tree], and Nia [devil] came and ate a manzana from that tree. Thereupon he was changed to a snake."

There are many stories of the difficulties that the Serkana (old ones) had to face. These ancestors were constantly plagued by great troops of Achu swike (a small, mythical black monkey) that tore their clothes and bit and ripped their skins. They could be thwarted only by taking refuge in the river, because the Achu swikes were afraid of water.

Then the ancestors were chased by huge, horrible, bear-like creatures called Wiop, and these animals in battle once forced them back farther and farther toward the edge of a great cliff, where many Indians fell off and were killed.

Curiously enough, the Cunas have always believed in evolution, but it has been evolution of a retrogressive sort. All mammals started out as men, and because of their disobedience to God and their wickedness they were punished by being changed into different species of animals. As a matter of fact, man and the alligator and the sea turtle were born to the Earthmother at the same time. Therefore, the old Indians say that you should not eat your brother, the turtle, and you should never kill your brother, the alligator.

Once Saikla Nipakinya of Mulatuppu tried to summarize Cuna history for me. "In the beginning the grandfathers came down from Heaven on golden plates, or sun discs. Bobo came to earth and where he landed they founded a town and named it after him, Bogota. He brought certain knowledge with him. Others came to earth and they named after them the towns where they landed, and each brought from Heaven some special message of how to do certain things, and how to worship God correctly. Nele Sipu, the white savant-seer, came down and taught us that all men are brothers. Ipeorkun came down and instituted the Inna Feast."

As he spoke, Saikla Nipakinya became more excited and more filled with emotion. "Emi [then] — Emi — Español! Tule Kinki suli [the Indians had no guns] — Español makke! [the Spaniard kills]." By the time he had gotten these words out he was shaking, and his eyes were filled with tears. He could go no further.

"Olopiliplele, the first man, had four sons," said my friend Manipekinappi, the Snake Man of Mulatuppu. "Their names were Káana, Inóe, Kutschuka [whose son was Olokanalilele], and Tonamnerkwa. Inóe had a son, Topekwa by name, and to him the Earthmother gave birth to the first snakes."

It appears that because of the extermination policy of the early Spaniards of Panama City, who were exploiting the territory south of the Cordillera, a general migration of the surviving Cuna Indians from the banks of the Chucunake River took place. They moved westward along the mountain summit trail and came down to the San Blas coast by the branch trails leading north, especially to Carti and Narkana where they settled along river banks near the seashore.

Although this general migration to the west and north took place in early colonial times, it would appear that the Cunas of Caiman, Arkia, Kuiti, and Kuti represent a much earlier movement toward the east, especially because of their extreme primitiveness and the appearance of Colombian place names in Cuna chants and legends.

It is not to be supposed that the Carti and Narkana trails are the only ones that were used, because today at least eight Indian trails lead across the mountains from the San Blas coast to rivers of the Pacific coast. Indians constantly use the ones at Armila, Akla (employed by Balboa), Tuwala, Sassarti, and Ustuppo.

Old Indians told me that most of the islands became populated after a great tidal wave that washed away some of the stream bank villages on the mainland. Careful questioning about this catastrophe makes it appear certain that it was not the tidal wave that followed the famous Krakatoa explosion of 1883, but one that occurred on September 7, 1882. No lives were lost because the Indians fled to the mountains. An hour later the villages near the sea were washed away, and the Indians, as usual, were afraid to rebuild on the ill-fated sites because of the presence of powerful devils that must have caused the calamity.

A mass migration eastward from the Narkana and Carti areas took place in 1907 and later, when the conservatives fled from the "foreign influence" and Christian religion of Padre Gasso, and also from the cruelty of the Panamanian Police who were sent later to force civilized customs immediately upon the Cuna Indians.

I am not certain of the tribal affinities of the San Blas Indians of Balboa's day, although they were probably related to, if not members of, the eastern Cuna group, called Cueva by the Spaniards, and at least two trails lead today into the Santa Maria de la Antiqua area of Balboa from the Sacred Mountain Tarcarcuna, a distance away of only thirty miles.

CREATION OF PLANTS, ANIMALS, AND MAN

The Cuna story of the creation of plants and animals follows a general pattern of religious belief that was widespread among tribes in both North and South America. The primary generalization of this belief pattern was once almost universal and stated that the sun is the physical father and the earth is the physical mother of man and the higher animals, as well as of some of the plants.

Possibly before this the Great Deep or Watery Abyss was conceived by the ancestors of the Indians as Creator of the Cosmos, and this original god may well have created the world to be his wife, as an early Egyptian account suggests for the Heavens. The Cunas say that originally God, Tiolele, was "under the earth," and that he created the World Woman out of his internal organs beginning with his heart," although the organs are placed in a "box" for development. The name here given to the World Woman is Olokunkwintili, a name usually applied to the World Woman's daughter. Another version makes the world out of God's "blood and soul." The Cunas say in some versions that the world when first created consisted of clods of red earth (the color of God's blood) very loosely collected together.

Presumably, the Sungod generally replaced the Great Abyss Creatorgod in importance and became the husband of the Earthmother in early religions. During four hundred years of Christian pressure, it appears that the emphasis on Ipelele, the Cuna Sungod (Olowaipippilele on earth) and Olotililisop, the Earthmother, has waned and Tiolele (now harmonized with Jehovah) has become more important. However, the sun is still called Tator (grandfather) and the earth is sometimes referred to as Mu (grandmother). There is apparently some confusion today between the acts of the Sungod and those of the Creatorgod. According to a Cuna version, with the male Sun "Tata" as their father, the female Earth "Mu" brought forth living creatures on a number of occasions.

At one of these births, say the Cunas, the Earthmother was delivered of triplets: man, the alligator, and the sea turtle. For this reason man should not eat the sea turtle, and until recently the Cunas, deficient in protein as they were, refrained from using the meat of that animal. Until recently they would not kill the alligator.

A universal prototype of reproduction to be followed by many animals and man was given by the Earthmother when she was childbearing, but her productiveness was different in that her progeny were not limited to one species. First she bore a boy, then she bore a girl. Next was born a pair of white turtles, then a pair of red turtles, and after that yellow turtles. Then other turtle species were born. After these were born black monkeys, then red monkeys. Then the Earthmother bore many plants. Among them were plantains, yucca, otoes, maize, and many others. All these plants and animals grew on the Paluwala or Saltwater Tree of the great Earthmother, that symbolized umbilical cord, placenta, and membranes.

There is a Cuna chant describing in poetic language the woman Olokukurtilisop (the Great Earthmother) who staggers along drunk, carrying a fish. She sings: "Paluwala, Kukurtiwala, Ko-

peti!" meaning "Saltwater Tree, Butterfly Tree, drink!" Thus,
the Great Earthmother associates herself, the Kukur (Butterfly),
with the Paluwala. Elsewhere in chants she is known poetically
as Achamommor (the big metallic blue butterfly).

Ipelele (the Sungod, known by his earthly name of Olowaipippilele) finds Olokukurtilisop, who leads him to the Paluwala.
Then begins the story of his attempts to cut down the Paluwala
beside the mighty pirea or whirlpool.

Ipelele is assisted in his task by a number of persons including
his brother Puksu (the Morning Star) who finally slays the fierce
puma, the enormous snake sixteen meters in circumference, and
the gigantic toad that guard this Tree of Life. Wherever chips
fall into the pirea they turn into inedible fish. Every night the
wild animals come up and lick the great gashes in the tree, pouring in their medicinal virtues so that each morning the tree is
completely healed. Finally, all obstacles are overcome and the
tree is cut down.

When severed the tree does not fall because its branches are
caught in the clouds; Ipelele remedies this by sending a chipmunk
to chop them loose. When the huge tree eventually crashes it
changes into saltwater which flows out to form all the oceans of
the world, while many animals and fruits fall from its branches
where they had developed to be caught in the golden net and the
silver net that Ipelele had prepared.

Related ideas of a symbolic "Tree of Life" were entertained
not only by many tribes of North American Indians, but they
probably also had a world-wide distribution in prehistoric times.
Among North American tribes various rites were performed for
the "tree," which was often preserved, sometimes to prove lineal
descent of the child from its "mother's" clan. Among the Cunas
the umbilical "tree" of the newborn child is wrapped in a banana
leaf and fastened to the twines of the head of the birth hammock.
After several days it is buried under a fruit or coconut tree, and
henceforth that tree and its products belong to the child.

When a veil from the Paluwala is found over the face of an
Indian baby, it is considered in many tribes as a special sign from
the Deity predicting a remarkable and often a significantly religious life for the child. To the Cuna it means that, should he
undergo the training prescribed by tradition, this child could
become a great "Nele" or religious leader among his people, with
extreme wisdom, magical powers, and clairvoyant, predictive abili-

ties. Alcibiades Iglesias, Director of Escuela Colman at Ailigandi, was born with such a veil.

My friend Manipekinappi, a native medicine man, who practices obstetrics in Mulatuppu, tells me that a large veil indicates a "Nele," and it must be handled carefully as a sacred thing. It must be wrapped reverently in leaves, and eight cocoa beans must be burnt as strong incense over it at high noon. It must be buried under the hammock of the infant or the mother. Cocoa beans are finally burnt again above the spot of its burial, and mother and baby are fumed with cocoa bean incense. If the ceremony is not carried out, the mother may die instantly.

I induced Chief Ikwaniktipippi to draw a picture of Creation for me. Centrally located in this amazing allegorical scene is a portion of the Earthmother's body with a rainbow above the "whirlpool," which indicates that after the storm of labor a child is born. High in the picture will be recognized the sun, moon, and stars, while at the top of the panorama is the Upperearth or Sun where Tiolele is. (But Tiolele here appears actually to represent the Sungod.) On the Upperearth are shown the five sacred plants whose seeds fell down to this earth: kai (sugarcane), opa (maize), upsan (cotton), mammi (breadfruit), and tarkwa (a fruit).

"First," said Saikla Ikwaniktipippi, "the Earthmother gave birth to two devils, Nia Tummakimakka who is the father of deformities and a Nia who is the father of insanity." These devils are drawn large and are flanked by Nuskesu and Mako, two great prophets who tried in vain to convert them and who in the end were contaminated by their wickedness. Above the head of Nuskesu is a fruit of the Paluwala Tree of Life. Four branches of the Paluwala Tree rise between these devils and prophets. Two rivers created by cutting the Paluwala descend into the Underworld designated by a nali, the shark symbol of evil. On these rivers men representing masar sticks (spirit bearing sticks placed in the grave to protect the soul) are taking a coffin in a canoe to the Underworld while other masar are bringing the organs and soul of a dead man on to the place of judgment.

The Saikla said this means that "as we were buried in our mother's womb, so upon death we shall be buried in the Earthmother." A Cuna story tells of the glorious rebirth of the soul from a golden box in the Underworld, the Earthmother officiating. Uan, the cemetery, is depicted in Ikwaniktipippi's picture with

the soul of a dead man (to the right of the shark) protected by
the Guardian of the Dead. Tekintepa (drawn large), a great
prophet and guardian of Cuna Paradise, is represented with his
two wives (drawn small) at the magic kuliwar tree that will "show
all the wicked things that a man has committed on earth." The
two wives stand in front of the tree. A flag bears siku (arrows),
naku (weaving bat), and achu (jaguar) "things that will defend
the soul." Eleven species of beautiful, golden Underworld flowers
are represented.

There are a number of details in the story of Creation and also
in Ikwaniktipippi's picture of Creation that are described by the
Cunas with stone age crudeness.

It appears that the Cunas although worshipping Sun and Earth
and fearing many evil spirits of the forces of Nature, of frightening
locality, of taboo objects, and of the Underworld, recognized other
"sources of power" (possibly along with a Creatorgod) which all
crystallized into the present concept of Tiolele or the Great Spirit.
He is now spoken of in a number of terms expressing different
attributes. It is possible that attributes borrowed from the earlier
Sungod enhanced the modern idea of the Great Spirit and vice
versa. Names commonly employed today by the Cunas are Tiolele
(the God Physician) and Pap Tummat (the Great Father).

IPEORKUN

"Yoo-yoo-yoo!" called out a young stranger's voice in the wilder-
ness near the ancient village of Akwapirmai on the bank of the
Tuile River on a mountain in Eastern Panama. The Cuna Indians of Akwapirmai ran toward the voice and found an adoles-
cent boy who had just descended from Heaven on a golden sun
disc accompanied by an impressive array of ceremonial equipment
with which to teach this group of people the will of God for their
lives. At his command the Akwapirmaians built a ceremonial
surpa in which hut the miracle boy sat down in solitude to sing
religious chants, while the demons of disease swarmed about him
and cried out, "Ipeorkun cananelepa yanelepa!" And the lowly
ones of the people declared, "It is Ipeorkun!" (The Golden One
Descended from the Sun.) Thus came Ipeorkun Kunkilel, the
great cultural hero of the Cunas who, almost alone, is credited
with teaching this tribe their strange way of life during his fifty
years sojourn on earth.

First of all he gave names to things and parts of the body. He gave the Cuna people a language. Ipeorkun first taught about God, how to cast out devils with tobacco, with flutes, with hot pepper incense, with cocoa bean incense. He taught how to chant for the dead so that the masarsticks would protect the soul on its journey to the sun. He then taught hospitality, kindness, and helpfulness one to another, honor to the aged, and how to serve God. "If you meet a man on the path you must always request his permission to pass," said he.

Ipeorkun instituted the coming out party of the girl and taught that it must be observed with maize beer and drunkenness. Without drunkenness at this feast Heaven cannot be entered. Intimacy must not occur in the daytime. "Birth," said Ipeorkun, "must take place in a special inclosure." He declared that when we kill the bastard child "we shed God's blood."

Ipeorkun assigned work to the men as follows: work in the forest, get food, fell trees, cultivate fields, spin, weave, make bird feather clothes, work gold, make bowls, plates, spoons, and nose-rings. The women must cook, raise maize, cut bananas, wash clothes.

Ipeorkun taught about the great lake in the mountain (Tarcarcuna) from whence all the then known rivers flowed. He ordered that villages should be constructed beside the rivers, kept neat and surrounded by flowers and herbs. He prophesied where the Cunas would eventually migrate.

He taught many religious songs brought from God, and sent Tata Maka-arkwenatti to Darien to tell the people his prophecy that a series of great Neles would descend often as newborn children from Heaven, to teach the Cunas more about God and his will for the lives of men.

So eight ipeleles came down. One came with his guardian Jaguar who carried an incense burner, flute, feather flute cleaner, tobacco incense, special wood from a tree, a knife, two calabash bowls, a spoon, and a white tree. Ipeorkun commanded that only a virgin should suckle such wonderworking babies from the sun, and the virgin wet nurses should eat only small fish. (Medicine was given to make them lactate.)

These ipeleles (wise ones of brilliance) were acquainted with all creation. Being clairvoyant, they knew of the evil intentions of certain people. All medical secrets were open to them, and they healed all diseases. They raised the dead with saptur (junipera) leaves, placing a cloth over the child four times and pouring medicine water upon it. They could attract wild animals to the

hunters, and make the fierce beasts tame. They spoke peace and
the raging hurricanes obeyed; the earthquakes ceased their destruction according to the neles' will. At their singing people came
crying from Heaven riding the wind, people as long dead as
twenty years. They could produce lightning and earthquakes.
They were friends of such terrible creatures as whales, sharks, sea
lions, dophins, alligators. They wrestled with evil animals and
devils. One went to the underworld with the guide of the Dead,
Paliwittul, and saw the legion spirits of the winds, the spirits of
earthquakes, and the spirits of the rain. Tiekun, one of the neles,
said that the doers of evil would be punished, and reported on
the evil sons of Olopiliplele (the first man). Then came Nuskesu
from Heaven and told the people not to kill children born out
of wedlock.

Ipeorkun told of the ancient struggle between the Gods and
their Children of Light against the Evil Ones and their Children
of Darkness. The Chief of the Gods sent Olowaipippile (the Sungod) and his followers, Mars, Suniplel (the Morning Star), Nikar,
Pukaliler, Olokaipipiler, Tuna Kupra, and Mako Ikwakinapiler,
who made war on those who had rebelled against God. Masar
Akpan was the leader of the Evil Ones. With him were the sloth,
the peccary, and the turkey, among others. The Wicked Ones
made pitfalls to catch the Children of Light and covered their
traps with leaves. Some Good Ones fell into these pits and were
saved by a sympathetic passerby. Olowaipippilel's people returned
good for evil.

There was a hand to hand combat between Olowaipippilel and
Tata Kuchuka, an Evil One. The wicked Kuchuka threw Olowaipippilel into a fiery prison, but Olowaipippilel knew the purpa
or soul of the fire and hence it could not harm him. The Puksu
(the Star Venus) pushed the daughters of Kuchuka through the
fire.

Ipeorkun wandered from village to village teaching the people.
He went to Nektup and thence to Puhuarkana, and there he died.
Thereafter Tata Make, his disciple, continued to preach the way
of life that the great cultural hero had instituted. To mark his
final resting place, Ipeorkun requested that there be placed on his
grave a great cross of gold.

BALBOA'S ADVENTURES

Juan de la Cosa served as a pilot for Columbus on the Santa

Maria during its famous voyage of 1492. In 1500-02 he accompanied Rodrigo de Bastidas and upon this expedition he carefully drew one wiggly line on a piece of paper. At the time that line was the only map in existence of the mainland of the Isthmus of Panama. The most notable feature on that map was a dip in the wiggly line labeled Urabá, denoting a deep gulf that appeared to be a very fruitful region watered by a wide river.

In 1509 Ojeda set out with three hundred men to colonize the dip in the wiggly line and he took with him the pilot who made the unilinear map for Bastidas. He struck the coast of Venezuela and sailed west suffering one tragedy after another. His pilot, Juan de la Cosa, was killed by a poisoned arrow in a fierce fight with the Indians, and many of the men he had left were weak from starvation and tropical diseases. The remnant, instead of proceeding to Urabá, stopped near the site of Cartagena, Colombia, and founded San Sebastian, where matters went from bad to worse. The colonists, lacking food, resorted to cannibalism. They despaired of the help that Enciso was to bring them in 1510, and the wounded Ojeda set out for assistance with the pirate Talliafero in the only navigable vessel that remained, leaving the other thirty-six men with Pizarro.

When Enciso's relief ships got under way, there were found two stowaways on board, a man named Balboa and his fierce dog, Leoncico. They were finally accepted as part of the expedition. When Pizarro's group of living skeletons were encountered Enciso was baffled, and nobody knew what to do. The human stowaway stepped forward and said he had watched de la Cosa make the wiggly line map, because as a member of Bastidas' expedition he had seen this coast before Columbus had seen it. He would guide them along the wiggly line to the fertile banks of the Tarcona or Darien River where there was a prosperous Indian town filled with food, theirs for the taking.

So they made for Urabá. On the shore they knelt and with outstretched sword and hand over heart they prayed to Santa Maria de la Antigua of Seville. Then shouting "Santiago" (St. James) they furiously attacked the Cuna defenders, with the two stowaways in the lead. It was a short but bloody battle, and luckily for the Spaniards these Indians did not know the secret of the poisoned dart. Many of Cemaco's warriors were slain and many were taken as slaves.

Balboa was the hero of the day, but he had to divide his honors

with Leoncico, who killed so many men and captured so many
prisoners that the Conquistadores voted him a share of the gold
and slaves equal to the other members of the expedition, and he
became the only rich, slaveholding dog in America. The other
dogs of the expedition received no consideration.

Balboa's friend, Hurtado, struck the jackpot by discovering almost $130,000 worth of golden images in an earthen jar, hidden
in a haystack. In a few days many of the Indians returned with
golden presents for the invincible, white war gods, and their
dragon helpers.

Enciso became jealous and made unbearable laws, whereupon
the colony mutinied and elected Balboa their leader. The latter
carried out a plundering expedition up the San Blas coast to
Careto where he slew, robbed, and captured, bringing back much
booty and many slaves. He brought back from Careto to Santa
Maria de la Antigua del Darien Chief Careta and his family.
These he treated with kindness.

After some days Chief Careta pointed out to Balboa that he
could do him no harm, so why should he not return to cultivate
his fields? He would seal his pact of friendship by giving Balboa
his daughter, Anayansi. Balboa accepted and soon made an expedition against Careto's rival, Comagre, who lived in the region
of Coiba near present day Ustuppo with Anayansi serving as interpreter and Careta supplying both men and food. Comagre capit-
ulated, and was told that Balboa's ransom would be all the gold
and food supplies that they possessed. Immediately, Balboa started
melting up the golden images and jewelry to divide the metal
among his men, when the chief's son, Pankiako, complained about
the destruction of beautiful artistry and craftsmanship, just to get
mere metal. His complaint fell on deaf ears because the gold-
thirsty Spaniards were not interested in aesthetic values. Ironically
enough, after robbing this Cuna town thoroughly the Conquistadores baptized their victims and gave Christian names to Careta,
Comagre, and a few others.

The young Indian Pankiako dropped a story of the treasure of
Dabaibe on the other side of the mountains, and he also told of the
Great Sea. Balboa and Pizarro were fascinated by the story of a
temple covered with plates of gold (Temple of the Sun at Cuzco),
while Pankiako said he would take them to the Great Sea.

From the point of Akla in 1513 the expedition threaded its way
along the jungle trail across the Cordillera of San Blas, plundered

mountain villages of their gold, and pushed on to the great ocean beyond, which Balboa christened the South Sea. On that side of the mountains the story of the Great Treasure and Golden Temple not only persisted but increased, and Balboa set his men and slaves to transporting across the mountains timbers with which they constructed vessels to explore the west coast and to search for the treasure of the Incas. With the first two brigantines built he conquered the Pearl Islands and explored the South Panamanian coast. It is said that Balboa crossed the Isthmus as many as twenty times.

Enciso had been shipped to Spain and he told his story to the King. Although, because of his new exploits, Balboa was named in 1514 Admiral of the South Sea and Governor of Panamá and Coiba, an order was also sent to detach him from the Darién colony at the Gulf of Urabá. The jealous Pedrarius had been sent out to replace Balboa in the Darien colony, and with a crafty message he enticed Balboa back across the mountains to Akla in 1517. When Balboa arrived, he and two companions were thrown in jail, tried for treason to the King, and beheaded.

After this the Cuna Indians who had become friends of Balboa were massacred by the forces of Pedrarius in a number of expeditions, and in return the Indians made life so dangerous that the whole Darien colony crossed the Isthmus and took refuge up the coast to the west where they founded the city of Old Panama.

The white man out of the way, the remnant of the Indian people settled back into their former way of life, poorer, wiser, their numbers severely diminished (from some 750,000 to some 10,000), and their minds filled with a horror of Spaniards.

SAN BLAS PIRATE COAST

One day in 1572 a noted slave smuggler, turned sea robber, sailed up the Thames River. He had just looted Nombre de Dios (Panama), captured a merchant vessel at Cartagena (Colombia), sacked Portobello (Panama), and crossed the Isthmus to Panama City where he took possession of three mule trains bearing thirty tons of silver. It was Francis Drake, the world's most famous pirate and fantastic prototype of them all.

Although England was not officially at war, Drake's daring accomplishments appealed to the British, who were beginning to dream of Empire, Empire that could only be achieved by breaking the Spanish-Portuguese world trade monopoly. Drake became a national hero. Queen Elizabeth made him an Admiral, and historians say that she gave him permission to raid Spanish possessions in the Pacific.

Drake's repeat performances were quite as spectacular as his curtain raiser. In 1577 he set out with five ships, lost three, became separated from a fourth, and with the last plundered Valparaiso, captured a richly-laden Spanish merchantman, and cut from their moorings all the vessels at Callao (Peru). He searched for the Northwest Passage up the western coast of North America and visited the Philippines and points in Asia, returning home in 1580. This time the Queen boarded his ship, knighted him, and received a gift of his plunder worth some $5,000,000.

Leaving his many daring exploits against Spanish shipping long enough to help defeat the Spanish Armada as Vice-Admiral of the British Fleet, he returned to his piracy and to Panama where he died of dysentery and was buried at sea.

Following his example that received such Royal favor, hundreds of dashing young Englishmen set out with wits, fire, and sword to win fame and fortune while contributing to the destiny of their native land, not much worried by the occasional bills posted at home that read: "Wanted for Piracy."

In 1635 Henry Morgan, the Welsh tobacco farm boy, sacked Portobello, rounded the Horn and captured Panama City, carrying away 175 mule loads of jewels and precious metals together with 600 prisoners.

All pirates underwent physical hardships and many met death by fire, sword, ocean wave, hurricane, starvation, and tropical diseases. Some returned wealthy. A few like Drake, Hawkins, and Morgan were knighted for their services to the Crown, giving Gilbert and Sullivan a happy solution for *The Pirates of Penzance;* namely, that they were *all* English noblemen and therefore socially eligible to marry the recently knighted Admiral's many daughters.

There was a sprinkling of Netherlands Dutchmen and French Huguenots among the pirates. The Dutchmen were getting back at the Spaniards for cruelty during their political domination of the Lowlands. The presence of French Huguenots injected the element of religious hatred deeply into the undeclared war on Spain. Besides, in those days any non-Catholic was considered a heretic by the Spaniards and a fit subject for the American branch of the Inquisition with its offices in Mexico City and Lima. It happened that most of the pirates were nominally Protestants.

Captured pirates were tried by the Inquisition and burned at the stake, not for their lawlessness but for being religious heretics. It is said that with a group of slain pirates the Spaniards once placed a sign — "Not because they are Frenchmen, but because they are Lutherans."

This religious hatred in pirate days is significant for our story because memory of it may have been one of the reasons for violent Panamanian opposition to the first Protestant missionaries in San Blas. Brutality was common among the pirates, such as L'Olonnais, 1650-1671, who ripped out tongues and sliced up prisoners with the sword just for the pleasure of it. L'Olonnais is reported to have marched down a line of eighty-seven prisoners with his sword and a whetstone, sharpening and chopping until he had beheaded them all. Nobody regretted it when he fell among the Indians of Panama, who ate parts of his body while he was still alive.

The Spanish merchantmen, under heavy naval convoy, left Seville, sailed for Santo Domingo or Habana, and then split into two groups. The one group proceeded to Vera Cruz and the other went to Cartagena, Nombre de Dios, or Portobello, and from these ports the cargoes were distributed by mule and boat to Colombia, Venezuela, and Ecuador, or to Panama City, Callao (port of Lima), Chile, and Argentina.

Thus, during pirate days the rich cities of Cartagena, Nombre de Dios, and Portobello were chief targets of the buccaneers as well as the rich, bulging cargo ships that visited these ports. The many uninhabited San Blas Islands, lying beside the sea lane between Cartagena and Portobello, became excellent hideouts for outlaw vessels and served as a base for their operations. Here, too, they could find primitive Cuna Indians from the mainland villages, excellent sailors and allies, that bore a fierce grudge against the Spaniards who had almost exterminated them. The Indians could be depended upon for food supplies and guides.

Tupak (Isle of Pines) was the only island of the San Blas chain on which there was fresh water; so this island became the rendezvous for the "Brothers of the Coast." Today there are two small Indian towns on the Isle of Pines (Tupak and Mammimutlu). The Colombian Negro smugglers of today with their canvas spreading tabulus, carrying coconuts and contraband, still stop and fill their water jugs at the three small streams that trickle down the Tupak hill.

Recognizing a four hundred fifty-year-old right of foreign sailors to this water, the Indian men of Tupak have not tried to bar them from the stream, but to prevent molestation of their wives and daughters by black mariners they put up a sign in Spanish that I figured out. It forbids sailors to go to the stream for water without first getting permission from the chief.

When Spanish trade to Portobello and Cartagena declined and almost disappeared under the scourge of the pirates, the impoverished cities of the Isthmus all but died, and the San Blas coast sank back once more into isolation and the ancient Cuna way of life.

NEW EDINBURGH

Because the Spanish had no political control over the fierce Caribe-Cunas the Scotch felt that a settlement on the Isthmus would divert much South American trade to the British Isles, and so, after much agitation, William Paterson set out in 1698 with a poorly-planned expedition to colonize the bay area just east of the Sassarti Islands and Akla. His colony of New Edinburgh was established on the peninsula of Alidonmutlu. It contained, among other things, 1,500 Bibles and 4,000 hair wigs.

Andrés, a Cuna Chief who had aided the buccaneers, assisted the Scotch to ward off the inevitable Spanish attack, but so many died of malaria that the colony was abandoned in 1699, some of the survivers making Jamaica and a few of them getting to New York.

A second Scotch attempt was made in 1699 but a Spanish force compelled Fort St. Andrew to surrender in 1700, because the English king William III would not protect Scotchmen since they were not Episcopal. Thus, the colony was abandoned permanently, and only a few bricks overgrown by the jungle are left to memorialize the fiasco.

THE CANAL

Columbus believed that the Caribbean Islands were close to the Orient, and so he searched for a passageway between them by which he might reach Cathay, especially because the Indians told him of a great ocean beyond the land. Others sought for a Northwest Passage to Asia.

When it became apparent that no such waterway existed across the Isthmus of America, Balboa suggested that a canal might be dug, and he and his men in dragging across the mountains from the Atlantic to the Pacific the timbers for several vessels must have wished for such a canal many times over.

In 1527 the Spanish at Panama investigated the possibility of a canal employing the Chagres River channel part way. In 1519 a Camino Real crossed the Isthmus, but at best muleback was a difficult and expensive method of transportation. Most people continued to think of a canal.

Von Humbolt spent the greater part of five years in visiting and exploring America, and upon his return in 1804 he published the account of his travels, in which he suggested nine possible water routes across the American continent. With the publishing of this account the world became highly Canal conscious.

In 1821 Panama declared herself independent of Spain, and asked to be included in the republic of Gran Colombia. Later she became a part of New Grenada. In 1838 the Congress of New Grenada conceded to Salomon et Compagnie of France the exclusive right to construct and operate a canal, railroad, highway, or combination of all three across the Isthmus of Panama.

In 1843 the French Government sent Napoleon Garella to study the possibility of a canal. Then came the Gold Rush, and three Americans were given permission to build the Panama Railroad, which was a great money maker. When the Gold Rush declined so did the Panama Railroad.

The United States Government became interested and made three naval surveys. With these the Atrato River region was pretty well ruled out. There were a number of possible routes surveyed across the Isthmus, several being near Mulatuppu and Akla. Men suffered and died of tropical diseases and exhaustion on these expeditions, and four of the "Virago" party of 1853 were killed by the Indians in the mountains near Morti.

The French renewed their interest and the Salgar-Wyse contract was signed for a canal concession of ninety-nine years. The aged but vigorous de Lesseps, who built the Suez Canal, took over the project and started work in 1880. He was greeted at Panama by the flags of many nations. That of the United States was noticeably absent, and President Hayes declared: "The policy of this country is a Canal with American control. The United States cannot consent to the surrender of this control to any European Power."

By 1888 sixty-three workers per thousand had died. There were 4,987 deaths, 1,018 of them from yellow fever. Then the project broke down financially, and the French courts of the early nineties were filled with investigations of mismanagement and scandals.

In 1895 the Compagnie Nouvelle was established under new management and the death rate was reduced to twenty-five per thousand.

In 1898 there was an attempt to sell the canal to President McKinley, but in 1899 the Morgan Bill was passed by the Senate providing for ownership, construction, and operation of a Nicaraguan canal by the United States Government, in addition to its complete fortification.

The shrewd Bunau-Varilla saw that with this American move his Compagnie Nouvelle would lose everything; so he got busy, especially in Washington. He wanted to sell the French rights to the Americans. He had to stop the Nicaragua project! He seized upon the volcanic disaster of Mont Pelée in Martinique to show the dangers of a canal in a volcanic country. Then he bought up pictorial Nicaraguan postage stamps bearing a picture of the Nicaraguan Momotombo volcano in full eruption, sending them to the United States Senators and later to many House members. The lawmakers got cold feet, just as Bunau-Varilla had hoped. Then Bunau-Varilla, almost singlehanded, planned a revolution for Panama. Since Bogotá was hesitant about agreeing to turn over rights to the United States, Bunau-Varilla sent Amador of the Panama Railroad to Panama with a proclamation of independence, military operations program, cipher code, and $100,000 out of his own pocket to get the insurrection going. Bunau-Varilla would remain in Washington to obtain recognition for the new regime.

The Junta had three hundred men organized as a fire brigade, and the Panama Police. They bought off General Huerta's Colombian Regulars for $50,000. General Varion agreed to surrender the gunboat Padilla for $35,000. Governor Obaldia was favorable; so he sent Captain Tascón (who could not be bought) to put down an imaginary rebellion, and he notified Bogotá of his action to make it look on the level. Bogotá ordered the gunboats *Padilla* and *Bogotá* to carry reinforcements, and General Tovar left Cartagena for the Isthmus with a battalion of riflemen.

Bunau-Varilla warned the United States Secretary of State of pending revolution in Panama and the battleship *Nashville* was sent to protect American lives and property.

When Tovar's riflemen landed at Colon, November 3, Colonel

Shaler, Superintendent of the Panama Railroad, which was interested in selling out to the United States Government, had moved most of the rolling stock away from Colon, and he apologized to Tovar for having only a couple of cars available. So Tovar and his staff took these across to Panama, Shaler promising to send his forces later. However, they were never sent.

When General Tovar suspected a trick, the Panama revolutionists locked him and his staff up and declared their independence. Captain Torres, who had been left with the Colombian Battalion at Colon, sold out, November 5, for $8,000 and returned to Cartagena. The *Bogotá* fired a number of shells on Colon, killing a Chinese and a mule, and independence was thus achieved.

De facto recognition was given by the United States on November 6 and official recognition on November 13. France, China, Austria-Hungary, and Germany followed suit shortly.

This account is highly significant for our story because the opportunity of working in Panama about the American Canal and elsewhere in the American Canal Zone has resulted in the presence there today of about two thousand Cuna Indians, nearly all of them men, who usually work there for several years at a time, living in the most horrible slum conditions, and then returning to their families. Often they take back the worst aspects of civilization, including syphilis, and as yet there is no settlement house or welfare organization of any sort to look out for them.

SAIKLA PALIKWA

During the years that followed the establishment of the Canal Zone, the Cunas became acquainted with Americans. The Cunas found a friendliness of spirit that they had not encountered in other foreigners. They had no tribal memory of persecution, slavery, or slaughter by the Americans. The Indians trekked into Panama along the mountain trails and they sailed into Colon on ivorynut boats and coconut boats. Some of them stayed to work a few months for the Americans in the Zone, and some, as seamen, discovered Nu Yak.

Contacts increased and fear began to abate so that in 1915 Colonel Gorgas could write, "In the ten years that we have been at work — the San Blas Indians have acquired considerable confidence in us, and have become quite friendly. They come to the hospitals very freely for treatment and surgical operations, and the men can now be seen almost any day in Colon trading. While the Indians recognize the overlordship of Panama, I doubt if the President, or any other white official, would be allowed to spend a night in the San Blas country, nor would they allow any official of the Canal Commission to spend a night in this domain."

Gunther in 1941 stated: " . . . the Cuna Indians in Darien have never been subdued and are still definitely hostile. All this within a few miles of one of the greatest engineering feats known to man!"

Of the many stories told about the amazing behavior of these half civilized Indians when in town the account of Saikla Palikwa is typical.

In 1925 a strange and eccentric barefooted Indian clad in golden earrings and a dirty old pair of flare-shank breeches strode down the streets of Panama City carrying a skinny and tattered red rooster by the legs like a bouquet of flowers. He brushed the guards aside at the Presidential Palace, climbed the stairs, went down the hall, and burst into the office of the President himself. "I have brought a present for you," said the Indian, poking the skinny rooster in His Excellency's face. Continued the visitor, "You are Belisarrias Porras. You are the President of the Republic of Panama, but that is nothing! However," he continued, pounding his chest with a fist, "I am Saikla Palikwa, and I am the Great Chief of all the territory of the Upper Bayano River."

The President appeared frightened and was not quite certain as to what was coming next. "And what can I do for the Great Chief of the Upper Bayano River?" he asked humbly.

"I have come from my powerful domains in the Upper Bayano to make an important request of you!"

"What is it?" asked the President with even greater timidity.

"Loan me five dollars!"

The President shelled out and Saikla Palikwa quickly took his leave, picking up a diplomatic cigar butt that somebody had inadvertently laid down on a marble-topped table in the hall.

So the Saikla issued forth from the Presidential Palace swelled out with pride in the success of his negotiations, clutching a five dollar bill in one hand, and puffing vigorously on a huge cigar.

AMERICAN INTERVENTION

It must be great fun to make a big bomber dive at an Indian

village, roar its engines like demons of hell to scare the primitives out of their wits, and then suck up a lot of dry roof thatch in its wake. If this were not true, it should not have happened so often to the island villages of San Blas, Panama, in recent years. Unfortunate as this practice may be for international friendships, it did have a salutary effect one day in early summer of 1951.

The men of Achutuppu had a fish wier for many years along the shore of their mainland territory, and those tarpon that failed to be trapped there swam up the coast where they might be caught in the wier belonging to the men of Mammituppu. This seemed like a logical and fair arrangement and so it had gone on for years without complaint. But one day the men of Achutuppu entered disputed territory and started to build a second fish wier, at the construction of which the men of Mammituppu immediately took offense because it would still more restrict their meager food supply. The men of Achutuppu, however, paid no attention to the Mammituppu argument.

To make their objection very clear, the Mammituppu men sneaked out one night and cut down a grove of coconut trees belonging to Achutuppu. In retaliation Achutuppu burned some grainfields belonging to Mammituppu.

Since interisland affairs had now deteriorated to an impossible level upon which arbitration was completely out of the question, it was decided to settle the matter as civilized people would do, by a resort to firearms. Accordingly, the men of Achutuppu, commandeering canoes, rifles, shotguns, harpoons, and what not, put out to sea to punish the men of Mammituppu. A lookout spied the oncoming flotilla and outdid Paul Revere with his frantic screams and his barefoot dash through the town. The men of Mammituppu seized all available arms, jumped into their dugouts, and pushed off bravely to defend their honor, their families, and their property.

Tempers ran high, and the war whoops could be heard for miles. Guns were being loaded, and men were being encouraged. Orators harangued the warriors of both sides, reviewing the arguments to prove beyond all doubt that their side was fighting for the right.

The dugout navies approached each other. Nobody thought of maneuvering, they were all so anxious to close with the enemy, and both sides rushed headlong into frontal attack as fast as their canoe paddles would carry them. Five minutes more and they

would be within gunshot of each other. Every gun was poised
for the first fusillade. At that exciting moment an American
bomber roared down from the blue. It skimmed so closely over
the two Indian navies that the men threw themselves flat in their
canoes to keep from being struck. A moment later the bomber
had disappeared.

In the Mission at Ailigandi I had listened to Alcibiades' radio
on that fateful evening two weeks previously when President
Truman stated that the United States, as a member of the United
Nations, had intervened in the Korean Civil War, and that word
had electrified the Indians all up and down the San Blas coast.
Both Achutuppu and Mammituppu had heard about the intervention in Korea, and a number of men from both towns knew something of the stupendous war power of the United States, having
seen units of its Navy pass through the Canal, and having worked
in Camp Clayton and elsewhere in the Canal Zone.

Automatically the two navies halted. The same idea struck both
sides simultaneously. "Somebody had reported their fish wier dis-
pute to the American Government and that bomber had been sent
by the Great White Father to warn them that the United States
was ready and prepared to intervene!"

"Why, both of their island navies combined with all their
twenty-seven rifles and shotguns would be no match for the armed
might of the United States! Maybe it would be wiser not to start
something they could not finish." So the two navies went home
without firing a single shot.

Some days later several Indians came to Alcibiades for advice,
and he said that because the new wier was on disputed land it was
not within the province of the two towns to decide the matter
anyway, but that the problem should be referred to Saikla Yapillikinya, the Supreme Chief of the Cuna tribe, who wisely took the
matter under advisement, without rendering a decision.

Achutuppu gave up the idea of building the new fish wier. During several months of anger the men of Mammituppu kept off
their island all Indians from other towns, and eventually peace
restored itself.

THE CUNA FLAG

An orange colored bundle of cloth caught my eye as I was
talking to the Chief of Ustuppo. We were seated in the Sunmakket Neka, and the cloth in question was lying on a horizontal

pole that braced the frame of the thatched roof. I guessed that it might be the Cuna flag that was born during the bloody revolution of 1925, and I suspected that Mr. Marsh, the adventurer, had played Betsy Ross, or at least had peeped over her shoulder and told her what to do.

"Ipua?" I asked as I pointed toward the bundle.

"Bandera Tule," said the Chief.

So I asked to see the Cuna flag. A naked boy shinnied up a vertical roof support, reached for the orange bundle, and returned to place it in my lap, after which the Chief told me a story.

In 1942 German submarines had been operating in Caribbean waters and everybody in the Canal Zone was jittery because they felt that the destruction of the Canal might be high on the list of Hitler strategy. United States Army planes were constantly patrolling the San Blas coast and signal stations on the mainland were perpetually on the alert.

Because Supreme Chief Nele Kantule resided at Ustuppo, the Sunmakket Neka of Ustuppo was virtually the national capitol, and accordingly, the Indians were flying their banner on a tall bamboo staff. The flag consisted of orange and red stripes surmounted by a huge black swastika.

Along came an American Army scout plane on patrol duty. Since those on board had never been Boy Scouts or Camp Fire Girls they had no idea that the swastika was an age old Indian symbol, and all they could think of was: "The Nazis!" Consequently they went into a nose dive, clipped off the flag pole with a wing, and radioed a frantic message to their home base in the Canal Zone: "The Nazis have landed in San Blas!"

The American military prepared at once to meet the threat, but found it to be a false alarm, although the boys swore that they had destroyed a Nazi flag. On the other hand, the Cuna Indians complained that their national emblem had been insulted without provocation. The American authorities explained to them that many Americans did not know about the ancient Indian swastika, but only knew about the Nazi one. And they warned them to keep their flag inside until the war was over.

"A council meeting was called," said the Chief, pointing to a yellow circle in the center of the flag, "and it was decided to superimpose the tribal nosering over the swastika. That is to distinguish it from Hitler's symbol, because it is well known that the Germans do not wear noserings."

Chapter III

◇ ◇ ◇ ◇ ◇ ◇

NATIVE RELIGIOUS BELIEFS

The Young Nele

A NELE OR savant-seer is so born, not made. Such super-natural abilities are special gifts from the Great Spirit. The potential nele is known at birth, because he bears an amniotic veil. In early youth the nele demonstrates his powers by predicting who is about to die and by performing other signs and wonders before the people. One such young nele of about fourteen years, Nel Pippi by name, lived at Carti. He possessed such occult powers that wherever he resided, there the devils, fearing what he could do to them, went on such a rampage that they threw sticks into nearby houses on pitch dark nights.

These sticks were thrown at people sleeping in their hammocks. Nobody ever saw the devils throw the sticks because by the time a "kwallu" was lighted the devil had the opportunity to run many miles. After a number of residents had been wounded thus in the head by the devils, the people of Carti asked the boy with such supernatural powers to depart from their coasts, but nobody ever dared to suggest that spanking the young nele might help. So he was invited to Ailigandi to undergo treatment to "reduce his supernatural powers." Many persons in Ailigandi were de-lighted with the prospects of developing this nele into a great spiritual leader who would do honor to their town and give them special favor with the Great Spirit. And old Mu was anxious for her granddaughter, Ankela, to marry the young nele so that he might live always at her house.

In order to carry out the plan of developing this nele, the Town Council of Ailigandi voted to build him a treatment house on a

48

small island visible from my room, and there every day for a month Manauwikinye, the albino Indian deeply learned in the ways of mental and spiritual abnormalities, was chosen to heal him. No sticks were thrown while the nele was under treatment on the island, but as soon as he was brought to Ailigandi to test the cure, then the devils began throwing sticks again on dark nights.

One morning before breakfast a young man of the town came to us to have his forehead patched up, the skin of which had been split wide open by one of those diabolical sticks. All the neighbor women said in the presence of their husbands that the devils did it because he had been mean to his wife. And even a government school teacher, husband to the chief's daughter, declared that it was actually the work of devils because no man could have thrown so accurately.

Alcibiades and I went back to the man's house with him and I asked to see the weapon. The family had found it on the floor in the morning. It was a veritable war club, and I remarked that in shaping it some clever little devil had made use of an excellently sharp pocket knife.

After half a dozen sticks had been thrown with varying degrees of success, the Town Council decided that the treatment had not curbed the nele's extraordinary powers to a point where the devils would not follow him about angrily, and so they asked the young savant-seer to leave the island before the devils began committing still more serious crimes, since the devils recognized him as a holy man of God and knew his power to cast them out and to do them harm.

When he was gone, all the people declared that it was now conclusively proven that the devils had done the stick throwing because as soon as the young nele left Ailigandi with his supernatural powers, no more sticks were thrown into houses on pitch dark nights.

Wooden Gods: Big and Little

At Tikantiki, near Playon Grande, there were several red streaks of dye and a basket reed knot on one of the central supporting poles that held up the thatched roof of the Council Hall. The ubiquitous gang of naked brown boys explained to me that these symbols were placed there by a nele during the ceremony of dedication. Farther inside was an image of a man fifteen feet high.

"He is the chief protector of the village and is used in devil exorcising ceremonies." They told me his name.

For several years the dilapidated protector god of Ailigandi, Olokatwalilele, has leaned against one of the stores near the wharf. He is about eight feet high and has taken part in driving devils from Ailigandi. As a matter of fact, it was he who many years ago ousted myriads of evil spirits off Ailigandi and made it habitable. God's wife used to stand under the shelter of a thatched porch at the end of the hut belonging to one of the Apsoketis, but recently she disappeared. A medicine man said she went up the river to drive away the devils.

About once a year in some villages there is a ceremony at which all the available devils of the island are rounded up and shipped out, but they have the discouraging habit of always slipping back into the village again, so that by the time six months have passed they have accumulated once more in significant numbers—causing diseases by theft of the soul, and occasioning all sorts of trouble. They are especially active during the rainy season.

For these community ceremonies an enormous wooden image is made to direct the exorcising, and about forty colorful images of fence post size are prepared to follow his orders. This large directing idol and those of smaller size are in the forms of various sorts of people and may represent distinct personalities whose influence is thought to be great. Thus, when World War II was over, the spirit of General MacArthur was selected to command the wooden men who drove out those evil influences that had come into Ailigandi because of the war and especially because of a detachment of the United States Army Signal Corps stationed on the mainland nearby. Uchu MacArthur was twelve feet high and had a uniform of baby blue with pink pockets. He wore German field boots and boasted an Iron Cross decoration. The Indians captured MacArthur's spirit by a ceremony, so that the image would be functional. Eventually the log dried and split, and, therefore, the defunct image of MacArthur was sold as a curio before I first visited Ailigandi. However, I located a dozen or more of his weatherbeaten and discarded assistants piled up like cordwood among some weeds on the mainland.

Among them was one fence post image all painted up as a Marine sergeant with huge yellow chevrons on his blue sleeves. From his daring appearance I imagined that he certainly could have raised the devil in his prime.

I intended to get a sample of the household variety of uchu, but nobody wanted to sell me one because they needed them all against disease; so Sosipippi said he would make me one eight inches high. He whittled at it off and on for two days. Then at dusk when the spirits were flying about most actively he prayed a "good spirit" into it through the holes he had bored in the proper position for the eyes. When the spirit was captured, he pressed little broken pieces of glass into these holes. This not only provided bright eyes but also locked the good spirit in. He said that this was a protector god for my family and really a dual purpose idol because he had given it a tar coat, which would keep away the disease devils.

Of course, when any wooden idol weathers and splits, the spirit seeps out and escapes, making the image worthless. Accordingly, some of the best uchus in my collection I found discarded and floating in the sea.

The smallest uchus I have encountered are two inches long and are made of hot pepper wood. One of these may be tied to the strings at the head of the hammock, or a collection of half a dozen may be worn as a necklace by children to ward off childhood diseases.

Atilio once gave me an uchu that had contained the spirit of Uncle Sam, and of course I wanted the unique story of its making. Atilio's father, Ikwanikinappi, had carved it early in the nineteen hundreds, and so we went to Ikwanikinappi to ask the story. Ikwanikinappi had taken a trip far down into Colombia where he obtained some wood of the sacred "Surukwala" tree. This is a type of wood that the Indians say grew in the Cuna "Garden of Eden" at Yeye, on top of the sacred mountain, Tarcarcuna, before the Great Flood that destroyed the world.

His having been to Panama undoubtedly gave Ikwanikinappi something of the following revelation:

"Who owns that big canal?"

"Uncle Sam does."

"Well, who owns that big building?"

"Same Uncle Sam."

"Who owns that big battleship?"

"Uncle Sam."

"Say, that fellow, Uncle Sam, must be about the most powerful man on earth."

"He is!"

Later Ikwanikinappi must have seen an American Government poster somewhere.

"Who is that serious faced, long haired old man with the sika on his chin and an eagle for a pet?"

"Why, don't you know?" answered his friend. "That is Uncle Sam!"

During his long trip home on the coconut boat Ikwanikinappi must have mused to himself:

"If I could only capture the spirit of that fellow Uncle Sam in an uchu, I would have a world beating medicine against disease!"

So the uchu he made is a good copy of the Uncle Sam's features that we know so well, and he has an eagle sitting on top of his hat.

CUNA UCHUS ARE NOT CATHOLIC SAINTS

When the Spaniards first explored Central and South America, they found so much in the religion of the Amerinds that super-ficially resembled Catholicism that they said St. Thomas, after visiting India, had sailed on to America and had converted the aborigines to Christianity. The idea was enticing because the Incas were found to have priests, nuns, and confessions. They used incense. Among many tribes there were saviors sent from heaven, even white and bearded ones, who preached morals and religion, and then went away promising to return. There were prophets. The sign of the cross was employed to subdue devils that possessed persons and places. There were heavens and hells, last judgments and punishments.

Not having delved very deeply into the details of these striking resemblances, the Spaniards of early days believed the story about St. Thomas, and their descendants still tell the Cuna Indians, much against the protests of the latter, that their uchus (medicine dolls) are really Catholic Saints.

The problem of the Cuna uchus has been attacked several times. G. R. Fairchild, Jr., visited the Sassarti Islands in 1924 and gave out the "Old Scotch Doctor" story. According to this, the physi-cian of Paterson's ill fated Scotch Colony at Ailodon Mutlu near Akla refused to leave when the Spaniards expelled the colony in 1699, casting his lot with the Indians. He healed among the Cunas of the Sassarti Islands for many years, and his ability was so revered that after his death the Cunas made images of him and brought them to the hammocks of their sick that his spirit might restore them. Cuna uchus were alleged to be copies of the "Old Scotch Doctor." The Scotch Doctor story pops up from time to time in the public press, as does the version that Cuna uchus are the image of a Scotch missionary. The proof is the finding of male uchus in the garb of the late eighteenth century.

The Catholic Saint interpretation was examined by Nordenskiöld (Ethnographical Studies 10, Göteborg), who noted that uchus were both males and females. He observed that exceptional uchus bear the form of angels with wings, and one was actually inclosed in a box with a cross on the cover (undisputed Christian influence). He commented upon the importance of the kinds of wood out of which the uchus are made.

My first experience with the employment of uchus led me to question both explanations. At Mulatappu, I watched preparations for retrieving Diomisio's soul. Elsewhere I have described the animal uchus used along with anthropomorphic ones at this ceremony. I reasoned that if many of the uchus were really animals, both the theories described above would be refuted. Maybe the nakkruses that accompany them are not Christian crosses at all, as the Indians maintain.

At the outset I asked Chief Ikwaniktipippi, who knows most about the old Cuna culture. He and other Cuna authorities insisted that the nakkrus is not a Christian symbol, and that the Cunas employed it long before the time of Columbus, although they now use the Spanish name and although the Spaniards always try to make them believe that it is the Christian cross. They are resentful of this allegation. Old Indians say that the nakkrus indicates the four cardinal points of the compass. This symbol may represent the old Sungod who controlled the four winds of heaven, a very common idea among many tribes of Indians. Thus, the presence of the nakkrus, that has all the power of an uchu, does not necessarily represent Catholicism.

There are other kinds of spirits besides those of anthropomorphic and zoömorphic uchus that are sent into the earth to retrieve the lost soul of the sick one — for example, the cocoa bean, the hot pepper, the yellow akwa nusa (stone mouse) that represents menstrual lumps of the original Earthmother (Mu, Olokukurtilisop).

It is rather difficult to distinguish between the use of uchus with a special chant to restore the soul of the ill person and the use of preventive "medicine" to drive away evil spirits attempting to attack the patient. However, among Cuna medicines one finds skulls of various animals used to combat and rout their evil spirit counterparts that normally reside in the underworld. Thus, the horrible spirit animals that crowd around and not only injure but succeed in killing one third of Cuna women in labor may be driven away by skulls of those corresponding animals in the collection of the remote control obstetrician.

Again, in nature, predatory animals may destroy certain creatures harmful to man; so if you have the spirit of the predator on your side, he may be used to attack certain other spirit animals (their natural prey) in the underworld. Thus the spirit of Wekko, the Snake Catcher, may be employed to chase devils in the form of snakes.

Uchus on certain islands, such as Ailigandi, Tupile, and Narkana, ordinarily have the forms of men and women in various garbs, whereas animal shapes are not present. However, this seems to represent a recent trend away from conceiving of many devils in the forms of animals and a growing tendency to look upon them as anthropomorphic.

Because of the animals present among the uchus at the more primitive island of Mulatuppu, I decided to look for zoömorphic uchus on other primitive islands. I went to Koetup accompanied by Peter Miller (teacher at Escuela Nipakinya on Mulatuppu) with the intention of examining for distinct types the largest collection of household uchus of which I had ever heard. Two years before, I had been permitted to glance at this collection of Kantule Olomikelikinya, but not to examine it. During my glance I estimated that there were about three hundred images in this group taking up all the space on a table that ran half the length of the large house. These uchus were very old. But alas, when I asked the Chief Aurelio Nukeli, he told me that the Kantule had died and that all his uchus had been buried with him.

However, the Chief of Koetup was very obliging and permitted me to examine all the large balsa wood uchus of the appeasement ceremony for driving devils off the island. These are kept from year to year on Koetup. (On most of the islands they are disposed of and new ones made for each exorcising.) The exorcising idols of Koetup were kept on a second story platform at one end of the Council Hall. The chief had a naked boy scramble up a pole to the platform and get out all the animal forms to show me. However, he feared the reaction of the curious inhabitants who began milling about asking questions, and so he would not allow me to take the uchus down to photograph them. He compromised by permitting me to take a slow exposure of them arranged on the platform.

The Chief identified all of the animals for me. They included three sulepak (eagles), two sulup (type of hawk), several no (hawks), several uisi (armadillos), a taim (alligator), a wekko (snake catcher), several achus (wild cats or jaguars), and an iskin (biting lizard larger than an iguana).

After the visit to Koetup we paddled to Tuwala where I told Supreme Chief Yapillikinya, of five years' acquaintance, that I wanted to find out if once there were animal forms among their uchus. At first Yapillikinya was reticent about discussing the matter because he thought I wanted to buy his collection of household uchus. When assured that I only desired to talk about them, he coöperated very well.

Saikla Tummat Yapillikinya said that the styles in household uchus had changed a great deal during his lifetime, and that formerly many of them had the shapes of birds and animals. Before the wooden ones, he said they had birds and animals of baked clay. Then he brought out his collection of well carved uchus made of special woods and neatly painted. They appeared to be people in all walks of life, especially prominent being sailors, soldiers, and policemen. He took me to the Council Hall where he showed me the town collection of large uchus for the community appeasement ceremony. The animals Yapillikinya identified as a sukku (sawfish), tapu (fish with inset teeth), ukka naipe (earth snake), taim (alligator), and the red alligator (presumably a spirit animal).

At Mulatuppu I asked an old medicine man about the kinds of animals formerly among the household uchus of his island. He replied that they included misi (housecat), taim (alligator), sapur achu (mountain cat), naipe (snake), and iwi (a horrible, grunting spirit creature in the form of an elephant that inhabits swamps and ponds).

Some uchus represent Indians, both men and women. As to the presence of persons of authority among the uchus such as policemen, soldiers, and other "fighting men" — they are chosen because of their aggressiveness and power. Among the household uchus the kind of wood from which they are made is important, as others have pointed out, especially prized being woods that withstood the cataclysmic times which the Cunas believe to have followed the Creation.

In my collection a household uchu in the form of Uncle Sam

is made of Surukwala wood that grew in the Cuna "Garden of
Eden" on Mount Tarcarcuna before the Great Flood. At Ailigandi there was a large uchu bearing the form of General Douglas
MacArthur, whose spirit had been captured and confined in it.
He was the leader of a band of uchus made to drive off the island
the evil spirit influences of World War II. These I have described
already. At Koetup there is the copy of the figurehead of a boat
called Mu Sekop (Grandmother Jacob) and she is the most powerful uchu on that island. At Mulatuppu the island protector is a
Kaopi (hot pepper man), who wears a tight fitting hat under
which he keeps hot pepper incense. "When he goes underground
to chase devils" said Carlos, "he runs right into their midst and
removes his hat. The smoke screen rolls out in all directions and
chokes the devils." At Ailigandi it is Olokatwalilele who protects
the island. It appears that these protectors are not Catholic Patron
Saints although Cuna men who have worked in Panama may even
call the island protectors "Nuestros Santos" in describing them to
foreigners.

The idea of retrieving the stolen spirit is a very old and a very
general one. It extends from South America to Alaska. It is undoubtedly pre-Columbian and bears no relationship to Christianity. As a matter of fact, if the image of a Catholic Saint is placed
in the household box with uchus, as sometimes happens, the Cunas
say that it creates confusion among them so that they cannot do
their work well. The Saint and Angel forms figured and described
by Nordenskiöld turn out to be so rare that, although a few Indians remember having seen one or two, I have never come upon
one.

My next act was to go to Mammituppu, a very primitive island
that seldom receives visitors. I gained entrance because the uncle
of my friend, Atilio Rivera (a teacher at Escuela Colman, Ailigandi), is Nele Yorki, the famous chanter of Mammituppu. It was
Nele's collection of uchus that I wanted to inspect. When we got
there Nele's brother was away chanting on another island and
had most of Nele's uchus with him. However, Nele said he not
only had wooden uchus of animal form, but also ones of baked
clay. I photographed three powerful armadillo uchus owned by
Nele's brother, which he kept along with his little wooden men.

How about the Scotch Doctor story? I inquired of the old men
on Mulatuppu (Sassarti Islands), all of whom were living there
at the time of Fairchild's visit. They never heard of the Scotch

Doctor, nor did their boxes show anything that could have been taken for the Scotch Doctor, save an occasional late eighteenth century costume, just as there were some uchus in the nineteenth century clothes, and some reflecting the twentieth century.

Because the people of the San Blas Islands originally came from the mountains, we should investigate the types of uchus in mountain towns that have had practically no contact with white men. It is also the old neles of the mountains to whom the young men of the coast have always gone to study and then returned to the coast to practice on their own islands.

I asked a mountain Indian newly come from Narkanti Tolla, who related that they had uchukana and suar mimmikana in the forms of animals in his town. Then I went back to Chief Ikwaniktipippi who said that the neles of Walla still teach about and use the animal form uchus. The mountain town of Walla is possibly the oldest Cuna town in existence.

Until recently Sokopti was considered the oldest mountain town, but today it is abandoned. Its inhabitants settled Koetup (possibly the Sassarti Island Fairchild visited). The neles of Tuwala (Sassarti Islands) studied in Sokopti. We have already discussed the animal uchus found in those two towns.

The Nele of Mammituppu (a population recently come from the mountains) studied at Walla and, as would be expected, animals are present among the uchus of Mammituppu. Chief Ikwaniktipippi says that about one hundred years ago at Okupsene (Playon Chico) there was a nele who introduced this form of service with animal uchus in the collection.

It all boils down to the fact that in time of need the Cuna will call on "every powerful spirit" he can think of to help "chase the devils of disease," or drive devils from his island. In former days the animal world impressed the Cunas even more than today, with mounting influence from Panama and the whole civilized world. Hence it is not surprising that animal forms are dropping out of household uchu collections today.

Taking all the above described evidence into consideration, I am forced to conclude that Cuna uchus are not Catholic Saints.

My Idol

A strange commotion was going on in a particularly large hut on the Island of Mulatuppu. Claudio and I noticed this as we made our rounds after school one day to visit the sick. Inside this hut everybody was working feverishly and everybody was very sad.

At the entrance of the hut sat our friend Ignacio, the Chanter against Sadness. He was chopping an idol from a fresh, white balsa log that glistened with watery juice where he had just stripped off the smooth, gray bark.

Over there to the left two men were shaping a pile of sticks and green, unopened palm fronds into crude nakkruses by tying on crossbars or by slashing the upright stems and thrusting crossbars through them.

At the back of the hut were three women with their bright molas, circular brass earplates, and huge, golden noserings. One was Ignacio's wife. They sat on stools diligently washing the family idols one after another in a medicine canoe half full of water, into which were cut pieces of magic leaves that gave out a pleasant aromatic odor.

By means of their finger nails the women were scratching spiderwebs, insect pupa cases, and dust out of the crevices on the idols. They were sloshing medicine water over each image and then inspecting it closely. After carefully washing and drying the idols with a cloth, the women painted them by dipping an index finger into a small calabash containing red seed-paint and then smearing it in splotches on the cheeks, streaking a noseline down the middle of the face for beauty's sake and making a nakkrus with it on the belly.

Somebody was thrashing about violently in a hammock suspended in the shadows at one side of the hut. It was Diomisio in a high state of delirium. Three women were holding him by his arms and legs as best they could, trying with little success to make him stay in the hammock.

Diomisio's emaciated old mother was bending over him weeping loudly and wildly, as she sang an improvised death chant to her boy.

> Soon it will all be over
> And you will feel no more pain.
> You will find rest from your troubles
> In Heaven.
> Yes, you have had a hard life, my boy.
> Hear me, my son, as I sing
> This final death chant to you!
>
> Yes, you have had two wives.
> The first was a good woman,

But alas, she has gone
To Heaven in childbirth before you.
Yes, she was a good woman
And she loved you dearly.

But the wife you now have
Has treated you horribly.
She has made your life
Very difficult. She does not
Love you at all.
She has never loved you.
Now you are dying and where is she?
She is at home with her relatives.
She will not care for you. She will not
Even sing you a death chant.
She does not want to see you
Or be near you
When you are closing your eyes forever!

But I am singing to you.
In Heaven you will remember
And will be comforted by the song
Of your loving mother.

Rows of small nakkruses were stuck in the sand floor under the hammock. An incense pot was among them. A two-inch uchu mimmi of hot pepper wood was tied to the hammock strings. About the hammock on three sides stood an army of huge balsa idols, four and five feet high. Some were armed with bows and spears. Between them were numerous "weapons" for fighting devils: spiny sticks and tall nakkruses massed in solid phalanx to guard the hammock.

We knew that Diomisio was a chronic carrier of malaria, but we did not know that he was sick. Nobody had come for medicine, his family being afraid of foreign influence. But Diomisio was deathly sick. He had been unconscious for three days, delirious and violent at times. Pasitto, the great Disease Chanter, had been called to chant therapeutically against the deadly weleket. He had come and was so insulted at the lack of preparations that he went away in disgust. He told the family to what underground city of the devils the stolen soul had been taken, but stated emphatically that he would not even chant to bring back the young man's spirit until after the much neglected family idols had been washed in his special medicine bath; a dozen new balsa log idols had been carved and hundreds of nakkruses had been made because this was a "poni tummati" (disease unto death), and the patient was in danger of dying even if the medicine chant was sung.

We expressed our deep sympathy and our desire to help, but I was an American and Claudio had been trained abroad, and foreign influence is always bad for a primitive ceremony! As we left to go home and passed the men working frantically at the open end of the hut, Ignacio arose with determination. He put into my hands a knife and a fresh balsa log upon which he had started to carve a face.

"Pe sobe!" (you make it) he cried as he grabbed his machete and another balsa to start a new idol.

I hesitated. But no. No, I could not tell them that I did not believe in all this foolishness! Since my Cuna vocabulary was limited, they could only deduce from my words that I was unsympathetic, which was certainly not the case. All their Indian friends and relatives were helping out in the dire emergency, and why should not Kilupippi, their American friend, help too? So because I could not make them understand without injuring them, and because I wanted to demonstrate my willingness to assist them in any way I could, I sank Ignacio's knife blade into the balsa and worked along with the rest. At one point the knife slipped and the idol's face eagerly drank in several drops of blood from my finger. In trying to wipe it off, I made the sacrifice appear even worse than it was. When my idol was finished, the family approved and it was taken to the company of its relatives by the hammock to do what it could to save the life of Diomisio.

When Pasitto arrived to chant against the devils who had stolen Diomisio's soul, he brought with him all his sacred stones and a huge retinue of personal idols in human form, taller than all the rest. He brought large, brightly-painted wooden birds and animals, idol weapons with sticky sap or poisonous juice running out of them, nakkruses, and spiny branches. Many of these big idols had been made especially for him by friends of his family when he had been "ordained." These augmented the already overpowering population of wooden characters that swarmed about to do the chanter's bidding.

All night Pasitto chanted the powerful exorcising verses that had come down by word of mouth for hundreds of years, calling upon the spirit of each stick and stone to help, and when Claudio and I visited him the next day the patient lay quiet and exhausted in his hammock with his eyes open. The faces of the family shone with relief and great faith in the Cuna way of life. It was costly — sixty hard-earned coconuts for each chant — but no matter, the renowned chanter had triumphed once more. The rocks and trees had obeyed him well.

They had wrestled with powerful demons many levels beneath the earth and with ones from Nia Yar Oloekinet in the mountains. They had snatched Diomisio's spirit from those terrible, thieving devils, and they had brought it back to him. He was lying clothed and in his right mind.

"How about some guanatol?" asked Claudio.

"Sure thing!" feebly replied Diomisio, who had worked a stretch in Panama, knew a few words of Yankee slang, and believed in American medical miracles as much as in the Cuna way of life.

We gave him enough tablets to last several weeks. Later, Pasitto confined him to his hut, ordering that he must take ceremonial baths daily for a month in order to strengthen himself against possible return visits by the devils.

As we departed I scanned the array of images by Diomisio's hammock and wondered what my idol could tell me about the underworld. I would recognize it by the blood stain on one cheek. I searched in vain because, alas, my idol was not in the final line-up. The Disease Chanter probably heard that Kilupippi had made it, and anticipating heresy and unbelief in his wooden army, he had summarily discharged the only foreign legionnaire among them.

SKY DRAGON

When somebody notices a bite being taken out of the moon, the word spreads like wild fire. He screams, "The Sky Dragon is eating the moon!" and all the Indians rush into their houses.

In mortal fear they remain indoors, under heavy penalty from the town council if they disobey. Even the missionaries are forced to stay indoors. They are all afraid that the Sky Dragon may succeed; and if he does, the world will come to an end.

Albinistic moon-children, who sin less than other people and hence are on better terms with Tiolele, are sent out with bows and arrows to shoot the Sky Dragon and to shout prayers to the Great Spirit on behalf of the villagers that they may not be destroyed by this horrible phenomenon of eclipse.

If you say to an Indian, "Why, you are crazy! Can't you see
that the wooden arrows never reach the Sky Dragon but drop into
the ocean two dozen yards off shore?" he will simply reply, "You
are the one who is crazy. It is not the arrow that goes to the sky,
but the soul [purpa] of the arrow. It flies straight to the moon
and pierces the Sky Dragon. You Waka [foreigners] are too un-
spiritual to realize this. And we have the proof that it is so because the Sky Dragon is always killed. It never has eaten up the
sun or moon completely, and as a consequence the world has never
come to an end at the time of eclipse."

Blowing Away the Storm

While dressing early one morning at Mulatuppu, I peered out
and saw Tiapilikinya, the famous medicine man, with a smouldering incense pot before him on the ground. Obviously he was up to
something. He was standing very still and erect, and he was blowing toward the sea through a hollow reed.

"What are you doing?" asked Claudio.

"Don't you see those black clouds over there? A hurricane is
coming, and so that it will not strike our island, I am blowing it
out to sea!"

Heaven Bound Canoe

At the time of death, the Cuna Indians tell me, the souls of
the various parts of the body seep out and unite to form one soul
that may stay for some time near the corpse. Indeed, it may linger
several days in the grave because it is tired from its last illness and
the death struggle. It may also be reluctant to depart from the
earth.

When it has rested, it collects the spirits of the many votives that
were placed in the grave, packs them into the ulu ikko or votive
canoe already afloat in the nearby river. It unties the mooring
string and paddles up the river, making its way eastward toward
the Rising Sun. After a number of days the spirit in its votive
canoe reaches the summit of the sacred mountain, Tarcarcuna, "at
the end of the earth." Then bravely paddling onward, it takes off
into the air and ascends higher and higher with steady strokes.

As the soul progresses it glances back from time to time and
notices that the earth is becoming smaller and smaller. The last
that it observes clearly is the view of friends and relatives who are

grieving. Smaller and smaller the world becomes until in a final glance over its shoulder the soul sees the "tiny earth rocking back and forth like a coconut husk upon the ocean waves." The soul now forgets its reluctance to leave the world and presses on with but the one thought of reaching Heaven. At length it moors its bark at "Pap Kastipir," the "wharf of Heaven."

But the difficulties have only begun. Stepping out of its canoe and going forward on foot, the spirit soon comes to a fork in the road. There it must choose the right or the left. To the left is the Road of Flowers and to the right, the Road of Thorns.

The left road is the one taken by the evil Piler, "who behaved wickedly toward his sister, his mother and his aunt" (presumably sex offenses). Because of his wickedness, the flowers disappeared and he soon found himself in the midst of thorn bushes that tore his flesh. Then he came to mud and swamps in which he floundered and became exhausted. After that he had to go through fire that burnt him, the sugar cane mill that crushed him, and past the eagles that rent his body with beak and talons.

But this was not all. After the eagles, Piler stumbled through the horrible land of the Snakes, where he was frightened and poisoned by serpent bites at every step. The land of the Alligators injured him further, then the land of Wild Beasts through which he had to fight fearful battles with horrible creatures that crippled him badly. Then because he mistreated the Iet woman who officiates at the hair cutting ceremony of the girls, he was cut in two by an enormous pair of shears. At last he came to the gate of Heaven only to learn that he must suffer many more years of torture before being allowed to enter the City of God.

Those who have been wicked on earth always choose the Path of Piler in the land above. The good always choose the Thorny Road to the right that leads directly to the City of Heaven. If the person has pretended to have learned the magic art of hypnotizing snakes, alligators, and other savage creatures, he must demonstrate it. He will suffer many times if he has lied and really cannot practice the art correctly.

Sitting with the records near the City of Heaven is the Great Judge, Olowikpalele, who tries the soul, and gives it free entry to Heaven if blameless or condemns it to delays, anxieties, or increasing punishments according to the degree of sins the person committed in the flesh.

One tantalizing punishment, the Indians told me, is to be allowed to disembark at the Pier of Heaven but be forced to remain on the pier for ten, twenty, or thirty years.

In the City of Heaven one stops to see his father and his relatives. He delivers special messages given to him while lying in the death hammock and distributes the gifts, especially of food and cloth, sent by relatives on earth to those already in Heaven. After resting from his long journey he goes to visit Tiolele (the Great Father). Probably at one time they would have said "Ipelele" (the Sungod.)

The soul observes Heaven to be the most beautiful city that can be imagined. There it lives in a wonderful house, takes delightful excursions in the Sunboat, and finds pleasures forevermore.

HEAVEN

"Would you be interested in what the Indian believes about Heaven?" asked my good friend, Saikla Ikwaniktipippi, of Ailigandi.

"Indeed, I would be!"

Nothing could have pleased me more than to learn about the Cuna religious beliefs, since most of the Indians who knew them thoroughly had been reticent to talk to me about them.

To hear of them at the feet of Chief Ikwaniktipippi was double good fortune because he, of all the Cuna tribe, knows their traditions best. Indeed, he studied kantule (chanting for the sacred feast of the debutante) during seven years and massar (chanting for the dead) for many years longer. He learned from the ancient Supreme Chief Colman and the highly famous Supreme Chief Nele Kantule.

"It would be difficult to explain to you about Heaven directly," continued the Chief; "so I shall draw you a picture. I shall draw it as my teachers taught me." I quickly provided paper, pencils, and colored crayons, and the Saikla set to work. Off and on for two weeks he bent over the task and I went to his cane-and-thatch house a number of times to observe the progress.

The astonishing allegory that resulted is reproduced among our illustrations. For a man who can neither read nor write,* Ikwaniktipippi shows an amazing native skill with pencils. His drawing

*Ikwaniktipippi's son, Jose, taught him how to draw his name for signing documents.

exhibits design, balance, proportion, action, and an excellent choice of colors. But more remarkable than all these artistic qualities is its sense of foreshortening, its conception of distance!

I wondered why the figures of animals and men at the top of the page are huge and detailed but then gradually decrease in size on down to tiny symbols at the bottom, save for the picture of the Great Judge who sits with the records. He is represented as being exceptionally large because of his great importance.

As a matter of fact, I studied this point for some time before it dawned upon me that Ikwaniktipippi's concept was correct. He was looking up to Heaven as he drew, and to view it his picture should be held horizontally above and in front of one's head, with the upper portion nearest one's eyes. Then, and then only, do the figures appear in perfect perspective commensurate with their distance.

Of course, I wanted an analysis of "Heaven," and the artist proudly supplied the following information: "Heaven is circular with beautiful zig-zag walls. The streets are directed toward the cardinal points of the compass."

At the top of the picture we find Manikwiskapilele and Olopipiailele, two eagles (sulepak) who examine at the gatehouse those persons desiring to enter Heaven. The examiners were once people who sinned and were punished, after which they were assigned this duty in Heaven.

The guard of the gate (Ikar opantur saikla) stands with a spear in his hand and a terrible dragon (achu) by his side to help him. "Even a Kantule Chanter for the Inna ceremony cannot get past this guard," the Saikla said, "unless he has dedicated his life to noble purposes." A good bird (sikwi nueti) sits at the right hand gate that is guarded by a second dragon (achu). A group of good Indians, who are not to be punished, blow upon their reed flutes with joy as they disembark from their canoes at Pap Kastipir (the Pier of Heaven) and enter the City of God, ready to parade triumphantly up its beautiful streets. A third dragon (achu) guards the left hand gate, where a gatehouse is also depicted.

At the upper left of the picture are six celestial policemen, with their cane symbols of office and a horrible dragon named Devil Nopenta, who see that a punishment is carried out. Here a young man is being cut up with gigantic scissors because, after starting to carry water for a girl's puberty ceremony, he quit the job and ran away.

Two men, at the lower left, are being punished for murder by being roasted in caldrons over the fire. Another man is being crushed in a sugar cane press for some unstated crime. Three who had intercourse with strange women during their pregnancy are condemned to be placed on top of trees from which they can never descend. As shown from left to right these will be placed on top of an Ule tree, a Kwipa tree, and an Urtak tree, respectively.

Below center is Olowikalele, the Great Judge. He sits in his seat of judgment with the personal reports at hand and has nak-krus symbols on his clothing. Flowers grow in profusion about him. Lights (presumably electric light bulbs!) hang from the ceiling.

At the lower right one sees a detention house. There several Indians, sitting on chairs, await the trial of their particularly difficult cases. Ikwaniktipippi said that their cases come under the classification of "Trees"; that is: either they (1) met an unnatural death by a tree falling upon them, so that it is difficult to say what the final score would have been had they continued to live and later to have died a natural death, or (2) they stole things off trees — such as coconuts, mangoes, calabashes, bananas, etc.

About the throne of the Great Spirit are lawns filled with beautiful flowers. Ikwaniktipippi uses for God the term Tiolele (the one above), but the situation suggests the Sungod.

Proceeding clockwise about his residence one sees houses for various categories of talented people, each bearing an appropriate identifying flag. These are (1) Inna Ceremony Chanters (flute and rattle), (2) medicine men (neles), (3) Chanters who know the hot pepper chant (kapur ikar), (4) men who know about the bird that eats snakes, (5) men who know the nakkrus chant, (6) men who know the cocoa bean chant (sia ikar), (7) women who sew well, (8) women who are good hammock makers, (9) diviners of the Inna Feast (diviners hat), (10) men who know about nature and living things, while (11) and (12) are reserved for men who know "other things."

The centrally located Tiolele sits on his elaborately decorated throne. Ikwaniktipippi said that the nakkrus symbols on his clothing and about him are not Christian symbols at all, but were used by the Cuna Indians long before the coming of Columbus; and, indeed, as we have said, the early Spanish explorers found so much among the Indian religions suggestive of Christianity that they declared that St. Thomas had visited Central and South America.

Tiolele has two houses filled with "protection." The one on the left is an arsenal stocked with bows and arrows. That on the right contains many dragons (jaguars, or savage dogs).

Ikwaniktipippi's picture of Heaven simply whetted my desire to learn more. I must have two more pictures to illustrate the Cuna afterlife! I knew that old neles described a "Sunboat" in which the redeemed take pleasure excursions and I knew that the soul may hover in the grave with the body for several days but that eventually it must set out in a canoe for a long and perilous trip to the sun.

Sunboat

I bargained with the artist and he promised. Almost a year went by with no results because Ikwaniktipippi had become deeply involved in politics, ceremonies, chants, and money making. At last, under the pressure of gifts, money, and the urgings of his son José, he functioned once more and produced the "Sunboat," on the wrong side of the same piece of drawing card that I had mailed to him the year before. Most of it was drawn while he was at Karti chanting ceremonially about the Cuna traditions.

Dominating the Sunboat scene is Olowaipippilele, who resides in the sun and is depicted in all his majestic splendor. He wears a headdress of feathers. To his left, bearing epaulettes and nakkrus badges, is Ikwaokinyapippilele, the archer, who with his keen shafts has just slain the devils of disease that are seen floundering in the water about the Sunboat. To his right, one may observe Putur, the construction engineer, who is about to "make something" such as houses or other buildings in Heaven.

In full view of the Sunboat are beautiful rivers, trees, and flowers. A number of stars are anchored to mountains at the periphery of the large circle, and Ikwaniktipippi identified number one as Sunip, number two as Oler, number three as Wikaler. "Wikaler," said he, "is the Nukwelokinaita or mother of the stars; number four is Olopurkaliler which represents a great constellation."

The occupants of the Sunboat are as follows: Kanir Ikwatuinkipe (the rooster) is a lookout. He not only peers ahead for trouble, but he also wakes up the passengers in the morning. Then there is Kiwikinya who is equipped with a long pole. His duty is to probe the water for dangerous coral reefs. Ikwapiekinya is the pilot. In front of the smoke stack is Olosookikilli, wife of the engineer Olosookikinya, who Ikwaniktipippi said on several occasions was down in the engine room. But by the time the picture was finished, he had come up on deck and may be seen leaning against the smokestack in a very tired fashion.

Up in the air are a sloth named Olopanalir, the medicine man of the outfit, and an iguana called Olopiskakwa, who is second in command and who "never smiles." Surprisingly enough, the Captain of the Sunboat turns out to be Nia Tummati (the Big Devil).

Offside to the right is "No nana," the toad mother. Her name is Kwelopunyai and she is the wife of Olowaipippilele, the Great Spirit. Offside to the left is Olopaitikinya (a Sulu monkey), who is really the son of Kwelopunyai by another husband.

Not being able to get any farther with Ikwaniktipippi in depicting the adventurous journey of the soul from the grave to the Sun, I tried Mastapeppi, a very old resident of Mulatuppu. His contribution was disappointing. He produced a Sunboat which is merely a modern American Battleship (such as he had seen in the Panama Canal) save that the big guns are replaced by searchlights.

JOURNEY OF THE SOUL

Nine months after producing the Sunboat, Ikwaniktipippi was again prevailed upon to undertake a picture of the travels of the soul in its ulu ikko or spirit boat.

Some items of the picture show celestial details already mentioned above, but because they are part of Ikwaniktipippi's explanation of his picture, I shall repeat them here.

The picture story starts off at the lower right corner with a cemetery scene having buildings (civilized style, with flags flying) instead of the thatched huts of the Cuna graveyard. At the wharf in the nearby river, a coconut boat, rather than a canoe, is moored, waiting for the spirit of the deceased one.

Apparently nothing of importance happens in the vast stretches of upper air between the sacred mountain, Tarcarcuna, and the Pier of Heaven, and for that reason Ikwaniktipippi does not separate the graveyard scene from Pap Kastipir. The City of God is hidden from Pap Kastipir by mountains and clouds.

Once arrived in the Upper World, the spirit, Dante-like, passes through the kingdom of animals where it is accosted by a bird named Kaymattar that says: "Once I, too, was a human being, but because of my wickedness on earth, I became a useless bird. I am eating worms and raw fish now!"

In the snake world a man who thought he was walking along the flowery road, is suddenly surrounded by thorns, and because he has the heart of a snake, he is punished by being bitten by a snake. In the alligator world a man is being chewed up because he has been bad.

Then come a deep gulley and the famous fork in the road already described. The flowery branch road that bad people always choose (to the left) is soon choked with thistles, and here one finds purgatorial punishments for sex offenses. On this road hangs an enormous pair of shears (molsikke). Here a man is being punished by the big shears for (1) "using little girls as though they were women," (2) sexually insulting the Iet woman who cuts the girl's hair ceremonially, (3) attacking the wives of the Kantule chanter of the Inna Feast, (4) abusing the women who gather reeds for the feasts and those who tie the gourd rattles for the Inna Feast. For these offenses the giant shears cut men up. Then the soul comes to the land of the eagle, where it may be torn to shreds. After this the soul sees a crowd of pretty girls under an immense, magic urtukku tree. With lascivious desire the wicked man will make a rush to seize one of the girls only to have the huge arms of the tree, "that acts like a human being," grab him and put him on its topmost branches. From there he falls down and is injured so severely that he does not think about the girls any more. Then comes the sugar cane mill, after which those insatiable men who attacked "old ladies and grandmothers" fall head first into an enormous hole in the ground.

Very wicked persons are then cast into Soosaikla, the Lake of Fire,* where they flounder for years and sometimes for eternity. The average person will get past this horrible place safely. After this there is a grove of saptur trees, used by the Indians for painting the skin of babies and girls ceremonially. A strong wind passes through these trees, and the fruits (filled with indelible, black juice) fall on the passersby.

At last, the wandering soul reaches Pap Yapi, the Gate of the City of Heaven (the place where the keys are kept), but the gate

*Soosaikla is kindled by Olosokikili, Manisokikili, and Ikwanai. The only one who can extinguish it is Olosokintili.

is locked. Here Ikwaniktipippi has depicted two tables at which
stand two great servants of God and the Devil. Their names are
Paliwittur and Niawenyo,* respectively. Both have a copy of the
personal records of conduct.

Between them stands the soul of a man who wants to enter
Patto Tiolele Neka, the City of Heaven. A stick in the man's
hands indicates that his soul is bad and will not be allowed to
enter. "He has fought, and was mean." Two sympathetic "mothers of men" have come to see how the trial will turn out. The
servant of God is hoping that the man's record will be good; the
servant of the Devil hopes that he can get him. If his record turns
out badly, the servant of the Devil will laugh at him mercilessly.
If he is saved, the servant of God will rejoice. Many souls are
waiting there to be judged and punished as there are two more
punishments inside the gate of the City of Heaven.

Two angels, actually the servants of God and the Devil whom
we met at the gate, are represented again, preaching a sermon to
the many souls newly arrived. "You are alone, and nobody will
help you. You individually will receive the consequences of your
deeds. You have come alone to this Upper World, and alone you
shall go to death and your punishments! For those who are good
it is good in Heaven, but it is bad for those who do not walk
straight. So treat each other honestly and do not be selfish. Think
of others, and treat your neighbor as a friend. The world is full
of bad men, but you must be good! This is the way to God's
Heaven, the Heaven of rest."

Then the servants await anxiously to find out where the soul
of the man will go.

RESURRECTION

When you put clothes on primitives, they look civilized. The
casual traveler will think that they are, but hats and shoes may be
donned in a minute whereas it takes generations to change folkways, beliefs, and superstitions. This fact was impressed upon me
when I made a life mask of Claudio.

Claudio the elder, who as a member of the Panamanian Police
was killed in 1920 near his home town of Narkana because of his
advocacy of advancing civilization among the Cuna people by

---

*Paliwittur means "one that protects." Niawenyo (one who teaches to steal) is also
called Nianopenta (one who causes jealousy) and Niatiopili (one who confuses).

force, had become something of a hero—a martyr to Cuna progress—because the tribe is now becoming civilized. In fact Claudio the elder is revered almost as a Saint by the young Catholic Indians of Narkana.

Since I believe that heroes are highly worthwhile from the standpoint of inspiration, ideals, and cultural cohesion, I agreed to make a terra cotta head of Claudio the elder, to be placed on a proposed cement memorial in Narkana, sponsored by the Catholic youth of that town.

Claudio, the native missionary, was born after Claudio the elder had been killed, and his mother named him for her lost, elder son. Curiously enough, the two Claudios looked much alike. Indeed, the wife of the elder Claudio thought her son had returned from the grave when she saw the younger Claudio after a number of years of absence at Bacone in Oklahoma. So, in order to have a model for the terra cotta memorial head, I decided to take a face mask of Claudio the younger.

Accordingly, I had him stretched out one day on a cot in his house at Mulatuppu. I was applying plaster of Paris to his previously greased face, and Claudio was breathing through two paper tubes. Because plaster does not harden well in the San Blas climate, I had to fan it for half an hour.

In primitive civilizations, there are pairs of eyes everywhere, and suddenly a pair looked in at an open door. Then a pair appeared at the other door. Then another pair, and another, and another. Finally, I counted twenty pairs at each door. But all these pairs of eyes have feet and tongues, and so soon the story had spread all over town.

Seeing what was going on they could interpret it in only one way: "Claudio, the missionary, has died! Claudio has died! And the great nele, Kilupippi, is performing magic on him to try to bring him back to life."

The pairs of eyes jammed the doorways and the tongues murmured and the feet stood still, and the forty witnesses remained in suspense. They strained their necks as I ceased fanning and began to slowly lift off the mask. A shout of triumph came from the doorways when a moment later Claudio sat up and opened his eyes.

Swift feet quickly carried the news all over town: "Claudio died this morning, but Kilupippi resurrected him, and now he is all right again."

WORSHIP OF ISHTAR

Man's first religion seems to have developed as an effort to explain the awe-inspiring miracles of the universe and especially those most bewildering riddles of life, namely: (1) sex-power, (2) death and (3) birth. Of these the miracle of *birth* was most important.

Apparently very early came the idea of an enormous, sexually turgid, ever-existent male Creatorgod, who produced the World-woman to be his wife, by a method now often considered as a perversion.

The Worldwoman or Earthmother in a very human fashion became the creator of all living things including plants, animals, man, and sometimes inanimate entities such as stars. The marvel of the woman in giving life was an old concept already in cave days because many terra cotta votives of pregnant women have been found in habitation caves. Fertility was due to the possession by a female of a Tree of Birth, sometimes spoken of as a sprout, which was the gift of Ishtar the Earthmother or of Anu the Creatorgod. When the secret of the male role in fertilization was unlocked, the original Creator of the Worldwoman was known as the begetter of the Earthmother's children. Great stone replicas of the Creator's phallos are still worshipped in India and many such statues are present in Central America.

The Earthmother later had a son who became the New Sun of Spring and replaced the older Sungod Shamash. In some of the American Indian religions as well as in Babylon the New Sun of Spring came into ascendancy. For example, the Sungod was all important among the Incas, Mayas, and Aztecs.

Religious emphasis on the sacred Earthmother as a source of fertility and developmental power, the great prototype pattern of giving birth, the guardian during life and the performer of resurrection after death remains among some peoples including the Cuna Indians of Panama.

The Earthmother has been worshipped under many names such as Ishtar, Astarte, Ashteroth, Aphrodite, Venus, Mu, the Snake Goddess, etc. For the sake of comparison let us briefly summarize the "Babylonian Epic of Gilgamish."

About 2,500 B.C. a number of already very ancient sagas of Sumeria and Akkadia were combined in a great epic poem and attached to the name of historical Gilgamish, King of Uruk in

Southern Babylonia. This poem became the chief literary production of the Babylonian religion, which had its emphasis on sex-love and sensuous Ishtar the Earthmother who bore and guards mankind. The "Garden of Ishtar" story in the Gilgamish epic is a masterpiece of sex-symbolism.

Gilgamish, the strong-bodied King of Uruk, oppresses the builders of his city wall until the gods hear their cry. Anu, the great God of Heaven, calls on Aruru the Earthmother to create a strong man to overcome Gilgamish.

Accordingly, Aruru the Earthmother creates the wild Engidu, half man, half bull, who is enticed by female nudity and sex from his grazing with the wild cattle, tamed and educated by a voluptuous young temple harlot of Ishtar the Earthmother. Gilgamish fights Engidu indecisively over the sex-favors of Ishtar the Earthmother, and the antagonists become good friends.

Engidu and Gilgamish set out together for the "Garden of Ishtar the Earthmother" on Mount Lebanon with its giant cedars and its rivers. They start to fell the Sacred Cedars and are attacked by the monster Khumbaba that guards the "Tree of Life." When Engidu touches the "door" among the Forests of the Garden, he becomes faint but, with the help of Shamash the Sungod, the heroes slay Khumbaba.

In the Garden Ishtar the Earthmother (Eve of the Bible) tries to get Gilgamish to marry her. He refuses because of her previous promiscuity; whereupon Ishtar becomes angry and calls on Anu the Great God of Heaven to create the Bull of Heaven to kill Gilgamish and Engidu. Gilgamish and Engidu return to Uruk. The Bull of Heaven is created, but the two heroes proceed to butcher the Bull of Heaven, and Gilgamish throws the "leg" of the Bull into the face of Ishtar. Her temple harlots mourn over the "leg."

Engidu takes sick; he says his female companions have made him weak, and he speaks in his fevered dreams to the "gate" in the palisade of the Cedar Forest on the Mountain of Ishtar the Earthmother. He curses the temple harlot who tamed him. Engidu dies, and there are strong suggestions that it is from venereal disease.

Gilgamish in great mourning for his friend goes to Mashu the Mount of Death at the earth's end. He passes through the mountain and comes out at the Sea of Heaven. There Siduri (another manifestation of Ishtar the Earthmother), cupbearer of the gods,

shuts her door and locks it. Later she directs Gilgamish to Ur-
Shanapi, captain to Utnapishtim (Noah of the Bible), who ferries
him across the sea to his master, the one who with his wife "has
found Life."

Utnapishtim tells of the "Great Flood" and how he saved his
family and all the animals in an ark that the vegetation God,
Enki, told him to build. When the flood came and killed all the
rest of mankind, Ishtar the Earthmother and Protector of All
Mankind becomes hysterical. After sending out a dove, a swallow
and a raven, Utnapishtim lands the ark on Mount Nissir. Utnapishtim relates to Gilgamish the history of the Patriarchs who
lived before the flood.

The wife of Utnapishtim asks what they shall give Gilgamish as
a parting gift, and Utnapishtim decides to tell him where to find
the "Plant of Life." Utnapishtim has Ur-Shanapi lead Gilgamish
to a lake of fresh water and Gilgamish descends to its bottom,
returning with the "Plant of Life" named "The Old-Man-
Becomes Young Again." Subsequently, as Gilgamish bathes in a
pit of cool water on his way home to Uruk, a snake steals the
"Plant of Life," eats some of it and becomes eternal. Gilgamish
is finally reconciled to his loss. Gilgamish then descends into the
Underworld to see his friend, Engidu, who tells him of the conditions of the Dead.

So far as we know, the worship of the Earthmother was the
only religion that ever became universal. A number of stories
from this religion have a world-wide distribution even today,
such as the *Quest for the Tree of Life and Water of Life, The
Fight of Two Heroes Against a Monster Guarding the Tree of
Life, The Fight Between the Gods, The Story of the Flood, The
Patriarchs Before the Flood.*

Occasional episodes of the Babylonian Gilgamish Epic that
spread before they were credited to the Hero King of Uruk are
found today scattered among Siberians, Indonesians, Eskimos,
Indians, Africans, and others.

Curiously enough, the Cuna Indians have a surprisingly large
number of the old Ishtar worship stories. They probably brought
these accounts with them when they migrated from Asia, possibly
as long ago as 4,000 B.C.

These same Mesopotamian episodes are in the background of
the Bible, the Biblical versions of which they resemble distantly.
It is interesting to note that the Spanish priest who first wrote

about the similarities between the Indian religions and Christianity was tried as a heretic and burned at the stake.

The Cuna Indians of San Blas have the principal units of the Gilgamish collection. They have Olowaipippilele and Pugsu fighting three monsters, a Snake, a Jaguar, and a Toad, that guard the Tree of Life. The two heroes cut down the Tree of Life, and its chips fall into the "lake" (God's Whirlpool) at its roots, where they become inedible fish. When the Tree of Life is cut down, its salty sap gushes out to form all the Oceans of the World.

The Tree of Life today among the Cunas is the Saptur tree, Genipa Americana, related to coffee and cinnamon. It bears fleshy fruits which yield a magic, black dye that wards off evil spirits. This dye was used by ancient hero shamans of the Cunas to resurrect dead children because it is from the Fruit of the Tree of Life.

The Cunas say that in Heaven there is a grove of these sacred Saptur trees and that two sacred monsters wander among them. The monsters are Achusimmutupalit, the jaguar-like monster with the long umbilical cord, and Achunipali, a monster described as a sphinx that has a "Golden Chain." However, the "Golden Chain" bears the name "olokwilotupa" which means "umbilical cord" and also "spirit bridge" of the afterlife.

The Great Toad is apparently Kwelopunyai, midwife to the Earthmother, and the Great Snake may be God's phallos.

Several Cuna heroes ascend to the various layers of Heaven, corresponding to the Underworld. Orkun, Pailipe, Nele Sipu, and Tiekun at different times descend to the several levels of the Underworld and report on the condition of the Dead.

The Cunas have four Destructions of the World including the Story of the Flood. The Babylonian account had four Destructions of the World including the Flood.

The Cunas have the History of the Patriarchs before the Flood, and one of them has the name Innoe (Noah). The pedigree of Patriarchs also contains Kaana (Canaan). Tat Opa corresponds to Adapa of Akkadia and Adam of the Bible.

Judging by Cuna correspondences that Chief Ikwaniktipippi explained to me, we may say that the Babylonian Garden of Ishtar in Lebanon represented the Earthwoman's enormous generative organs in childbirth. The Giant Cedars reaching to Heaven represented the Plant of Birth or Tree of Life. Four Rivers of Life flowed thence, the Tigris and Euphrates being identified in the Bible; whereas, the Jordan and Litani are implied. The Jordan and Litani soon end in salt water (Salt Sea and Mediterranean), and the Bible suggests that the rivers from the Garden of Eden actually became oceans, flowing around Ethiopia and Havilah.

The Cunas still make a picture comparable to the Garden of Ishtar identifying the Tree of Life as the umbilical cord and foetal membranes of the great Earthmother at parturition. The Lake (God's Whirlpool) is her vulva. The Rivers of Life (Water of Life) are streams of salty amniotic fluid shed at the time of childbirth. Khumbaba (the Guarding Monster disc) is apparently the Placenta with an exaggerated umbilical cord emerging from its center and draped in such a way as to outline a horrible carnivore-like face. This probably became Ishtar's Lion in later Babylon, and it may be the Jaguar fought by Olowaipippilele and Puksu of the Cunas. The Cunas have a mythical, shaggy-haired mountain monster "like a jaguar" named Achusimmutupalit with a long umbilical cord. Furthermore, the placenta is called the jaguar. In recent times the Cuna word achu (jaguar) has been applied also to domestic dogs, and no Cuna now dares to kill a dog lest its angry spirit return to injure women during childbirth.

Cuna medicine men say that during pregnancy the spirits of the friendly whales bring back salt water from the ocean, which is really the Water of Life or Amniotic Fluid of the Great Earthmother, and they infiltrate it into the amnion of the developing embryo.

The Babylonians represented Holy Persons as having the head and wings of an eagle or vulture. Pre-Columbian Cuna graves yield such bird-beaked figurines in gold, and Cuna medicine idols today have similar enormous bird beaks. Some of the ancient figurines hold a sacred umbilical cord that may be used as a spirit bridge in the afterlife because both spirit bridge and umbilical cord are called "olokwilotupa," as we have stated above.

As civilization progressed in Babylon, it would appear that many beliefs in the Earthmother religion became symbolized, and with this change the original connotation was sometimes lost. However, the primitive peoples of the world such as the Cuna Indians have zealously guarded the true concepts of the Earthmother religion, and if they will discuss their religion at all, they will tell you frankly some of these meanings.

I sent a copy of the Akkadian Tree of Life and Water of Life symbol to my friend, Chief Ikwaniktipippi. He knew what it was. He said it had something to do with umbilical cord of birth of Achusimmutupalit, the shaggy jaguar-like monster of the mountains. I sent him the symbols carved on an archaic altar of Ishtar from Sheba in Southwest Arabia, and he gave me the interpretation because the Arabian symbols are identical with those used today by Chief Ikwaniktipippi to record the Cuna chant about the Earthmother. The interpretation was something as follows: "To the Sungod, who, after six matings with semen from God the Creator, was conceived in the womb of the Earthmother and born in the Earthmother's Holy Chamber."

Thus, if you want to know the original meanings of symbols in the ancient Ishtar religion of Babylon, you may (with considerable caution) ask a medicine man of San Blas.

Chapter IV

◇ ◇ ◇ ◇ ◇ ◇

INDIAN MEDICINE

SNAKE BITE MEDICINE

WHEN I VISITED Mulatuppu for the first time everything was unusually quiet. There were no children playing. There was no shouting or laughing. The Town Council had forbidden Claudio to beat on the oxygen tank he had salvaged from the sea to call the children to his new school. There could be no singing at the new Sunday school and there could be no playing of the little portable foot-pump organ that Claudio had brought with him. The reason was that a man had been bitten by a poisonous snake.

The night before I arrived all the people of Mulatuppu had been corraled into the Council Hall by the police where they were required to "drink medicine" for the man who had been bitten. The idea was to spread out the poison and hence the pain and danger over the whole town rather than keep it concentrated in the "bitten man." Each person would suffer some of the pain for the man, and the strength of all the people in the town would be called into play to overcome the poison. Even Claudio, the missionary, was forced to join the town in drinking medicine for the victim.

Manipekinappi, the Snake Medicine Man, according to professional custom, was not eating or talking to anybody, nor would he do so until either the man had died or else was well on the road to recovery. Manipekinappi was out in the mountains before dawn every day, and he labored until dark ceremonially gathering bark, and roots, and leaves, and then applying them to the patient in his isolation hut that stood on stilts out in the

78

ocean. And while at the isolation hut he was constantly singing to the patient his therapeutic chant, the symbols for which he had spread over eight pages of his notebook in pencil and colored wax crayon.

After two weeks the man began to recover, and Manipekinappi decided to test the cure. This was done by putting him for a day in a hut nearby where a house was being built on his native island. If the sound of the swishing thatch, the dragging and bumping of frame poles, the noise of digging pole pits, the "chop, chop, chop" of the machetes, and the joking and laughing of the workers did not make his leg feel worse, he would be allowed to go home to his hammock. But if these things bothered him, he would be returned to his isolation ward far out in the ocean.

Manipekinappi was not a young man and his endeavors began to tell on him, so that when the horrible swelling of the man's leg finally began to be reduced and he was brought back to Mulatuppu to test the cure Manipekinappi was exhausted.

The test showed, however, that the man was actually getting well. Next day the children laughed and played once more, the oxygen tank was hammered at the school with usual vigor, and the pump organ was played. The huge conch shell of a cooperative was blown to tell the townswomen that a new batch of brilliantly colored cotton cloth had arrived during the night on a windjamming tabulu or coconut boat. The Medicine Man broke his fast.

Proudly Manipekinappi walked the streets of Mulatuppu, and he was congratulated by all. His prize patient was getting well from a poni tummati (disease unto death).

That evening Manipekinappi brought the three traditional white hen eggs because he wanted to propose friendship with Kilupippi, and I gave him a pipe in return. And so we became "Aimar nueti." Of course, there is a slight catch in becoming "friends." Your friend has the right to ask favors of you which you cannot refuse, but this is recompensed by his being honor bound to do favors for you in return.

Next day Manipekinappi brought his medicine notebook to me. He was so proud of his recent success with the snakebite case that he wanted me to enlarge a picture that he had drawn on the inside cover depicting the Earthmother in the act of giving birth to the first snakes. He wanted it made large so that he could hang it up like a doctor's diploma in his hut.

That was a big order, but I set to work with India ink and water color pencils, finally producing something so colorful and attractive that all the visiting medicine men from other islands came to admire it and my fame as a medicine artist spread up and down the coast. The whole family was so proud of my picture that his daughter copied it onto a gorgeous applique mola.

But where you find gold it is wise to dig; so several days later Manipekinappi came back with his notebook. This time he wanted me to "modernize" the picture of snakes from which he sang his therapeutic chant about all the different kinds of "snakes." This classification included various insect larvae, dragon flies, centipedes, and "spirit snakes that fly through the air," in addition to the orthodox varieties.

After that he wanted the eight pages of his snake medicine chant "modernized." I saw that I would get little else done in Mulatuppu if this continued because other medicine men were already looking about for three white hen eggs. But I agreed, and spent three days doing nothing else but copying in India ink and colored pencil.

Of course, Manipekinappi was delighted and so he asked what he could do for me. I replied that in return I would like to have his original medicine drawings, and he agreed. My request was really a heavy one because his medicine pictures were sacred and should normally have been buried with the Snake Man upon his death.

After that, Benito, the understudy of the Snake Man, brought his notebook and I "modernized" several pages for him.

Various medicine men who were from other islands admired my handiwork at Manipekinappi's hut and expressed how nice it would be to have their medicine pictures modernized too, but, alas, they did not have their notebooks along!

The real test of faith, however, came from a famous Snake Woman of Morti who had descended from her mountain village with her husband and was so thrilled when Manipekinappi showed her my medicine pictures that she came right over to Claudio's to negotiate "friendship" with me.

"Kilupippi has made medicine pictures for Manipekinappi and for his student, but I was the teacher of Manipekinappi, and therefore he ought to make some pictures for *me!*"

Margaret, Claudio's wife, translated her words for me although I had a pretty good idea what the Snake Woman was talking about.

I replied that I would be happy to make medicine pictures for her. "Just bring your notebook to me and I will copy the symbols for you!"

"But I do not have my notebook with me. I left it in the mountains at Morti."

"In that case we shall have to wait until you bring it down on some future visit."

At these words the Snake Woman of Morti was greatly dejected. "You are an American, aren't you?"

"Yes, I am an American."

"But I thought that Americans knew everything! And I supposed that all you would have to do would be to sit down and see in your mind the symbols that are in my notebook!"

ART MEDICINE

Suppose you are a Cuna Indian youth who has just wakened with a vision for your life. In your dream you had become an artist. The brown, barefooted townspeople were crowding about you and your handiwork saying: "Poo! Karpa nueti" (What a beautiful basket). And the women who own many coconut trees were whispering "We should have him marry our daughter."

You lie in your hammock and relive the vision until dawn when father calls: "Son, we go fishing."

That evening by the light of a flickering kwallu and over a calabash of "op tuttu" (new corn drink) you confide your dream to your mother who is fanning the fire. She adjusts her golden nosering and agrees that to be an artist, in addition to mastering the necessary crafts of the village, would be very nice indeed.

It is not too difficult to get old scraps of paper and pencils from the coconut boats with which to practice, but if you really want to become a talented artist you must follow the Cuna tradition. You must pay an Indian medicine man to develop your natural artistic powers. He may also suggest a special treatment for your kurkin (knowledge) or one for your nika (drive). But let us settle for the development of artistic powers. So the deal is made.

High up in the jungled mountains behind Anasasukun there grows a tall, magic tree called "sapi karta" (printed paper tree). Its leaves are smooth edged blades with a shiny green upper surface. They are of a lighter color underneath. During the wet season there is nothing unusual about this tree, but in the dry months the invisible fingers of Nature mysteriously draw pictures with India ink on the lower surface of the sapi karta leaves. Slowly the pictures seem to delineate themselves with strong ebon lines. Whose hand guides the spirit paint brush that moves over most if not all of the leaves of this tree? "They belong to God," said a medicine man reverently to me. When the miracle pictures are completed the leaves fall.

The medicine man gathers up the strange pictures, a prayer on his lips. As he does so, he notices a great variety of designs all based on an isometric spot surrounded by three or four concentric circles. They remind him of the active water sketches generated when naked Cuna boys drop pebbles into a quiet pool. Sometimes the central dot is near the tip of the leaf. Sometimes it is anywhere to one side of the mid-rib. Occasionally there are two and even three centra, irregularly placed. This condition results in a strikingly beautiful design. To the Indian this is an inscrutable miracle of God, but to the scientist it is probably a parasitic fungus, the internal mycelia of which come to the surface at intervals to form their heavily pigmented fruiting bodies.

These leaves are placed in a medicine bath and the water is applied to the eyes of the patient, accompanied by the burning of cocoa bean incense and the singing of a therapeutic prayer. As is usual, the ceremonial bathing of the eyes with medicine water must be carried out "under the care of a physician," for if it is applied without his guidance the patient will go blind.

Old Indians who became artists in this fashion tell me that "sapi karta ina" is excellent medicine and they declare their testimonials with the fervor of patent medicine devotees.

But what are some of the artistic values that "sapi karta" will help us to master? The chief fields are:
1. Making medicine picture writing.
2. Basket and fire fan weaving.
3. Wood carving.
4. Hammock making.
5. Painting the picha makkalet, or woman's loin cloth.
6. Modeling the sia nala incense pot.
7. Stringing the arm and leg beads.
8. Sewing the applique mola blouse.

The first two of these arts are generally for men, the rest for women and girls.

Back in the days of the pirates several of the buccaneers described the Cunas as a body-painting folk, addicted to occasional cannibalism just as Europeans were a few centuries before. At that time the Cunas adorned themselves with figures of trees and animals in red, yellow, blue, white, and black. The red and black still persist in Cuna face decoration but this has degenerated so badly that it is scarcely an art any more.

We shall give illustrations to show something of the problems in the fields of art remaining today.

Medicine pictures are a fine art dependent usually upon neat, unshaded lines forming certain symbols, understood by all medicine men to represent the same medicinal plant or other object.

Cuna wood carving consists mainly of producing walking cane symbols of public office. Some of these are very elaborate. A favorite design bears wekko, the snake catcher, on the head with a snake wrapped about the staff. One ailigandi official's cane is surmounted by a pelican, and below it, totem pole-wise, a monkey. Today these canes are usually coated with bright-colored enamels. Many uchus are crude, but some of them are actually works of art.

Basket making includes both the utilitarian and the aesthetic types. At least three common weaves are used for large, half-bushel containers with forehead strap to be carried upon the back. There are several half bushel types: the open weave for coconuts, the tight weave for carrying earth and gravel. There are enormous baskets for storing maize.

The pipi or fire fan is of a simple basket weave and its designs show great variety.

Today hammocks are made almost exclusively by grandmothers for their grandchildren. They consist of blue stripes on white with designs so simple and fine that at a distance one can scarcely detect them.

The painted picha or loin cloth is almost a thing of the past, but I was able to locate a woman at Mulatuppu who still made pichas, painted freehand with indigo by means of a crude fiber brush already described.

Only one or two Cunas in each town make the sia nala any more, a crude, hand-moulded pot whittled externally with a knife. It bears no decoration. We must imagine that at one time pottery was more highly developed, and we know from burial artifacts that some ancient Cuna pottery had incised borders. Only one woman on the coast still makes the ceremonial mete jar.

Designing arm and leg beads is a very laborious process because the complicated cuff consists of one long strand wound round and round the arm or leg is such a fashion that a design, preconceived when the beads were strung, is reproduced when the strand is tightly wrapped about the arm or leg. The favorite colors are orange lines on a yellow background with a dark blue border consisting of one row of beads.

Of the applique mola blouses there is now no end of variety. Many years ago the body painting gave way to the painted picha and it, in turn, was followed by the mola of older girls and women. It is worn with a printed sarong. In another chapter we have described its interesting evolution.

So if you were a Cuna youth or maiden that woke up with a vision of becoming an artist, it would be to your advantage to have your favorite medicine man search the mountains above Anasasukun. It would be advisable to listen carefully to his medicine chant. It would be necessary to bathe your eyes in his medicine water in which lie contrasting magic leaves from the "sapi karta" tree.

BIRTH

One day I entered the hut of my friend Manipekinappi, the Snake Man of Mulatuppu. I found that important person sitting on a low stool beside his medicine collection. A large caldron of water stood before him. Into this caldron he was seriously grating powder from each member of a bundle of dried sticks by rubbing them with a rough granite rock.

Soon an old woman came in from the next hut, adjusted her big golden nosering, and whispered something into his ear. In a very businesslike fashion he got up, took a package of leaves from a shelf, and with the granite rock grated some of them into the caldron. He dipped a calabash into the liquid and gave it to the woman, who took it and disappeared.

We conversed for a few minutes and another old woman stood by the Snake Man. She cupped her scrawny hand beside her mouth and whispered into Manipekinappi's ear. The Snake Man arose, took from his shelves a bundle of thorny, bifurcated plant stems and untied the withe with which they were carefully bound. He grated each stick about twenty strokes with the rough granite over the caldron. Then he sought out a huge, rusty fishhook from among the motley contents of a fancy figured basket and scraped it in like manner. Finally, he gave the woman a calabash of the dilute mixture and she shuffled out of the hut with it in her hands.

I noted the thorns and fishhook and knew that they are used symbolically against sharp and intense pain. I saw that Manipekinappi was not administering the medicine himself; so it must be for a woman whose disease is very private. I witnessed two old women serving the sick — they must be midwives. I observed that the patient was in the next hut that also belonged to Manipekinappi. Putting all these observations together, I deduced that the Snake Man's daughter must be having a baby.

Manipekinappi continued to scrape sticks and stones vigorously over the caldron, and he worked so hard at it that beads of perspiration stood out all over his brown forehead.

At length, a little cry was heard coming from the patient's hut. Manipekinappi rested the backs of his hands on his hips and looked up with a knowing smile. Nature had triumphed in spite of his superstitions — although he believed that his ministrations had complete control over Nature.

When a baby is born and washed, it is occasionally possible to see it, and once the familiar little cry is heard, the curious neighbors begin asking that eternal question: "Ipua, ua soet, ti mimmi?" (What is it, a fisherman or a water carrier maiden?)

But what went on prior to the little cry? From the time of conception until parturition the expectant mother has been visiting the inatule (medicine man) almost daily and he has prescribed most curious medicines to do various things. He tells her what she must do to make the child strong and what she must not do that would otherwise mark or harm it.

For example, most Cunas do not want an albino child, and their tribe has the highest incidence of this unfortunate variation in the whole world. They believe that an albino child results from the father or mother having gazed too long at the moon during the pregnancy, and hence albinos are called "ni mimmikana" or moon-children.

So to prevent the child from being an albino, the inatule burns balsa wood to charcoal and gives this in water to the mother to drink two months before parturition to "upset" any possible albino tendency. He administers balsa charcoal for one month after conception to produce very dark children. If he gives the white tip of the balsa fruit in quantity to drink, an albino will be produced, but if he gives it sparingly it is "good for the pregnancy." The father is warned against various plants and animals, such as kikir (the octopus), because looking upon or handling these taboo objects will mark the child.

For a price the medicine man will scratch the top of the skull of a male dwarf deer (Koe pepe nikka macheret) over the medicine bath. And he will sing a special medicinal chant with it, too. This is excellent for the child's development. Of course, scratchings from the skull of Achu kinnit (the red jaguar) accompanied by the appropriate chant makes the child powerful and strengthens the mother.

And the parents will want the child to be talented; so the inatule suggests a treatment with the skull of tias (the otter). He can administer this skull powder in water two ways with appropriate medicine chants. If they choose the first chant the inatule will make the child into a good hunter. If they choose the second chant he will make him into a clever fisherman.

At the time for delivery the hammock of the expectant mother is surrounded by canoe sails, and three old midwives are brought in to sit and smoke their pipes by the expectant mother's hammock. They must watch the process of birth, but must not assist it. And, of course, for modesty's sake, the medicine man dares not witness the birth of a child! He simply sits it out at a distance and maintains remote control while the old women inform him from time to time how things are going. He prescribes accordingly. "The contractions are like those of a snake," whispers a midwife. So he washes the wooden image of a snake in water and sends the water to be poured upon the woman's belly. Later another midwife comes to him and says, "Now the contractions have the form of an alligator." Accordingly, the obstetrician places an alligator skull in his medicine canoe and instructs the midwife to have the patient drink half a calabash of the medicine water. Again the medicine man may decide that it is time to use his akwa kwile or jumping stone. This disc-shaped granite stone is supposed to increase the contractions of the mother and make the baby jump, because the activity of the child is thought to assist in the process of birth.

If the labor continues normally and the child's head appears, a midwife deftly slits the mother's hammock and the child is expelled through this opening to plunge into a canoe full of cold water from which it is fished out by the midwives and washed.

It is wrapped up in a cloth and given to its mother, who cuddles it as every woman would, and endearingly calls it "An koe pippi" (My little fawn).

A sad commentary upon this procedure is, however, that one third of Cuna women now die in childbirth.

At Ailigandi the scene was much the same. Old Upikinya's daughter was having a baby and he was assisting the birth *in absentia* with his sacred sticks and stones, fishhooks, and what not. All had gone well until a midwife whispered in his ear that the baby's hand, arm, and shoulder had appeared and that the process of birth had stopped. Realizing that he was old, and that he had only his life to lose for breaking the powerful taboo of tradition, Upikinya rushed to his daughter's side, turned the baby around, and thus saved the lives of his daughter and granddaughter.

Complaints about the wickedness of his action, and threats of what should be done to him, even to sentencing him to death by a poisonous plant, reverberated about the town for more than a month, but the matter settled down and he was not brought to trial. One thing that helped the men of Ailigandi to forget his crime of lifesaving was that shortly thereafter Upikinya found a rather rare weed in the mountains that produces vomiting, and since the Indians believe that there is nothing quite so healthful as a thorough regurgitation, for several days he did a very flourishing business until the weed was all used up, and everybody was delighted with his contributions toward public health.

SHALL WE KEEP THE BABY?

Cuna women have always been taught that babies die because they become too hot. The medicine man has magic stones called "akwa nusa" (stone mice) and the cocoa bean chant for keeping down a fever, but the most practical way is to drench the child's body with cold water and expose it to the cold wind. Because of this practice, many babies die at a very early age.

Claudio and I were called into a hut. The two-weeks-old baby was gasping. Its breathing was congested and its chest was heaving with that deep down appearance that denotes pneumonia. "The only thing that can possibly save it now is ikko ina (needle medicine)," we announced. The woman said, "No, I would rather see my baby die than to have a needle stuck into it!" So the baby died two days later and was buried, as customary, in the sand floor

of the hut. The mother asked us for nails to build a little box
to put it in.

Up the street that same evening Faustino called us in to see his
baby of the same age. It, too, was dying of pneumonia.

The mother said, "I want to keep my baby girl, but you cannot
put a needle into it."

"But your baby is dying now and ikko ina is the only thing that
can possibly save it. Indeed, even if we do inject it, it is very
likely to die anyway."

"I want to keep it!" said Faustino, the father.

"So do I!" said old Mu, the grandmother. "Say the word,
daughter; let us take the chance with ikko ina."

And finally the daughter murmured a reluctant "All right."

Claudio and I went home and cooked up the needles in a
saucepan. We got out the penicillin and returned to the dying
baby. When the needle was inserted, the baby was too feeble
even to cry. As soon as we went home, a little girl in the house
was sent to call the famous Ome Nele (medicine woman) of
Careto.

"Will the ikko ina that Claudio gave do the baby any good?"

Evading the question the woman replied, "This child is suffering from three diseases at once. It has the O poni or disease of
its lungs. It also has a dragon in its throat that gives forth that
loud, gurgling sound when it breathes. And its third disease is
that the old Mukana (magical grandmothers in the underworld
who watch over development and birth) in the land from which
it came are trying to take it back."

"But that is not what we asked. Will the ikko ina do the baby
any good?"

The woman nele was on the spot. If she said it would live, and
then it died, her prediction would be false. On the other hand,
if she said it would die, and then it lived, again her reputation
would suffer. So she wisely replied in cautious terms, "I think
that the ikko ina may possibly do it some good."

Next day the baby looked brighter, but it was very weak. That
afternoon it nursed for the first time in three days. That night
we injected it again, and the next day it was on the road to recovery.

On the fourth day it was nearly well; so I designed a shirt to
be worn by the baby to protect its chest because tiny Indian
babies wear no clothes. I wanted it to be a thing of pride so they

would keep it on the baby, and for that reason, I had them applique the father's initial "F" on the front like a college football sweater because neither the baby nor its mother had any name. The woman nele was impressed.

PUTAMAYO

The Indians have been cheated so often by white men that they seldom can put anything over on them any more, but almost any charlatan of their own race can dupe the Indians because they trust him. That was the secret of Putamayo's success.

Putamayo was a big operator whose real name nobody knew. They simply called him that because he hailed from the mountains far up the Putamayo River Valley in Bolivia. He kept his hair fairly long and wore a white under tunic and a robe of black alpaca wool girded with a cord. About his neck he carried a great weight of beads. He spoke convincingly excellent Spanish, and he had with him a young and beautiful Indian girl, who was the "come on."

In her most charming voice she said: "Some have declared that Putamayo is a charlatan as they said of Christ, but this is not true. He is a Holy man of God and he heals by faith exactly as Christ healed. Yes, like Christ, much of the healing that he performs is by miracle. Reject him not, but come unto him and believe!"

Putamayo had a big bank account in Panama and traveled by airplane. He had worked the heathen islands of San Blas for several months and did very well, according to all accounts. Alcibiades usually protected Ailigandi from such persons but once he went to Panama on an errand and Putamayo slipped in. All the sick of Ailigandi opened their hearts and their pocketbooks to the rascal and he took them all in.

For example, one man had an aching molar tooth. Putamayo said some magic words, made a few passes about his face, and suddenly pulled a scorpion from the man's cheek to dangle it before his astounded eyes. "This is what was causing the trouble in your jaw! Seven dollars, please!"

One of his most spectacular medicines consisted of little, flat, fossil snail shells. When you placed them in a calabash in a little lime juice, they crawled about like living things. This was due to the pushes of tiny bubbles of carbon dioxide gas produced by the reaction between citric acid and calcium carbonate.

Putamayo quickly went all over Ailigandi, collected an estimated $300, and departed before Alcibiades could return.

A month and a half later Alcibiades accompanied me to the Catholic island of Narkana, the town of his birth, and there I examined, weighed, and measured twelve moon-children. While we were at the airstrip on the island of Narkana waiting for a plane, down came a plane containing Putamayo and his beautiful companion.

The Chief of Police, who was married to Alcibiades' sister, was standing nearby and a conversation took place. Then the Chief told Putamayo that he could not practice his healing art in Narkana in view of ill reports from several islands down the coast.

"But, gentlemen, you have me all wrong. Everything is completely on the level."

The charmer in her most appealing manner turned on the Chief and pled for an honest test of his methods to be made right there in Narkana. "But why should you cast out a Man of God without a fair trial? Your sense of honesty and fair play forbids it!"

However, the Chief of Police was adamant, and ordered them both back into the plane, but they defiantly took their time about it. Putamayo owed a woman from another island for board and lodging, and she came to the field to collect. Putamayo placed a pack of his belongings on the ground and untied the leather thong with which it was secured. He drew out two boxes full of aluminum Catholic medals and gave the woman one of each kind to pay his bill, saying that they would bring her much more good luck than if he had paid in money. The girl climbed into the plane.

The Chief of Police was becoming impatient.

I thought that maybe here was a dramatic shot and started to pull my camera from its case. Putamayo observed this action, suddenly bolted to the plane and started to scramble in.

The Chief also saw my move and asked: "Photographia?"

"Aye!" said I.

Then the Chief made Putamayo climb out again and pose for my rogues' gallery photo. But he was equal to the occasion and turned on his most affable smile!

Chapter V

◇ ◇ ◇ ◇ ◇ ◇

STRANGE CUSTOMS

GIRL'S PUBERTY CEREMONY

THE EVENT to which all girls look forward suddenly took place. Maria became a lady. Ordinarily the family would have kept the matter a tight secret for several days, but it occurred in Dr. Iglesias' Sunday School, and in accordance with a universal human failing, the word spread like wildfire. Some thirty-five or more classmates could hardly get home fast enough to spread the story of what happened to Maria. The young lady's family decided to make the best of a bad situation and to carry out the puberty ceremony at once.

The puberty ceremony of the Cunas is one of their most sacred rites. The great cultural hero, Ipelele, the Sungod himself, instituted the rite for his sister. The great Ipeorkun, a Shining Golden One who descended from the sun, instructed the Cunas in the details of the ceremony.

In compliance with these ancient, heavenly instructions, Maria's father made the matter known to the Town Council of Ailigandi on Sunday night. Then father and mother visited the family huts on their side of the town. "Tomorrow we ought to work in the house," said the father in cryptic language. "I have business to attend to tomorrow," said the mother, and the neighbors understood. On Monday morning before dawn the forty men of the town took their canoes and paddled to the mainland. They walked the path to the forest in search of leaves of the urhwa that resemble those of the banana tree.

Soon after daybreak on Monday morning, the group of men returned from the forest and quickly converged on the home of the new yakwa. I followed them. Each man carried two urhwa leaves in his right hand. Within the house a framework for the surpa or bathing inclosure had been erected previously. In the center of it stood a three-pole wigwam covered with a blanket. The lady was already sitting on a log seat hidden in the wigwam.

The men handed their leaves one after another to an official of the ceremony within the inclosure. He quickly bent their stems and arranged them to form the walls of the surpa, by hanging the bent stems inward over the horizontal poles of the framework. Having delivered his leaves to the official, each of the participants sat down on especially prepared benches to be served a chocolate drink by old Mu, grandmother of the young lady. Instead of using calabashes, Mu, who enjoys outdoing her neighbors, served the chocolate in Chinese rice bowls from Panama. At this point the ceremony calls for playing the tetenono armadillo skull flute, but that was omitted. (In fact, nobody knows how to blow the tetenone any more on Ailigandi.) Small conversation was indulged in for a few minutes after which each man greeted the hostess and departed.

A dying Cuna or one about to die has clairvoyant powers, and after he is gone his predictions are much thought about, if they turn out to bear any resemblance to future events. Such a prediction was repeated excitedly all during the five days of Maria's ceremony. Several weeks before, another of Mu's granddaughters had died in childbirth. Just before she died she had predicted that Maria would become mature in the streets of Ailigandi and that groups of old women would be huddled together all over town talking about the public occurrence of her most private of events.

For five days the new yakwa spent most of her daylight hours in the wigwam within the surpa inclosure, where she was almost constantly bathed by old Mu, who conducted the ceremony. I noted that some of Maria's girl friends with red makepa on nose and cheeks were kept busy each day bringing water in calabashes from the ocean and pouring it into a canoe just outside the house. Others carried it from the canoe to Mu when she needed it.

Before dusk on the fifth day, I went with Alcibiades Iglesias to see the sacred ceremony of bringing in the saptur fruits. After a long wait a canoe containing a man and a boy drew up to the island shore near the house of the yakwa. The boy Antonio had on his cheeks large red spots painted with makepa seeds. The man, still in the canoe, hoisted a basket of saptur fruits to the back of the boy, and helped adjust its headstrap. Antonio intentionally allowed several fruits to fall into the canoe, probably for the family of the man. Then he came to the house of the new yakwa. Within the house he allowed one to fall to the ground, from whence it was snatched up quickly by an old woman and tossed over a high board fence that separated the ceremony region from the rest of the house. Then she wiped out the spot where the fruit had originally landed by making a cross mark with her finger in the sand.

At this time the man came to the house armed with a shotgun. Before entering the house he fired the gun into the air. Then with the boy he entered the surpa where they were met by Mu. The boy filled his pockets with saptur fruits to be given to the townspeople, as the occasion of a puberty celebration is the only time at which saptur may be gathered.

As a matter of fact the town was starving for saptur. Babies and girls had gone unpainted against the devils. Men who had seen snakes had not been able to cut their great toes and paint them with saptur to render themselves invisible to serpents. Feminine beauties all over town could not add that final touch to their gorgeousness, namely, the vertical, saptur noseline.

Old Mu took half a dozen saptur fruits and put them in a basket that hung on the inside of the surpa wall. At this point, Alcibiades and I left the front door of yakwa's house from where we were watching, before we could be ordered away. The most holy rite of the puberty ceremony was to follow, namely, the cutting of the saptur fruit. No foreigner and no Indian not following Cuna traditions dares witness this rite.

But we know that Mu cut it properly in accordance with Cuna tradition, and that night she painted her granddaughter with black saptur juice from head to foot. This would make Maria unattractive to devils who might otherwise steal her soul, thus inflicting upon her some lethal disease before her haircutting ceremony, her coming out party, and her marriage.

Two men were sent to the river to seek a pair of Suknan crabs. If they have great difficulty in catching them, yakwa will have heavy labor at child-birth. If the captured crabs fight, yakwa and her husband-to-be will fight each other. If the male crab dies in one day, the husband will die in one year. If the female crab dies in a day, yakwa will die in a year — always a day for a year.

If the she crab escapes from the clay pot in which they are kept, yakwa will trick her husband and have another lover unbeknown to him. In the clay vessel there is a sacred stone, probably akwa nusa, and white maize to soften yakwa's menstruation.

Next morning the black Maria, looking quite unattractive to devils, and to everybody else for that matter, set about her usual tasks quite embarrassed by it all. I met her as she brought calabashes of water from her canoe to the house.

"An pe wakar wilup sai," said I, hoping against hope that I could get a rare portrait of the newly painted yakwa.

"Suli!" she replied, and the tone of her voice as well as her word meant "No!"

"Suitumbo," I returned, taking a chance on dollar diplomacy, whereas the customary price for posing is ten cents in Ailigandi.

With that inducement, Maria buried her pride and agreed to pose. I had scarcely opened my camera before we were surrounded by a sea of irate women who sensed what was going on. They threatened Maria. They threatened me, and they threatened to smash my camera. Maria realized that after this moment her chance to pose at that price would be gone forever. She could only become a lady once. So she stated to the crowd that she, now a woman, had the right to pose for a picture if she wanted to. She defiantly stuck to her decision. I focused, clicked the camera, and got out of the melee as quickly as I could. The picture of the black yakwa is good, but Maria's expression shows that she was not in the least at ease when it was taken. Her face is tense from having just exchanged angry words with the women of the town who felt, not without reason, that their religious ceremonies are too sacred to be photographed for wicked foreigners to gape at. Surely, Ipelele and Ipeorkun would not have permitted it.

INNA FEAST

Old Upikinya, the Ailigandi medicine man, was not wealthy; but he had saved up his money for the day when his granddaughters must be introduced to society with the great expense and ceremony that were traditional in the Cuna tribe. And now the time for honoring one of them had come. The young lady had her puberty ceremony and her hair-cutting ceremony behind her, leaving only the extravagant coming-out party or inna to separate her from social acceptance and marriageability. Upikinya knew that it would be difficult especially because he had lost his wife the year before, and she had been a spouse who would have helped him greatly with this arduous matter.

A month in advance the date for the inna had been fixed at the Council Hall, and since then preparations had gone on with increasing vigor. For two weeks many men of Ailigandi had caught fish, and the women had smoked them on wooden frames over the cooking fire. Other men combed the mountains hunting four-footed game. Still others assembled yucca roots, plantains, bananas, and rarer fruits to be laid aside for the period of the ceremony. Some of the foods could not be preserved and had to be gathered at the last minute.

Manitikinappi, the famous inna maker, set about mixing the mash for the maize-sugar cane beer that must ferment during two weeks. It must be prepared in fourteen jars inside the inna hall and each jar must be covered with banana leaves, bound at the neck with a reed.

Friends and relatives on neighboring islands must be invited; a kantule and other officers of the ceremony must be consulted and bargained with. All this Upikinya and his sons-in-law arranged — of course, with the coöperation of all the in-laws who lived together in the big cane and thatch house they called home.

On the afternoon of the thirty-first of July, Upikinya, accompanied by his two sons-in-law, came ashore from a canoe so enormous that they could not beach it alone; so I helped them. The canoe was loaded with materials for the approaching inna. In it were four large packs of banana leaves and two mysterious bundles eight inches square, wrapped in banana leaves and bound with supple vines.

Later I met my friend Upikinya, who took me by the arm, as usual. He said he would paint the order of service board at eleven o'clock and at tat yoroku (sun overhead) they would start drinking. He requested that I come to taste the inna. Then he told how some Americans came to an inna and drank and drank until they became mummu.

When the drinking started I observed that Upikinya was wearing magic, red makepa paint that drives away the devils which swarm about the town during inna feasts trying in particular to get into the sacred service of the inna hall. His makepa took the form of two diagonal cheek stripes and a vertical nose line.

Early next day (August first) I met Upikinya. He was now

wearing a nose line of black saptur and a short vertical line of
the same material on the wings of his nose. Upikinya had recovered from his first day of drinking; so he took me lockarmed
to the front of the Ipeorkun kapir neka hall where he bade me
look aloft to see the hooked poles daubed with spirals of makepa
to which would be suspended the newly completed marriage hammock woven for his granddaughter. He led me nearby and
pointed with pride to the hand-hewn board painted with red and
black pictograph symbols that indicated the order of service. He
then escorted me inside the drinking hall which was crowded with
visitors and humming with noise and commotion. The men were
congregated at one end of the hall and the women at the other,
partaking of traditional premasticated corn drink. Many were
wearing red cheeks and black nose lines. Upikinya informed me
that tomorrow he would sing Machiolosuilipippiler, the hot spearpoint chant, which I was anxious to hear.

He showed me two other buildings where preparations for the
feast were going on, one with two huge iron kettles and great
cooking fires. A number of women busied themselves with food.
There was much fruit, smoked fish, iguanas, tarpon, rabbits, deer,
and agoutis. Many people were sitting on benches about the
walls. Finally, Upikinya led me to a small, especially constructed
reception hut to meet and congratulate his granddaughter. Then
we parted.

At nine o'clock I slipped back to the reception hut to present
the young debutante with a scarlet silk scarf. I found her sitting
in a hammock with one foot resting on a stool, winding a string
of bright orange and yellow leg beads about her ankle.

At eleven I returned to the drinking hall. I recognized a woman
visitor from Achutuppu, who boasted a bright red nose line and
scarlet cheeks. There was a procession of participants that wended
its way to the drinking hall. First came the officials of the ceremony with the leading man carrying a lantern, an incense pot,
and a string of fibers, the purpose of which I did not know. Following him came old Upikinya, owner of the feast, swinging two
sianala incense pots and several ropes of soft black ceremonial
warsuit tobacco. They entered the hall followed by a great crowd
of people.

The officials took their places on six low seats at the side of the
drinking hall. Facing them were four seats occupied by servers.
The two sides of the square were formed by long planks laid up-

on small sections of logs. The order of service boards and the inna jars completed the fourth side of the square.

Before anybody sat down two servers with calabashes of red makepa and fiber brushes quickly painted nakkruses on all the seats, after which they daubed makepa on the faces of each of the participants. Everyone received cheek lines or spots.

Servers with drinking gourds rushed back and forth from the great jars to the celebrants who swallowed the liquor as quickly as possible. Their running to and fro symbolized the many trips of the three midwives to the house of the medicine man before the debutante was born. Behind these servers were other acolytes armed with ceremonial warsuit tobacco ropes two feet long. They lighted their rope cigars from a sianala and blew on the hot end forcing the smoke through the sides of the rope into the faces of the seated guests. One after another they gulped it down. The alternate shocks of alcohol and nicotine must continue until the participants succumb. Indeed, it is said that if one does not become drunk at inna feasts he will certainly never go to Heaven.

At the inna feast the kantule chanted symbolically about the miracle of reproduction and the development of the girl who has come to maturity and now is eligible for marriage to reenact once more the eternal mystery of the perpetuation of life. Many details of this chant describing reproduction and development would be consided pornographic in other cultures, but not to the earthy Indian. To him, the chant is sacred. It merely describes with complete frankness the strange and miraculous facts of life.

At 1:00 P.M. I returned to watch the progress of the feast. The drinking hall was swarming with drunks, thickly chattering, staggering, sitting unsteadily, vomiting, falling over. The unconscious were being laid out in hammocks suspended at the two ends of the hall. Many were falling asleep. Groups of three or four were swaying about arm in arm, trying to keep awake. Others, still sober, were struggling to get the more mummu members of the family home. Some of the women were very drunk and reeling. The participants were now a seething mass of disorganized humanity, droning and crooning incoherently rather than speaking and singing.

Three members of one family were rushing their gray haired, old grandfather home as rapidly as possible. Old Tator, unconscious and face down in spread eagle fashion, was being carried by two women each holding tightly to his arms at the shoulders,

while a man ran between his thighs holding on to his legs as if
they were the handles of a wheelbarrow. Women were staggering
in the streets. Frightened children were crying as they clung to
their drunken fathers and mothers. One woman visitor from another island who passed out had been laid in a canoe on the seashore and sloshed all over with cold water from the ocean until
she revived. She was fighting with her fists, kicking and screaming frantically for her mother.

At 4:00 P.M. I again returned to the hall. Only a remnant of
the celebrants were there wavering about. Six hammocks were
all occupied by drunks, two with one person, two with two, one
with three. In a hammock near the entrance of the hall lay the
the genial old host, Upikinya the Medicine Man, as limp as a
rag and as unconscious as a stone.

Two drunken boys who had worked in Panama laid hold of
me, called me "pal" and tried to demonstrate their knowledge
of English. But they were so unsteady, so thick-lipped, and so
confused in their ideas that I could not understand a thing of
their loud, inarticulate mutterings. After a time a drunken Indian angrily pushed us out of the hall saying that he could not
stand foreigners and foreign languages, and that the drinking
hall was for Indians and the Indian language.

Next morning (August second) at seven, Upikinya, in green
shirt and black bow tie, came to my home to fetch me. I had not
finished coffee; so we gave him a cup and a slice of bread. Then
taking me by the arm he led me to the inna hall. Things were
relatively quiet. The old kantule was sitting in a hammock surrounded by a crowd of men on low stools. He was blowing
quaint, plaintive notes on a kammu tummate flute. Several additional groups of drunks were huddled together attempting to sing
chants. Others, their ears dulled by the alcohol of the inna
kantiki, were trying to listen. Manitikinappi, the albino medicine
man, was brokenly holding forth with the thrilling tales of Cuna
heroes.

Upikinya went with me to the cooking house to have his spear
heated to demonstrate his occult power over the effects of fire.
Thereafter, at the drinking hall I sat between him and his middle-
aged son, who was to sing the Machiolosuilipippiler Ikar with his
good, clear voice. But the son was unsteady and so drunk that
he soon forgot the chant, became nervous, and shed tears. The
old man arose, went over and sat down on the other side of his

son where he rasped the chant near his ear that he might learn it.

> With a fire fan they cause the fire to kindle.
> The Red Lord begins to light,
> The Great Red Lord begins to crackle,
> The Great Red Lord begins to roar,
> The Red Lord begins to blaze.
> Machiolosuilipippilel [the little savant-seer boy with
>   golden points],
> Machiolowitinapippilel [the little savant-seer boy
>   with the golden palm handle],
> Into the Red Lord the spearpoint is placed.
> Machiolosuilipippilel begins to change his color.
> With the sacred stones Kana [the medicine man] is
>   hardening his hands,
> Kana turns his heart toward the great water con-
>   tainers in the underworld,
> Kana turns his heart toward the great sources of water.
> The spearpoint is taken out,
> Kana is sitting waiting for Machiolosuilipippilel,
> To Machiolosuilipippilel he turns his face.
> Kana wipes Machiolosuilipippilel with his hands.
> Machiolosuilipippilel is being rolled between his hands.

Then they called for the heated spear. The crowd backed away in fright to produce a corridor through which the server came running, holding the spear in his hand, its glowing point extended before him. As father and son grabbed the spearpoint and started to roll it across their hands, it fell from its haft to the sand in front of me. There was a vain scramble of father and son to pick it up. They grabbed at it unsuccessfully. That gave me a chance; and, as I could see that it was not very hot, I picked it up moving it swiftly from one hand to the other. Upikinya quickly pronounced the demonstration a failure because the spearpoint was not hot enough. The helper covered the point with sand and thus recovered it. The old man, having lost face, walked out of the drinking hall in shame with the spearpoint inserted in its haft.

Some of the Indians had been drinking and carousing all night. Those still able to stand were swaying through the streets in groups of two and three, dim eyed and garble tongued. A wave of seven or eight, all holding on to each other and talking noisily, came staggering up the street, while the few pedestrians scurried out of their way.

The chief's son told me that his father, Ikwaniktipippi, had the whole town in to see the brightly colored plaque I had made of the Cuna hero, Ipeorkun. He is credited with most of the culture, including institution of the inna feast, although some give Kammim credit for the Inna. This morning Ikwaniktipippi knocked himself out completely by drinking half a pint of Christian whiskey from Panama, and I helped two women who were struggling to carry a drunken man home.

At five-thirty they were feasting at the inna hall. Later in the evening a representative of each family participating would take home a portion of food for use of the household the next day. At seven in the evening I peeked in on the festivities for a last time. Thirty-six women were dancing wildly, two by two. They were progressing counter clockwise in a circle, slapping their feet, clapping their hands, and bowing this way and that. The rhythmic clanking of the many silver half dollars that composed the necklaces on their chests almost drowned the familiar sounds of the kantule's chant and his gourd rattle with which the time was beaten. The marriage hammock was tied aloft to the striped wooden hooks. Under it the kantule was chanting while his kamsuet assistant was shaking the rattle. Then the pairs of dancers did much the same step as before, first bowing and clapping toward each other and then away from each other.

After this they danced the Kutili. With right arm over the shoulder of the one on the right, left arm under shoulder of the one on left, they formed a huge circle that progressed. They barked twenty-seven times and all knelt toward the center. Outside the ring several servers, faced each other holding calabashes of inna in their right hands. They barked five times, three times, gave a long yell, and then consumed the liquor. Finally, the dancing stopped and the kantule sang the sacred yoe that ended the feast.

Next morning I went with my camera to the drinking hall and asked for Upikinya, because I wanted to take some pictures. An old woman said nothing, but she pointed. Old Upikinya was dead to the world, with another drunk laid beside him in a hammock. A dozen others were strewn upon the floor just as they fell. Because these were my friends who would resent having their pictures taken while drunk, I refrained from making photographs of the hall, except a snap of some inna jars and the order of service board.

MARRIAGE

About sun-zenith (tat yoroku) on the second day of the inna feast when the adults of the town are flushed, loose-lipped, and unsteady, suddenly a group of a dozen young men come swarming down the narrow streets calling, "Sui! Sui!" (the husband, the husband). They are half-carrying, half-pushing a struggling young man. When he stalls, one of them seizes him roughly by a sensitive member and drags him along. The poor fellow doesn't want to get married, and besides, nobody has told him who is to be his bride!

During the previous night the parents of a marriageable girl communed quietly together. "It is high time that our daughter should marry. She is already thirteen and if we do not get a husband for her soon, nobody will want to look at her. Besides, there are few good providers like José on the island; and if we want to secure him for our daughter, we shall have to act quickly, because somebody else might get him at this very inna feast!"

So the two slipped into the darkness and sought a certain hut where they talked with José's parents. After the cocoa-filled calabash of hospitality had been passed, and the weather and health had been disposed of by light conversation, they got down to business.

"Your son, José, must marry somebody, you know, and our daughter is young, beautiful and clever. They would make an excellent couple. Don't you think so? Two years ago our daughter had her puberty ceremony. She was buried in the ground up over her waist in a specially constructed hut and deluged with cold water for five days. Shortly thereafter she had her haircutting ceremony. Then last year she celebrated her inna feast; so this year she is ready for marriage."

"What you say is true, and your family has many coconut trees, and your sons-in-law do get along well with José."

After a time the parents of José said yes, and the bride's father and mother returned home triumphantly. And this is why José is being dragged through the streets so roughly, and why the young men are yelling "Sui! Sui!"

The crowd rushes José into the designated house and dumps him into a particular marriage hammock. Somebody grabs the bride, who was quite unaware that there was going to be a wedding, and ties a cloth over her head so she will not see what she

is getting into. They carry her rapidly to her marriage hammock
and deposit her on top of José. A burning balsa log from the fire
is placed under the hammock which is swung back and forth
vigorously for a minute. Then the cloth is taken off the head of
the bride.

The young couple, much embarrassed, jump out of the hammock and run to opposite sides of the hut where they pull off
their clothes and take a shower from inverted calabashes of water.
All the men who had an active part in the ceremony bathe along
with the groom.

The bride gathers up all the empty calabashes, and the laundry,
and paddles her canoe over to the river, while the groom runs
away and hides. At dusk the father-in-law must start searching
for José while all the old women of the town tease and taunt him.

"You'll never find José, old man; he's entirely too smart for
you! Did you get into something when you hooked José! He'll
get off the line if you don't watch out!"

And so the old man wanders half the night looking for José.
At last, José, who is hungry, tired, and bewildered, comes out of
hiding and stands in the moonlight on the seashore and there his
father-in-law finds him. The old man pleads with him to come
home. He tells him that he needs rest and that he has a hammock
for him. He tells him that he needs food and that there are crabs
and rice at home cooked and waiting. Finally, José gives in.

For several days this game is played; but since nobody will
help José, to try to get away from it seems futile. And yet, José
can actually cancel the marriage at any time until he condescends
to go with his father-in-law to the forest, cut down a balsa tree,
and lay a log therefrom before the mother-in-law's fire as a sign
of submission.

After several days José hangs around his old home less, and at
his new home more, and he usually sleeps there. He converses
with his bride from time to time and is asked to lie in the marriage hammock with his bride. But this privilege is simply sex
tease because they must lie side by side on their backs all night
with their arms at their sides, squeezed together tightly by the
natural pull of the hammock. By the light of a flickering kwallu
the mother-in-law keeps vigil to make sure that they abide by the
premarital rules of chastity.

After four or five days, José gives up and goes to the forest
before dawn to cut the balsa tree that is to seal his troth. When

he returns, all his friends and his bride's friends rush out to greet the couple who are now legally married. And all those who were uncertain how it would turn out breathe a sigh of relief. The bride goes to her mother-in-law's house and brings back José's personal belongings.

Once the marriage has been sealed with a balsa log, the young couple must get acquainted. They go to the bride's family plantation together. They must take long walks in the forest. They help each other with the duties of daily living and usually they fall deeply in love. They are teased by everybody because of their coyness, awkwardness, blushes, and outward signs of affection as their post-marriage courtship progresses.

ON THE TOWN

The town of Ustuppo has a charming municipal hospitality that I have not experienced elsewhere on the San Blas coast. After a visitor has been in Ustuppo for a couple of hours he must go to the Sunmakket Neka, for politeness' sake, to be questioned by the townsmen about his health, family, business, his trip, and what his purpose may be in coming to Ustuppo. If he is a stranger, the chief may make friends with him as he did with me on my first visit, by offering him the gift of seven or eight white eggs in a broken calabash. Of course, the stranger is expected to reciprocate in cigarettes, tobacco, a necktie, or some other present.

After some time a woman slips into the hall and speaks to the chief, who smiles and says that dinner is served. The visitors go by twos to the house of the woman where she and her associates have prepared a meal at town expense. They sit on low tree-trunk stools to eat from the same large dish with a big spoon and their fingers. There are broiled fish, coconut crabs with fat-gland sauce, toasted plantains, cocoa drink, corn drink, salt and hot peppers for condiment.

I have enjoyed this hospitality several times. The Ustuppo specialty is coconut crabs, but I have also been treated to delicious koe or dwarf deer, recently taken off the taboo list.

Of course, I always remembered the ladies who had prepared the meal. Once it was with a card of bright buttons apiece as presents, and to their leader I gave a string of beads. The old lady who received the beads smiled very graciously behind her big, golden nosering and said: "Tios pinsaet." This was a generous "Thank you" because it means literally "You think on God," but intimating much more: "Because you think on God you have been so generous as to give me this present without the thought of being paid back!"

SELF DEFENSE

Ignacio had been hunting on the peninsula of Sukunya that juts out at a sharp angle from the mainland and helps to bound Scotchman's Bay. There his flare-eared Indian hunting dog chased a rabbit into an enormous hollow log and the dog went right in after it only to become helplessly wedged. Ignacio had no axe along. The Indian tried everything he could think of to dislodge his dog but in vain, and when night came on he was forced to go home in his canoe alone and leave the animal to die. Ignacio was very sad and could scarcely be comforted.

Three days later another Indian came to Mulatuppu and said that he had seen a strange dog in the forest near Sukunya, and he wondered if it might be Ignacio's. Hope rose in Ignacio's breast and he decided to make the trip with his wife to Sukunya, half-a-day's journey away, if the wind was fair. This was my chance to see another part of the coast; so I asked permission to go along.

Ignacio's wife prepared kaisak (cornmeal and sugar cane), roasted plantains, and bananas; and I took along sandwiches, roasted palm nuts, canned fish, saltine crackers, and apricot juice. We borrowed Claudio's big canoe, and the chief lent us sails. We piled our provisions into the canoe and were off shortly after dawn.

Down the coast we sailed, past Golden Island that the famous pirate Wafer described so well, then past the towns of Tuwala and Kupa, then past a huge devil infested ishi tree, a landmark on the mainland shore. The wind from the sea became cold and contrary, and we plied the paddles. Then it began to rain a tropical downpour. Ignacio and his wife paddled on, and it was all I could do to keep the canoe bailed out with a calabash. Next we passed the unfriendly island of Koetup. We were in the middle of a cloudburst as we went by the historic point of Akla, with its mountain path by which the Indians led Balboa to show him the Pacific Ocean.

At Sukunya we were cold and shivering when we pulled the canoe ashore and started carrying our supplies to Ignacio's work hut. Ignacio whistled, and his lost dog came bounding to greet him. There were tears of joy in Ignacio's eyes as he knelt down and patted his pal.

We built a fire in Ignacio's hut, dried our clothes and ate our provisions, sharing generously with the hungry creature we had come to rescue. After resting a while and gathering the mangoes, coconuts, and papayas that had ripened we headed our canoe homeward, and again the chilly torrents poured upon us.

Just west of Sukunya we went ashore during the cold rainstorm, and Ignacio showed me where there were some flat, square, red bricks in the ground. We were on the site of the ill-fated Scotch Colony, and this was what was left of Fort Saint Andrew; so I gathered up several bricks to plaster into my fireplace in the States.

Eventually the wind died down, the clouds blew away, and we roasted in the tropical sunshine. We dripped with sweat as we paddled on and on. As the sun was setting, again there arose a cold wind in our faces. This time it was from the mountains, and again it brought a tropical storm. It struck us as we glided through the traffic opening between the poles of the Mulatuppu fish wier, rounded the back end of the island, and moored our canoe at the shore behind Ignacio's hut.

In our absence rumor had been busy. At the town council that night Ignacio was attacked in a powerful speech for having neglected his duty to work for a town project that day in order to take Kilupippi on a picnic, for which he had been paid a sum variously estimated at ten to fifty dollars.

After he had been censured severely in the charges, Ignacio arose and his oratory was superb. "Many of you men have been to Panama and have earned big money during a number of years, and while you were there you men paid one dollar a year to the Mulatuppu town treasury. I have never gone to Panama, and I have never been absent from my duty to the town in my whole life until today, except when sick in my hammock! And you who have made big money in Panama for many years while neglecting your duty to our town now dare to criticize me for my actions today! I have no children; I have only a dog, and for this reason he is as precious as a son to me. He is my helper. One day he brought me both a rabbit and a dwarf deer. A few days ago my dog, in trying to get a rabbit for me, became lodged in a log, and finally I had to leave him there to die. I was very sad. Several days later, when I heard that he might be alive I went at once to rescue him. What would you have done, you who accuse me? And you charge me with receiving an enormous sum of money to take Kilupippi along. Kilupippi did not pay me one cent, but went along because we are friends. What would you have done for your friend and your helper?"

The accusers remained silent.

EAR-PIERCING CEREMONY

One day Claudio and I went to the house of Olopiaite the Kantule. He was squatting by a pot of coals, fanning them into orange flames that lapped up about a glowing iron spearpoint.

"What are you doing?" asked Claudio.

"I am getting ready to perform a piercing ceremony."

"Tell us about it."

"This is an ear-piercing ceremony that is observed only here at Mulatuppu and across at Tupak [Isle of Pines], and it is accompanied by a ceremonial chant. We have this ceremony for piercing the nose and ears of the first-born girl in the family. In this case it happens to be my daughter's baby girl. There will be inna drinking with it, too! First we shall pierce the baby's nose and ears. That will cause her much pain. And her mother, my daughter, has already had much pain in giving birth to the baby. But you see that my son-in-law has not suffered at all, and it seems only fair that he should share the pain of the family; so we shall punch holes in my son-in-law's ears too!"

"That does sound rather interesting."

"Yes, but alas, it is a ceremony that is rapidly dying out. It is very unpopular with the young men!"

THE WRONG BRIDE

At one marriage I attended the groom was very indignant because he said that they had married him to the wrong girl. "She is not the one I wanted!" he complained. "And I'm going to call the marriage off. I shall never carry the balsa log to her mother's fire!"

"Well, what is wrong with this one?" asked Alcibiades.

"I don't want her because she's an old maid and the whole town will laugh at me for marrying an old maid."

"But she's *not* an old maid, she's only sixteen. What did you want, anyway?"

The disappointed groom replied, "I wanted one thirteen!"

This was not the end of the story. For a day or so the bride was angry at the rebuff. For a number of days the groom swore that the marriage was off, but as I looked from my window one morning at dawn a canoe quietly glided up to the shore and out stepped the groom with his father-in-law. In the canoe was a balsa log and an axe.

By now many pairs of eyes were watching through the cane walls of the houses nearby. The young groom shouldered the axe and started up the shore. Everybody's heart sank. He hesitated, returned to the canoe, and with a "beaten dog look" on his face he threw down the axe. He shouldered the log. Thereupon everybody rushed out of their houses and congratulated the young couple. The last time I visited this family they had two children and were very happy.

I knew a young man of Ailigandi who actually rebelled against the *vinculae matrimonii* and ran away from the sharp tongues of his wife and his mother-in-law. He hid on a coconut boat and went to another island.

At the council hall of the other island the chief and officials asked, "Why are you here? You are newly married and you must have run away from your wife." Nobody dared to take him in and nobody dared to feed him. After three days of exposure and starvation the young man managed to get back to his home island where he was afraid to face his mother-in-law. He found his father-in-law and asked him to intercede, but the father-in-law replied, "I should say not! You know how old Mu is. She would take my head off. You'll have to go to her yourself."

The starving prodigal went home and old Mu pounced upon him. "You have disgraced our family. Never in all time has a husband in our family run away before. Of course, *I shall not take you back!*" Old Mu stuck her pipe in her mouth with a determined thrust, like Pansy in the L'il Abner cartoons, marched out of the house, and said to the neighbors, "I'm just going to let him stew awhile!"

By fear, hunger, and anguish of soul the young man was tormented for several hours more, and upon Mu's return he was very willing to promise never to run away from his wife again. And you may be sure that he kept his promise.

LICE AND THE SCIENCE OF PHYSIOLOGY

One Sunday afternoon in Narkana I saw two Indian girls with

marcelled hair. They wore delicate golden earrings such as are purchased in Panamanian jewelry shops, golden necklaces with a gold cross pendant, golden bracelets of the most modern design. One had on a green silk gown of the latest New York fashion. The other was dressed in comparable style. They both wore new high-heeled shoes. They must have been living in Panama and had come home to Narkana for a visit.

There they were, representing the epitome of sophisticated civilization, sitting together on the log that served as the threshold of their modest thatched home. They were indulging in the ancient Cuna sport of catching and eating each other's head lice, a primitive folkway which they had not yet given up.

A related incident occurred one day at Ailigandi during my stay. The gossips were busy. The story was that a government school teacher had just beaten his wife, and the women of the town were enraged at this almost unheard of behavior. Of course, everybody was trying to find out why he had done so.

It appeared that the teacher had caught his wife in the act of picking lice off the head of a neighbor woman and eating them. He did not find fault with this procedure, which is a time honored custom, except that the host was skinny and the science of physiology teaches that a skinny person is likely to be a sick person. If she wanted to eat lice, that was all right, but in the future she would have to pick them off a fat woman!

MODESTY

I had only been in Ailigandi a few hours. The Indians were trying to find out what they could about me. And since olfactory stimuli are depended upon as a routine test of things by primitive people, Upikinya the Medicine Man thought nothing of slipping up quietly behind me and sticking his finger in my armpit, after which he smelled his finger.

The more serious calls of nature are answered traditionally by squatting in the ocean up to the waist, followed by an adept washing with the heel. Often today, the men make an attempt at modesty by sitting upon the edge of their canoes some distance off shore. Women who are surprised in the act, instead of quickly covering their bodies, simply hold their clothes over their faces to prevent identification.

The sense of modesty is less developed in little girls, although they sometimes employ the shore behind the dugouts. In the boys, who run naked much of the time, there are no inhibitions whatsoever, and they often stand proudly side by side on the seawall straining themselves in hilarious distance competitions. When the school bell rings at Ailigandi the boys make a bee-line for the wharf or seashore for a moment before going inside to their classes.

Clothing is worn through a sense of pride of ownership more than through a sense of modesty by a primitive people, and for this reason one does not expect to see them clothed at all times. Accordingly, in the house women and young ladies may often wear merely a loincloth and men usually wear pants, but boys almost always remain naked and girls frequently do so. Men often bathe naked in the town streets as do the girls and boys by holding calabashes of water over their heads so that the water sloshes down over them in all directions much like a showerbath. Young ladies and women usually bathe and swim at the river after doing the daily washing, filling the calabashes, or gathering fruit.

When strangers are on an island one never sees nakedness, except in boys. I remarked about this radical change in behavior of the little girls. The reason, I was told, is that little girls running about naked in the house are often scared by their fathers who say slowly: "Someday a great-big-white-man-is-coming, and he has a-great-big-knife, and he is going-to-stick-you-there!" Whereupon he makes a sudden dive with his finger at his daughter's pudenda, and she grows up with an innate fear of all white visitors. Again, it is customary when a little girl runs naked in the house to sneak up behind her and slice the flattened hand upward between her thighs just to make her scream and run. A counterpart of this sport among boys is the creeping up and suddenly snatching playfully at each other's genitals.

Two curious sex practices, found everywhere in the Cuna tribe, are started in tiny baby boys by their mothers who pull at them rhythmically to keep them quiet. I have seen a row of women at Mulatuppu thus quieting their baby boys in church. This leads to the habit of mild sex stimulation with the fingers, so universal and done so unconsciously that one can hardly take a group picture in San Blas without catching a man or boy demonstrating this habit. The other practice is that of sitting upon a stool, chair, or bench with one foot placed over the other and shuttling the knees together and apart rhythmically to produce mild sex stimu-

lation. This is sometimes done by the hour, and if one attends a
town council meeting he will see many pairs of knees in motion
simultaneously, accompanied by much saliva spitting. The spitting is common among all Cunas, but the knee shuttling, although
observed in girls and women, is more prevalent among the men.

SEX TABOOS

The Cuna children are kept in as absolute ignorance about sex
and child-birth as possible. A boy who has become wise will be
beaten with takke, the poison nettle, at the council hall if he
reveals to anybody what he has found out, and his auditors can
be punished for listening. This is one of the severest Cuna taboos.

Chickens do not lay eggs in the normal fashion. They find
them spontaneously generated under their wing. The yellow
yolks present in turtle eggs deposited on the shore or encountered
in the uteri of sea turtles are not called eggs. They are referred
to as okup sana (meat of the sand), and on some islands they are
dignified by the name sarsep. When Indians have a dog it is
usually a male. But occasionally a bitch is kept. At whelping
time she is hustled away in a canoe to the mainland and when
the pups are brought back to the island, the ever present crowd
of curious children is told that the mother dog found them down
by the sea.

And of course, as in any country, Cuna children ask the inevitable question, "Where do babies come from?" Mother is afraid
of breaking the taboo and is likely to tell the child to ask father.
When it does ask its father he describes how the men, working on
the mainland, find the new babies sitting on the horns of koe,
the dwarf deer, and how they bring them home to their wives.

When the ill-fated aviator, Mito Vanderhans, made his daily
trips along the San Blas coast a few years ago, carrying cargo, mail,
and Indians, he became so popular that the story developed that
he brought the babies in his Sourkukwalet (airplane); and children used to pester him with requests for baby brothers and
sisters.

This birth taboo is so strict that a married girl usually goes
through the horror of her first pregnancy without knowing what
is wrong with her. Not even her mother will tell her that she is
to have a baby.

Shortly before I arrived at Mulatuppu the story got out that foreign visitors brought the babies in their suitcases, and accordingly, a girl who had been married a month previously and whose sister had just had a baby, under the greatest secrecy, remarked to me very innocently: "Now that I am married I would like to have a baby. Did you bring any in your suitcase?"

Sometimes such ignorance is fatal. A girl at Ustuppo who was highly pregnant was allowed to answer the calls of nature alone, at night, in the sea. When she did not return home one night a search was instituted. The next morning her body was seen floating in the ocean, but the baby to which she had given birth was never found.

Sex ignorance, however, is not confined to brides. I know a young Cuna man whose bride constantly complained that something must be wrong with her husband because she just simply could not tolerate his painful attentions. When they had been married six months, the husband vented his rising wrath upon his wife for not getting pregnant like the other girls who married at the same time. The fights between them became so severe that Alcibiades investigated the matter and found out that the husband's knowledge of female anatomy and physiology was so distorted that it would be absolutely impossible for his wife ever to have any children by him unless he changed his tactics.

Kill the Chickens

One day a woman came to see the chief of Ailigandi shortly after dawn.

"I had the most horrible dream," she said.

"What is it?"

"I dreamed that the chickens on this island have a disease that will spread to our children and kill them all!"

"Horrible," chorused the town fathers. "This woman has dreamed that all of our children are going to die because of the chickens, so the chickens must all be killed at once!"

The boys of the town rushed out with big sticks and in a matter of minutes some one hundred and fifty dead chickens were floating in the sea.

The Burial of a Little Girl

It is the rainy season. Savage bolts of fire, a hundredfold, rip jaggedly across the blackness of night to illuminate the landscape, while our island shakes violently before stupendous rolls of thunder. The heavens open and great torrents of water pour down the palm thatch. Then come malaria mosquitoes and the hand of death is laid heavily upon the Indian village.

One after another children of the village are stricken with high fever and pain and are laid in their hammocks while their fearful mothers constantly drench their delirious heads and burning restless bodies with cold water in which have been placed magic leaves. Crude red nakkrus crossmarks are smeared on their foreheads and chests to ward off the demons of disease. A box containing the forty wooden idols of the home is dragged up under the head of the hammock. Douching with cold water continues and, as a result, pneumonia sets in to belabor the breathing. The fever mounts to impossible heights and a kapurtule medicine man or chanter is called.

This specialist sits all night on a low stool beside the hammock of the sick one, stirring and fanning his ka, or hot-pepper incense, in its clay incense pot. The pungent, choking smoke rises and fills the house. Passersby in the narrow street gag and cough because of its fumes. By means of his powerful medicine chant the kapurtule sends the spirits of the uchu mimmi idols and hot pepper far underground, perhaps to the eighth level beneath our world, to search for the spirit of the sick child that has been stolen by devils. His efforts are in vain and finally the tortured little body lies still.

A sister quietly slips between the cane walled houses to the home of the massartule or death chanter. Loudly the family express their lamentation to the corpse both day and night as they sit in their hammocks crowded about the small frame. A calabash shell is placed over the child's head to keep evil spirit-birds from pecking at it. His pot of cocoa bean incense before him, the massartule sings a twenty-four-hour death chant while against the hammock strings lean four painted and plumed massar sticks. Other massar are stuck in the ground in a row on either side of the death hammock. Into these the massartule prays good spirits to protect the child on its road to heaven.

After dark, Claudio (the young native missionary of Mulatuppu) and I hasten through a cold drizzle to enter the death house of a nameless little girl who was our friend. We stand with bowed heads for several moments among the mourners that are gathered about the child's hammock, quite uncertain of our welcome. We extend our sympathy to Densi Chak, the father, who straddles a nearby hammock mute with the shock of it all. By the light of a flickering kwallu, he is fumbling with a crumpled fragment of paper that says: "Nacio una nina el 8 dia del mes de. . . ." It is a certificate improvised by some literate Indian on the proud day of her birth, and her father is trying to learn just how old his little daughter was when she died. But because he cannot read and knows nothing about calendars, we figure it out for him.

We go to the other side of the hut where lies her little brother on the point of delirium, attended by their grandfather, Olopiaite, the famous inna kantule, who sings the most sacred long-chant for the coming out ceremony of the debutante. Yes, it is weleket (malaria), too; and with tears in his eyes, the old man, whose medicine chants failed to save his granddaughter, gladly accepts the white man's metaquinin that we offer, and he promises to follow instructions.

Exhausted though they are, the family of the dead child and their close friends prepare abundant food and food drinks for the funeral, because burial is an all-day event and the many friends and relatives must be fed at the cemetery and the grave-diggers must be feasted.

They arrange their canoes to go to uan, the cemetery. While being conveyed to the graveyard in a canoe, the cloth wrapped corpse, lying in its hammock, is surrounded by veiled women mourners who continue their chanting. As uan is approached a shotgun is fired, some believe, to frighten away devils. Others say to notify the town.

The graveyard is on the mainland, up the river near the farm plots. It is actually a village of palm-thatched huts where the grave diggers have already been at work carving an elaborate sepulchre in the red clay. The death hammock is hung up in a nearby hut where the mourners continue their lament up to the moment of interment.

On the hot, sunny afternoon that Olopiaite's granddaughter was buried, Claudio, Ignacio the Chanter against Sadness, and I, on a hunting trip, wandered up through the cemetery carrying a couple of .22 caliber Winchester rifles. We came upon the burial party and the stricken father thanked us on behalf of his wife and himself for our kindness in coming to visit his little daughter in her hammock the night before. We again expressed our sympathy, and the father said sadly: "We have no bird for our little

daughter to take to Heaven with her. Won't you please shoot a
bird for our daughter?"

Because I was not armed, the father asked me to rest on a seat
with the mourners while Claudio and Ignacio searched the trees
of the vicinity. Later, the father inquired if I had ever seen an
Indian funeral, and to my negative reply he invited me to stand
on a little hillock from which I could view all that went on.

A huge terra cotta censer is lowered into the grave for a few
minutes to sanctify it and cocoa bean incense puffs up in great
clouds. After this, a gravedigger arranges dishes and cups in a
small, low-vaulted antechamber carved in the sepulchre wall on
the right hand side. In a second small antechamber at the head
of the sepulchre, he places a covered sewing basket containing
money, jewelry, and other prized possessions of the deceased
child. He adds a tiny woven fan bearing an Indian swastika.
Four massar sticks or spirit ladders (massar arsan) are stood up
in the corners and additional ones are placed with the child in
its hammock. There is an olokwilotupa or braided cord to serve
as a spirit bridge. A dozen short splints (ukkurwar) with a little
banana-leaf bundle of chicken meat (purkwet suar masi) at each
end are arranged on the floor, together with similar splints bearing little bundles of cloth (suar ki purkwet mas anwalet). A
miniature canoe equipped with paddles is added. These accom-
panying objects are thought to become enlarged in the afterlife.

All afternoon my friends popped at parakeets and banana birds
in the tall trees without success, but just before the muitikket
covered the sepulchre, Claudio brought down a white-faced parrot
to accompany the little girl. This act of kindness was greatly ap-
preciated by her parents, because it was considered as a good omen
for the arduous voyage to Apya or Heaven in the Sun that the
little spirit had before her.

Finally, the hammock is suspended in the sepulchre with its
face directed to greet the Rising Sun, that Glorious Grandfather
of the race to whom its spirit must return. At this point a strange
procedure was carried out. The little brother, though very ill,
had been brought along to uan. Panic stricken and screaming
with fright lest he be buried alive, he was lowered into the sepulchre and forced to sit and then to stand for a short time upon
his sister in the death hammock. Upon inquiry, I was told that
this was done so that he would not forget where his sister was
and commit the horrible error of someday asking, "Pia punolo?"

(Where is my golden sister?), because this act would bring about misfortune for her journey to the Sun.

After this, the calabash on the child's head is quickly removed, smashed, and thrown away. A ceremonial string of red and white cotton threads is tied lengthwise and around the death hammock. Thick rails are rapidly fitted into a ledge of clay at the top of the sepulchre to form a roof over the grave. The white wrapping cloths are laid upon the sticks and then the extra clothing of the child is spread above that. Over these is packed clay which is trampled down solidly. When the interment has been completed there is laid upon the grave a fresh, green banana leaf about which the grave diggers sit, on low wooden stools, to eat their feast of rice, chicken, and food drinks.

A symbolic animal's foot, woven from basket reed, is inserted into the earth above the grave in company with the skull of a howler monkey, to scare away the devils. A string is stretched from the grave to a miniature canoe afloat in the river ready for the long trip to Apya. A second strand is strung from the grave to a tree across the river. This forms a spirit bridge by which the ancestors, who cannot cross water, may come to commune with the newly departed, because the soul may be tired or reluctant to leave the body and may linger a number of days in the grave before setting out upon its journey. Wooden seats, food, drink, and possessions may be left on the grave for use by the occupant or its ancestors' spirits. An old lantern may be lighted from time to time above the grave for a year.

Finally, a hut is built over the grave if it was not dug inside an already existing family burial house or uaneka. From time to time during the day the uncle of the little girl fired a shotgun into the air to scare away evil spirits, and a final shotgun blast announced to the village that the burial had been completed.

The Crime of Burning Old Medicine

Bright, sharp, restless tongues of fire in crimson and gold leaped skyward as they licked their way eagerly through the piles of mangrove brush outlining the shore of a small island. The dry, twisted branches crackled and hissed loudly as roaring flames consumed them and sent great clouds of gray smoke spinning and ever spreading through the lazy air. The heavy odor of the conflagration penetrated the nearby town of Ailigandi, where people stood on the shore to watch the smoke and fire.

At a safe distance from the flames and radiating heat stood a
husky young Cuna with a machete in his hand. It was Jud,
newly returned from Bacone Junior College in Oklahoma, and
he was clearing off a small island in order to show the boys of
Escuela Colman how to raise pigs, goats, turkeys, and chickens,
because animal proteins are sadly deficient in the Ailigandi diet.

But the watchful eyes of the witch doctors noted in this project
an opportunity. They went to the leaders of the town and convinced them that burning the brush would result in calamity for
the whole town. Epidemics would spread in Ailigandi and many
would die because the devils of disease and the spirits of their
dead were angry at what Jud had done. Previously this had been
an abandoned island and the medicine men of Ailigandi had
deposited there old bark, leaves, and roots that had been used in
treating diseases. There they had thrown the corpse of a man
who had been killed for being a sikwikolo. The schoolboys found
his skull.

Said the witchdoctors: "Not only will devils and spirits in general be angry, but especially the souls of those who have died of
the O poni (tuberculosis), who have been treated in vain with
some of this medicine. They will manifest their anger in Ailigandi!"

With such dire possibilities before them, the town council of
Ailigandi decided to appease the spirits. Each inhabitant was
assessed ten cents and Alcibiades was fined a dollar and a half
because he was responsible for the boy's actions. The money was
to pay the apsoketi for his ceremonial chants.

For two days the men sat in the council hall smoking tobacco
ceremonially. The long ropy ceremonial cigars were smoked
backward by the apsoketi, and appeasement chants were sung.
On the third day each family in the town set out by canoe and
planted "medicine" all along the shore of the small island and
along the path to the mountains that followed the bank of the
river. The medicine against the spirits consisted of little colonies
of uchu mimmi idols of balsa and nakkruses made from palm,
spiny sticks, roughbarked sticks, and sticks that oozed adhesive
sap. Some of the idols were armed with miniature bows and
arrows, and some had spears.

With these idol colonies were small calabashes filled with
smouldering hot pepper incense. Some calabashes were loosely
stoppered with a corn husk that allowed the smoke to ascend and

choke the devils but would not permit the devils to put out the fire in the calabash. There were also set up shells of large sea snails, ground down at the edges and filled with water. Thus, when once the spirits were started on the run by the hot pepper incense which they just can't stand, they would not fall exhausted along the way. Instead, they could stop and drink water at one of the snail shells and then be able to run on again.

The town council warned everybody not to go near the river or the island for twenty-four hours, until the devil chasing would be over; and the witchdoctors said that if anybody broke that taboo, his face would become twisted with paralysis.

Several days later I landed at Ailigandi and decided to take some pictures secretly of the fresh idol colonies on the shore of the little island and up the river. All went well at the island and nobody saw me. But as I was photographing a particularly interesting group of idols among the tall rushes by the river, suddenly there rose up before me in the weeds one of the witchdoctors. I had visions of my camera being smashed and of my being expelled from Ailigandi by the town council. Definitely the witchdoctor had me on the spot.

As luck would have it, I happened to look at the witchdoctor's hands. In one of them he held a couple of dozen little spears that he had been stealing from the idols. So here was my chance.

"Ibua?" (What are those?) I asked, pointing to the tell-tale spears.

"Ina nueti," (Good medicine) he replied with the sheepish grin of a boy caught in the act of stealing jam.

"Pia niakana?" (Where are the devils?) was my next question.

The witchdoctor's mind clicked quickly. If he should report my taking pictures, I would probably reveal his stealing the little spears. We had better call it a draw. So the witchdoctor, with a sweeping motion of his arm and a nod of his head, replied, "Yala ikar pa naoe." (They went up the mountain path.)

"An wakar wilup makke?" (Then it is all right for me to take pictures?)

"Eye." (Yes.)

With this the witchdoctor withdrew.

But this incident of insulting the spirit world is not unique. There are many similar cases. For example, one day at Arkia an Indian accidentally set the cemetery huts afire, and the flames swept over them in no time. Naturally the Serkana, or spirits of

the ancestors, were very angry; and the town had to do something
at once. So Yapilikinya, the Supreme Chief of the Cuna tribe,
was sent for and, with seventeen days of chanting, he was able to
appease the ancestors for the harm and insult of burning the city
of the dead.

THE DEVIL'S ACRE

The matter was put to a vote at the council hall and a majority
wanted to invite Claudio to start a private Christian school at
Mulatuppu. But where could they put it? The island was badly
crowded, badly crowded except that big uninhabited space belonging to the powerful dragon-devil (achu) who lived with many
lesser devils in the enormous, thorn-covered ishi tree on the eastern shore. Everybody was afraid to go near there at night, and
closeby was Niaya, a terrifying hole in the bottom of the sea, where
anything might happen.

"Well, how about the devil's acre, anyway?"

At last it was decided to build Claudio's house in a coconut
grove on the devil's acre, on a strip belonging to Ignacio the
Chanter against Sadness, although to get to it one had to pass by
the dangerous ishi tree.

The house was built, and Claudio, Margaret his wife, and their
tiny baby moved in, while the Indians sat back to see who would
win out — the Lord or the Devil.

One month went by and nothing catastrophic had happened at
Claudio's house. Even the baby was in the best of health.

"Just give that devil time!" said some. "You'll see!"

Two months passed and all was serene at Claudio's house.
There were beginning to be doubts. Three months went by safely
and the inactivity of that horrible old dragon-devil became the
talk of the town. At the council hall some became so bold as to
question the witchdoctor, Morti Nele, from the mountains.

"Why does not the Ishi Achu destroy Claudio and his family,
who obviously are on his property?"

"Do you suppose that the dragon-devil is getting old and de-
crepit, or is he sick, or what is the matter?"

"He certainly doesn't appear very active. Do you think that for
a price, you could handle him now?"

"Well, for a price, yes. At least, I could try it," agreed the
apsoketi.

So the apsoketi's fee was raised, and the procedure was begun by the men of the town smoking ceremonial cigars at the council hall on the first day of the rites while chanting went on.

On the second day the scene of the ceremony moved to the devil's acre. Here the apsoketi stirred up the coals in his incense pot and poured ka (hot pepper) upon the glowing charcoal. A continuous cloud of poisonous fumes was generated that rose and spread out among the broad branches of the ishi tree. The big dragon-devil and all the little devils began to sneeze and choke. The apsoketi danced about the tree, puffed on a twenty-four inch cigar with the fire end in his mouth; and, between puffs, he sang his powerful devil-exorcising chant. Claudio watched from his window because they said he had too much foreign influence to attend the ceremony.

While the dragon-devil was choking, the apsoketi suddenly seized him by the tail and started pulling him this way and that, trying to dislodge him from his home. With a zeal that would have done credit to Saint George or Beowulf, he wrestled mightily with the dragon, and the sweat flowed from his brown face and body because of the strenuous exertion.

By noon the apsoketi announced that he had pulled the dragon-devil down to about seven feet above the ground. By sundown he had been forced deep underground into a subterranean cave and the apsoketi had piled huge rocks over the entrance. Finally, the apsoketi charged the dragon-devil that he must stay there forever. Without difficulty he got rid of the small-fry devils and told them that he was putting their string or "spirit bridge" (by which they got in and out of the ishi tree) over on the mainland. Then the Indians came out with their axes and cut down the enormous ishi tree, thus giving Claudio a safe place nearby to put his basketball court.

When I first visited Mulatuppu several months after this incident, the great ishi tree lay where it had fallen, and its leaves were still flourishing in the humid, tropical climate. I sawed off a section of a limb as a souvenir, which proceeded to put out buds and to develop five leaves, like Aaron's rod. The Indians were still afraid of the ishi all that summer. A year later I saw a man making a canoe from the ishi trunk, and I witnessed an excellent basketball tournament between teams from five islands. They were using the court located upon the devil's acre.

THE COCONUT GROVE HIDEOUT

A Sunday School had been conducted for seven years at Achu-tuppu when I went there with Claudio, Margaret, Atilio, and several others. It was a lovely sunshiny Sunday afternoon, and we had a fine trip over in the small gasoline powered boat, *Niisk-wa,* that several Indians had found and sold to Alcibiades for twenty-five dollars and a shotgun. All went well until we took off our shoes, rolled up our pants legs, jumped into the water, and waded ashore. We carried with us the little pump organ and started for the sunmakket neka, or council hall, where we were to hold the meeting.

Everything appeared strange and abandoned. Where were the naked boys and half-clad girls that usually swarmed about us, laughing, joking, and asking questions? Where were the braver ones who always vied with each other to hold onto Kilupippi's hands? We saw very few children, and those we did observe were straight faced, avoided our presence, and did not speak to us. Something was wrong. Suddenly near the sunmakket neka, two policemen stepped out from behind a hut and barred the way with their horrible, poisonous takke nettle stems, symbolic of their office.

"Go back to boat! No Sunday School today! Make no sound on music box! Must have no foreign influence on island!"

"What is the matter?"

"Apsoketi namnakke." (The witchdoctor is chanting.)

A ceremony was under way for exorcising devils off the island. Upon inquiry we learned enough to be able to put together the rest of the story. Measles, mumps, and whooping cough were cur-rently epidemic at Achutuppu, and as a result a number of deaths had occurred. Devils of disease had concentrated upon the island and were up to their old trick of stealing spirits. The frightened townspeople had met in the Council Hall and had questioned the apsoketis: "Why this unusually severe infestation of the island by devils?"

The apsoketis stirred their pots of incense and went into a trance that carried their souls into the spirit world underground in order to find the answer. After communing with the occult powers they returned to the presence of their townsmen in the sunmakket neka and announced: "The devils of disease have per-fected a hideout in the coconut grove on the end of the island,

and from there they raid the town of Achutuppu to steal spirits. There must be an exorcising ceremony at once to drive them away! And it must be a big, expensive ceremony, too — the long eight day ceremony. Nothing less can dislodge them."

The town fathers weighed the matter. The five men who jointly owned the coconut grove were found guilty of harboring devils on their property and were fined the sum of two hundred dollars for their crime. This was exactly the amount demanded by the apsoketis for their therapeutic services and the long chant.

We had come to this island in the middle of the ceremony, and nobody wanted us, lest our presence with its "foreign influence" should cause all their expensive efforts to be wasted.

The five owners of the coconut grove were rendered bankrupt. Because as long as the trees stood the devils could return to their hideout, the men decided to cut down the grove and go out of business.

On my next visit I found the enthusiastic young men of Achutuppu, under Atilio's direction, playing baseball where a year before the devils of disease had maintained their hideout.

Chapter VI

◇ ◇ ◇ ◇ ◇ ◇

CUNA STORIES AND CHANTS

CUNA LITERATURE

IF ONE makes a casual visit to San Blas, he is not likely to be aware of Cuna literature. As a matter of fact, some persons in the past have felt that these Indians were so primitive that they had no literature at all. However, the Cunas, like all Indians, are great orators; and they prize the art of convincing speech so much that they eat certain song birds (sikwikolo) for a number of weeks under the chanting and ceremonial guidance of some famous nele in order that they may become great speakers who can mould public opinion to their desires.

The white man has had difficulty in getting at this Cuna literature simply because these people are so jealous of their literary productions that they do not want to give them away. A Cuna Indian may spend as much as $50 in order to be taught a particular story, and religious chants pay big dividends. So when an American ethnologist breezes in and says to a chief, "Saikla, now let's just sit down here and you recite to me all the stories you know, and I will write them down," the chief thinks to himself, "You're crazy if you think I am a big enough fool to sit here and give you for nothing the stories that cost me $500!"

As a matter of fact, many of these stories are considered so beautiful and so sacred that they cannot be related by speaking, but can only be told in the framework of a ceremonial chant. They can only be sung! Some of them are too sacred to be heard by children.

"And after all," thinks the saikla, "our stories are none of that impolite, uncultivated, snooping foreigner's business. He would only take them to America, sell them, and make a million dollars!"

After this reasoning the chief finally replies, "I don't know any stories." However, the Cuna Indians have a rich repertoire of narrations and chants filed away on the collective memory shelves of the tribe.

During my first visit I was unable to collect anything worthwhile, but during the past two years Alcibiades and I have managed to obtain more than twenty productions, and we have scracely scratched the surface. One might classify Cuna literary efforts somewhat as follows:

1. Medicinal chants, to be sung while medicines are being administered.
2. Chants for driving out devils.
3. Ceremonial chants.
4. Poetic gems.
5. Ballad chants, usually with a humorous twist.
6. Historical chants about the ancestors (serkana) or the divine messengers.
7. Stories about what horrible thing happened to somebody at some particular devil-possessed mountain, tree, river, rock, or whirlpool.

Most literary efforts reveal the deeply religious nature of the Cuna people. They often point a moral, or like the JUST SO STORIES of Kipling, end up with: "And that is why . . ."

There are stories about the strange Ansu people who live under the sea and whose beautiful daughters marry the sailors from sunken ships. There are never-ending serial episodes about the adventures of such young heroes as Nika Sapinkwa (the young nephew). There are many humorous tales about the somewhat stupid old grandfather (Tator) who is always having slapstick comedy tricks played upon him by Achu (jaguar), by Usu (agouti), and others. Occasionally, Tator, like Donald Duck, in a stroke of pseudo-genius, gets back at his tormentors. The ballad chants are especially full of practical jokes played by one character upon another. Each animal character is called "friend." We shall recount several of these literary pieces in order to demonstrate their nature.

Sosepippi sings a beautiful chant about Wekko (the snake-catcher) and Naipe (the snake). The Indians believe that all birds and animals worship God, sing praises to Him, and bow resignedly to His divine will, even though that submission means death for

them. In Sosepippi's chant the snake-catcher sings to God, and
the snake is willing to engage in fatal combat. Sosepippi wrote
out the pictograph symbols of this chant for me.

Wekko Naipe Epokwa

At daybreak Wekko [the snake-catcher]
Sits upon a lofty mountain;
He surveys the landscape in all directions;
He fills the whole world with his melody.

He chants to the rising sun:
"Now, Tata, Glorious Grandfather,
You are taking possession of the day!

"All things become brighter and brighter.
Now you are coming to show me your face!"

He has hunger and therefore he sings this song;
"Great Spirit, I believe
That thou wilt provide me good nurture
This day!"

High up in the mountains
Wekko is calling to Naipe [the snake],
Because he is searching for food.
Then Naipe glides out
And the bird flies down to the snake.

They converse with each other;
They decide to have a battle.
"Let us see who will win
In the end!" they say.

At once the fight between them begins,
And because Wekko is a kinkitule [literally **sharpshooter**
        with bow and arrow]
He firmly grasps Naipe
With his eight piercing talons.
Then Naipe sinks his golden fishhooks
Into the flesh of Wekko.

Wounded Wekko retreats for an antidote,
But the medicine once applied,

He swiftly returns to the fray;
He fights again!

At the long last Naipe succumbs
And Wekko whirrs him up with the wind.

Yes, the Great Spirit has made Wekko
A sharpshooter
And has ordained
That Naipe shall be his food!

Kipplo Ikar [the Way of the Kipplo] explains why birds migrate.
It is a charming little chant of somewhat ballad quality.

Kipplo Ikar

When the season of migration arrives
The kipplos call to their friends
Saying: "Let us go and fight with other birds!
We are ready to go fighting now!"
At the end of the earth [Mount Tarcarcuna]
Hundreds of different kinds of birds
Have gathered together for the struggle.

The kipplo, who is king of all birds,
Has many hundreds under him
And they are ever prepared for battle.
They are very brave!

Not one dares to say "no" to the kipplo
When he calls: "Let us go and fight!"
For he is their king.
At the demand of this bird
All kinds of birds
Go to Kikipipalu, their assembly field.
The smaller birds carry
The calabashes of ina [medicine] for the others.

First they reach the Buzzards' Field
And they call out to the buzzards,
"We are ready to go and fight!"
But the wives of the buzzards reply,
"My husband is injured and cannot go."
Then the little kipplos go inside the houses

To look for them, to see whether or not
They tell the truth —
When they enter the buzzard houses
They find the buzzards covered up with cloth.
They were not injured at all;
They were only hiding themselves.
And because these kipplos are such roughnecks,
They just kick them and kick them
And make them get up and go to fight.

When they arrive at Tarcarcuna [the sacred mountain]
They all congregate there and
Encourage their soldiers by saying
"Make yourselves strong!"
Although they are all very brave,
They usually drink medicine
To make themselves even stronger.

Once arrived at Mount Tarcarcuna
They station the soldiers
In their proper battle positions.
The humming birds are selected. They are the scouts
To lead the attack,
Because they fly so rapidly.

When all is ready
They start fighting,
And many are injured.
They had taken along mula [the buzzards],
To care for the injured, but when the wounded died,
They turned and ate them up.

And that is the reason why
The buzzards will eat meat
No matter how rotten, (for they will eat anything).
And that is the reason why
You will see birds every year
Going toward the rising sun to fight,
And the kipplos are the leaders among them.

My friend, Saikla Ikwaniktipippi, sings to his grandchildren a number of beautiful chants. Among them, Swirintitti (the partridge) and Tulup (the crayfish) are most interesting. Both show creatures created as food for man, bowing to divine will even though it may cost their lives.

Swirintitti — Swirintitti

Because Tiolele [the Supreme Deity] cares for us,
He provides us a well-protected home
And good food in the midst of the forest
Near Man's plantation.
Yet, because God has created us for man's food,
We are in constant danger.
What a sorrowful fate
To become food for these human beings!
Swirintitti — Swirintitti.

These human beings are always eagerly searching
For our little ones until they find them.
Swirintitti — Swirintitti.

Whenever these human beings steal our little ones,
I think to myself:
"How can they take care of my little ones
As their mother does?"
Swirintitti — Swirintitti.

They will only give my little ones
Scrimpy corn meal.
Swirintitti — Swirintitti.

As I sit on my nest near the plantation
Looking down at my little ones,
I can see and hear these human beings
Approaching with machetes.
Nearer and nearer they come — beware!
Swirintitti — Swirintitti.

In a tall tree my soul will be angry
At these human beings for their intrusion.
Swirintitti — Swirintitti.

What can I do but grieve for my fate
And the fate of my little ones?
The Supreme Deity has created us
As food for human beings.
Swirintitti — Swirintitti.

These human beings cannot care
For my little birds as I can.

They will raise them on scrimpy corn meal.
There is nothing for me to do
But to find another companion
And build another nest.
Swirintitti — Swirintitti.

Friendly companions have seen
My fear and my flight.
Swirintitti — Swirintitti.

They joined me in anger
Against such intrusion.
Swirintitti — Swirintitti.

I have found another companion.
Swirintitti — Swirintitti.

We will build our nest together.
Swirintitti — Swirintitti.

Tulup Ki Namakket (Song of the Crayfish)

Machiolotietipippiler is talking to his family;
Father crayfish is chatting with his wife:

Because Tiolele created us for the human family,
What shall we do? We cannot help ourselves,
For that is our fate.

Father crayfish is talking to his family:

Tiolele is good to us; he has given us
A dwelling place in the earth. He has created
Holes in the clay, and within these holes
We have made our habitation. We show our silver claws
And we close them for protection.

God has given us warning that when
The Sun in all its glory arises,
The wives of men will be coming,
Rattling their calabashes and making sounds:
I hear them coming over the surface of the earth.

The human beings are coming
While making noises with their canoes.
I hear them coming over the surface [of the water].

Father crayfish is talking to his wife. He shows his silver claws. He closes his silver claws.

Father crayfish says:

> If the wives of men see me, they will certainly
> Put their hands into the hole to capture me.
> He shows his silver claws. He closes his silver claws.
> The wives of men are coming, while making noises
> In their canoes. Woe is me, my evil fate, woe is me!
>
> Wives of men, when you saw me
> You came after me. You became excited
> And you shouted: "There is a crayfish in there!"
> Then you got a cloth to catch me.
> You put your hands in my hole.
> If I could somehow slip around them,
> I would be all right, and if I could find
> Another hiding place I would be secure.
> If I simply drift with the current
> It will be safe for me.
> When I find another hole I will be safe.
>
> The wives of men put their hands into the hole.
> I slipped around them and escaped.
> They are shouting: "Where did the crayfish go?"
> I drifted down the river with the current.
> They all are saying: "Where did he go?"
> I got under the leaves of a tree and drifted.
> I found another hole. I entered the hole
> That I found.
>
> Woe is me, for I left my wife
> And I left my children behind!
>
> Since Tiolele has created us as food
> For human beings, what shall I do?
> How can I help it, how can I help it?
> Woe is me!

RE SIPEP

Re Sipep (the Giant Coconut Beetle King) is a story that is typically Cuna. Big balls of gold are not too unusual in Cuna stories, and I was told as a historical fact in the Sassarti region

that once a Cuna king kept high up in the hill on Koetup a ball
of gold so heavy that men could not roll it down. Of course,
some of the color of the Re Sipep story is adopted from civilization. The wording is much as Peter Miller translated it for me
from the recording tape.

Once there was a King Beetle who had three charming daughters, but the youngest was the most beautiful of all. The King
made a proclamation that the man who could sing the magical
chant to roll two large balls of gold to a certain place would have
the right to marry his youngest and most beautiful daughter.

The tarantula came to the King and said he knew the chant
and that he would roll away the gold. He began to chant, and
he chanted and chanted until he became so hoarse he could chant
no longer. Yet the gold did not move.

He decided to go and see an inatule who would operate and
fix his throat. The doctor told him that there were certain things
he should not eat, such as pieces of sugar cane and pieces of
plantain skins. The inatule operated on his throat and sent him
home.

The tarantula was so accustomed to eating these forbidden
things that after a while he became so hungry that he had to go
back to his old habit of eating the very things the inatule had
warned him not to eat. However, he decided to try again to move
the balls of gold. The tarantula started chanting again and all he
could say was "Norr, Norr," his voice got so terribly hoarse. It
began to rain heavily and the King became very sad because the
gold did not start rolling. Finally the tarantula had to give up.

Then came the beetle (probably a ladybird beetle) with his
friend, Olor, the rain beetle. The beetle started to chant and the
gold started to roll a little. The gold was so heavy that no one
could move it. He continued to chant and the gold kept on rolling until he rolled it right to the door of the house where the
king wanted it to be. The beetle chanted again and the other ball
of gold rolled until both balls were inside the house.

The beetle said to the King, "Now are you going to give me
your daughter?"

The King, realizing that the tarantula could not do a thing,
felt that he should be punished for deceiving him by saying that
he knew how to chant to roll the gold, when he was unable to do
so. So he called his guard and commanded that the tarantula
should be beaten with some heavy cords. Eight of his big officers
came and started to beat the tarantula, while the beetle and his

friend, Olor, looked on. The tarantula was angry because he suspected that Olor, who was a singing insect, had helped his friend to win in the chanting; so he vowed vengeance. He cried when they beat him with the cords.

After the tarantula was punished, they gave the youngest daughter to the beetle for his wife and made a big celebration.

The tarantula said, "I'm going to beat this beetle up." The beetle said, "How can you beat me up when I rolled the gold and you didn't?"

So the beetle and his wife went for a walk. The streets were filled with the people who were celebrating the wedding — cockroaches, rats, etc. While he and his wife walked the streets he could see the tarantula looking at him with angry eyes. Meanwhile the cockroaches were rattling the chairs and the rats were beating the drums. The cockroaches' daughters, who were the maids of honor, were also in the parade.

Olor, who had helped the beetle chant in the rolling of the gold, was given a band of gold around his neck, and that is why he always has a golden appearance. The other beetle had yellow (golden) spots on his back.

It became time to go to work and Olor, who was head of the gang, with his friends, the conejo pintado, and the bob-tailed achu (possibly the lynx), and the beetle who had won the princess for his wife, got together some food and some corn-drink, which they took along in calabashes to eat and drink at midday.

Olor told them, "If you hear a yell about mid-day, you will know it is time to eat." About nine o'clock as the sun was up they heard a shout. The friends asked, "Who is calling?" The beetle said, "Someone must be calling me; I must go and see."

The beetle gets hungry very easily; so he went to the brook where the food was stored and ate a part of it while the others went on working. He returned to work and after a while he heard another shout and said to his companions that he must go and see who was calling him. He went back to the place where the food was stored and finished eating it all.

When the noon hour came, they all went to the brook to have their lunch and found the place empty of food. The beetle said, "Somebody must have eaten our food while we were working." The bob-tailed achu said, "I believe you were the one who stole our food, for it was you who went away from us each time we heard a yell."

Of course he denied it; so they decided to conduct a test to find out who stole the food. Each one of them was to lie face downward in the heat of the sun, and the one who perspired the most would be the guilty one.

It was a very hot day. So Olor said, "We will make this test and the fellow who is guilty will show some evidence in his skin." The beetle, who was next to the bob-tailed achu, started to sweat, and he began throwing his sweat over on the achu. Then he said, "Let us wake up and see who is the guilty one." The bob-tailed achu was the one found full of sweat, and so they said, "Oh, you are the guilty one," and they reprimanded him for playing such a dirty trick. The bob-tailed achu was indignant and said he had not done it, someone else had eaten the food.

They returned home and found that the tarantula had been doublecrossing the beetle with his wife during the beetle's absence.

The rain beetle said to his friend, "I will help you out. This is a dirty trick." When he found the tarantula chatting with his wife, the beetle got so mad he made a big rumpus and started fighting with the tarantula. The tarantula got the best of him in the fight and so the poor beetle was defeated.

The bob-tailed achu, seeing that his friend was defeated, said, "I will help you out. I am going to eat this tarantula." So he ate him up. The beetle's back was broken in places because of his fight and he fell against the stone floor several times, because, unfortunately, he was very badly beaten. The father of the princess did not know anything about the fight that had taken place.

The following day they went to work again. The bob-tailed achu couldn't find his clothes, as it seemed somebody had stolen them, and so he had to go without his clothes. They again took the food and drink they would need, and they stipulated that under no circumstances should anybody give a yell while they were working. After a while the achu gave a yelp. He said "I have to go because my wife is sick, and I must go home to see how she is." Instead of going home, he went to the place where the food was stored and drank from the beetle's calabash and threw the calabash into the stream.

The beetle decided he too would play a trick and he said his wife had bought him a new file for his machete and he was going to get it. He went, and drank the calabash of drink belonging to the bob-tailed achu and also threw away the calabash.

Then they all went down to the brook at noon and each blamed the other for throwing away their calabashes, and they began to quarrel. So the achu decided to take the matter to the King to be settled.

They told the King and he called a meeting. They also summoned the tarantula to the meeting to be punished for his misbehavior with the princess. They called two policemen and the beetle started to accuse the tarantula* in the presence of the King's guard. The beetle said that the tarantula had beaten him up for the sake of his wife. So they (the court) decided that the tarantula should be put in prison for about four months. The King scolded the bob-tailed achu for throwing away the calabashes of his companions and warned them all that they should behave themselves.

Meanwhile the princess became ill. She said the tarantula had beaten her, and that was why she had such rheumatic pains. The King was quite angry about it. Finally she died, and the poor beetle lost his wife. Bemoaning his great loss, the beetle went wandering among the big rocks near the river and while struggling between these huge stones he hurt himself and died of a broken heart.

ACHUSIMMUTUPALIT

One day as I returned by canoe to Ailigandi from Ustuppo with Alcibiades and Seferino Colman (whose father, Supreme Chief Sam Colman, did not want him to learn to read and write) we talked of Indian traditions. Seferino is steeped in Cuna lore and while we paddled and sailed he named the horror places along the coast where the devils abide. He told the stories of what fates had befallen different individuals near each particular diabolical bastion. He said that in the chants to bring back the spirit of the sick there are mentioned in sequence all of these places along the whole Cuna Coast to which devils may have taken the spirit.

The spine tingling stories about these locations are taught to the children. They have all listened to the one about the famous Nele Powwow and his family that were sucked down along with their canoe and swallowed up by the pirea whirlpool between Narkana and Naluneka. They know about the fishermen whose

---

*It will be remembered that the bob-tailed achu has already eaten the tarantula. I commented to the Indians about this contradiction and was assured that "this is exactly the way it is related in the chant."

canoe was wrecked by the big devil living among certain jagged, jutting rocks between Ustuppo and Ailigandi. They have heard how those fishermen were immediately eaten by sharks. Typical of these devil stories is the one about Achusimmutupalit and what he did at Kasnun (Rotten Hammock) Mountain on the mainland near Ailigandi.

Once upon a time many years ago two men were walking in the mountains. Night overtook them while they were on top of Kasnun and naturally in order to sleep they strung up their hammocks between two trees, the one hammock above the other. At midnight when it was pitch dark there was heard a blood-curdling shriek like the voice of a fire siren in Panama and a mighty whirr of enormous wings like the sound of the propellers on an American bombing-plane. After this all was silent.

The man in the lower hammock called to his friend but there was no answer, and because he had no way of making a light he shuddered in his hammock until day break.

When it became light enough to see, the man in the lower hammock found a pool of blood and the head of his friend ripped off at the neck. His body had been devoured by Achusimmutupalit. The man was so filled with fear that he ran down the mountain and never returned to get their hammocks, that were left there to rot, for which reason the place is called Kasnun.

Because of this tragedy whenever Cuna Indians must camp overnight in the mountains they always hang up their hammocks in a ravine, to save themselves from Achusimmutupalit, the shaggy-bellied monster who sweeps the pitch black mountain-top trails at midnight in search of victims.

MOLI, NIKKEPKWA EPOKWA (THE TAPIR AND THE CHIPMUNK)*

Many years ago, the animals wanted to climb Paluwala, the enormous salt water tree, because halfway up that tree there were rich fields of corn and fruits and many other kinds of nourishing food. Friend Usu (agouti) climbed, Friend Sule (monkey) climbed, Friend Wetera (mountain pig) climbed, and Friend Moli

---

*Other versions of this story exist, and it will be noted that the tale is based on the sacred account of Olowaipippilele, Olokukurtilisop, and the Paluwala or Umbilical Cord Tree of Life.

(tapir) climbed. But one after another they fell down very hard on their rears and that's why all these animals have humped backs.

Having failed to climb the great Paluwala, the animals took counsel together and decided to chop down the huge tree. First Friend Usu tried and tried, but finally had to give up. Friend Sule tried his best but became exhausted. Then Friend Yannu (wild pig) and Friend Wetera (wild mountain pig) tried but all in vain.

Then Friend Moli attempted it and actually after the greatest effort succeeded in cutting off the immense trunk of the Paluwala. But the Paluwala did not fall. The great branches of the Paluwala and the enormous vines that twined about the branches were caught in the clouds.

It was decided that Friend Nikkepkwa (chipmunk) must be the one to climb the Paluwala and chop the vines and branches loose from the clouds, but Friend Nikkepkwa did not want to go on such a dangerous errand. No, he would not go! They all pleaded with him, and finally Friend Moli promised that if Friend Nikkepkwa would ascend the Paluwala, chop loose the branches and vines and thereby prove himself to be a man, he would give to Friend Nikkepkwa his beautiful daughter to be his wife.

To this Friend Nikkepkwa agreed and soon he disappeared into the high branches of the Paluwala armed with rope, machete, and axe. In a short time those below could hear the "tok-tok-tok" of the axe as the invisible Friend Nikkepkwa chopped at the branches and vines. Finally, the great tree tottered and crashed and all observers fled to safety. Down came the enormous Paluwala that turned to salt water and formed all the oceans of the world.

Nikkepkwa's friends rushed up very sadly to look for the body of the poor little wood chopper who didn't have a chance. They searched and searched and searched everywhere, but alas, no Nikkepkwa was to be found. At last they had to give up the search, and all the animals set out for their homes, weeping as they went.

When Friend Moli came home he saw that nobody was about, but as he entered the house he found that Nikkepkwa was already in the marriage hammock making love to his daughter.

Friend Moli said, "Ai Nikkepkwa, we all thought you were dead. I knew you were a fast worker, but I did not know that you were quite that quick. How in the world did you get here so soon?"

"Well, that is very simple," replied Friend Nikkepkwa. "When the great Paluwala tree crashed, I jumped and here's where I landed."

Chapter VII

◇ ◇ ◇ ◇ ◇ ◇

DARIEN

REPORTS ABOUT Indian towns on down the coast toward Colombia were so conflicting that I decided that I would have to make a trip to the Gulf of Urabá to learn of any possible moon-children in the region, especially because some scientists thought that they did not exist in that part of the tribe.

Ignacio wanted to take me to Urabá, but the town council of Mulatuppu would not let him go because of the controversy about his trip to Sukunya. However, he had a friend named Taniu in Anasasukun just a quarter of a mile below the Negro town of Pito, and the coconut boat would stop at Pito. So Ignacio dictated a letter of introduction to Taniu, and Claudio wrote it on his typewriter, signing it for him.

Armed with this letter I made my way to Tuwala by dugout soon after dawn and caught the coconut boat that had anchored there the night before. The chief of Rio Cedra, a small town of the Carti Region, and Supreme Chief Yapilikinya were taking the coconut boat as far as Careto where Yapilikinya was to spend a week chanting about God in the council hall.

It was beautiful weather, with bright sunshine and a blue sky with cottony clouds suspended in it. We sailed smoothly in the quiet water behind the Sassarti Islands and then turned left at Punta Escoses to feel the choppiness of the open sea. Yapilikinya, who knew my interest in Cuna history, pointed out and named the peaks, bays, and rivers for me as we went along.

"That fog-covered mountain over there behind Akla is Poyala [Foggy Mountain]," said he, pointing to what some American

137

cartographer had prosaically christened on my map "Mount Vernon." "And that huge rock cliff is a place where the Spaniards used to get stone for building, and they split the cliff the way you see it now. And that rock peak at the end of Scotchman's Bay is Ipeyala [Stone peak], and there is a long story about a medicine man who was killed there by many snakes that attacked him. This point of the peninsula is called Alidonmutlu and the Scotchmen once had a fort there."

Captain Peterson put in that broken pieces of pottery are still found at Akla, where Balboa was beheaded; and I told him how I had dug up some bricks at Alidonmutlu, the Fort Saint Andrew of the ill-fated Scotch Colony.

We made Careto before dark and, as I was not allowed to go ashore, I could not see the present town, which hides behind a coconut grove; but I did photograph from the deck two previous sites of the town nearby, each abandoned because of the devils of disease that bring malaria.

Captain Peterson and I were leaning on the rail enjoying the beauties of the sunset when the Indians had finished trading their coconuts for staples and trinkets, and Serin, the sooty black weighing man, had put away the steelyard. The three crew members were back on the poop eating the fish they had caught during the afternoon, together with yucca roots, wild rice, and coffee.

"The Indians on the shore in this region," said the Captain, "do not perpetuate themselves because of the severity of malaria and are constantly replaced by individuals who migrate from the mountain villages."

"This is a very historic spot," said I, "and this town was an ally of Balboa, wasn't it? I wonder if ————?"

"I know what you are thinking," smiled Captain Peterson, "and about ten years ago I tried to answer that question. I realized that nearly every family here had come from the mountains to Careto in recent years, and there was only one old man who could possibly have been descended from Balboa's friend and father-in-law, Chief Careta. So when I got a chance I asked that man." He said, "No, there are no old families of Careto left. I have been here longer than any other person in town and I came from the mountains as a boy!"

The bright sunset faded to yellows and browns, then changed to gray and leaden hues. After this came the dark and it grew cold. Captain Peterson gave me a tarpaulin and an army blanket.

A loaded coconut boat is much worse than a cattle boat, and the stench of the vile, nauseating fumes of fermenting copra makes sleeping almost impossible. But in order to get some rest for my tired body I spread my tarpaulin over the reeking forward hatch, because the remainder of the deck was occupied by pigs, turkeys, iron kettles, and Indians. I lay awake thinking of the treachery of Juan Alonzo and Balboa at this place, and of Anayansi, daughter of Saikla Careta, and the part she played in the history of the Spanish Conquest of the Isthmus.

Next day about 2:00 P.M. we came to the Negro town of Pito, and an Indian walked along the shore to Anasasukun to deliver my message to Taniu. But unfortunately he was away working in a coconut grove. Getting no reply I decided that before dark I had time to walk some ten miles to the Pito River, and so I set out with my camera. The river kept moving farther and farther away every time I met a stray Indian along the shore, and I was about to give up, when I chanced upon one who carried several unhusked coconuts, and a machete. With him was a boy.

He said, "Just beyond the next coconut grove." At this I took courage and gave the boy several bright plastic airplanes from my pocket, with which toys he was well pleased. In the coconut grove I heard above me the flapping of huge wings, and several screams that came from a defiant golden eagle which I had disturbed; but by the time I secured a club it flew away.

Beyond the coconut grove was a sandy shore, that filled my shoes so that I had to remove them; but the fine sand was so hot on my bare feet that I had to walk in the water, and then the waves tried to wash the sand from under my feet and make me lose my balance. After that there was a stretch of blue granite gravel that bruised my feet, and a swift, clear stream that I forded with difficulty. After that there was another coconut grove with a barbed wire fence and a Spanish-speaking Negro in a huge sombrero who was burning up coconut husks. He pointed out the Pito River to me and told me that the men lived up the river several miles.

I stood on the bank and drank in the memory of history, for this was the river at which Balboa had found the Cuna Indians panning gold. But because the Spanish thirst for yellow metal was the cause of their almost complete extinction, the Indians are still afraid to pan it today, although they will buy crude gold-plated jewelry from Negro goldsmiths, whose source is the Pito River.

A group of gold panning Negroes live in a settlement up the river, finding enough gold dust to take it to Pito once every two weeks where they trade it in at the two grog shops for whiskey.

I walked back to Pito and found the small store of Gabriel Capech, who was about seven-eighths white — thin, curly haired, gray eyed, wrinkled-faced, sallow, and unshaven. Serin said it was illegal to deal in gold, but if I would use his name, I could get some dust from his friend. I wanted to see what Balboa's gold looked like; so after mentioning Serin's name I spoke about gold to Gabriel who searched me through and through with his steel gray eyes. He quietly unlocked a strongbox, removed some ancient apothecary scales, and carefully weighed out a castilliano of the yellow powder, about enough to fill a dental cavity.

Leaving Gabriel's store I was stopped by a young Negress who was accompanied by a mulatto child. The Negress asked if I knew a white man by the name of Marson. "He is the father of my little girl. He said he would come back to us. She is now five years old, and he has not returned. If you meet Mr. Marson in Panama, tell him we are still waiting."

Because Pito is a Negro town, nobody would take me in. So I sat by the seashore on a tree stump and meditated upon the disadvantages of being a white man in a colored world. Then at dusk the sand flies came in clouds and reminded me painfully and perpetually that my white skin was also thin.

I had slapped sand flies in the dark constantly for about four hours when a colored man took mercy on me and invited me to lie on his porch nearby. The porch had a roof of thatch and a rough wooden floor with gaping cracks between the planks. Several members of his family lay on thin, loosely-woven straw pallets spread out on this floor, and they were protected from the voracious sandflies by two smudges of tar and coconut shells under the porch, the smoke of which filtered up between the planks. A kerosene slut flickered on a shelf that was fastened to the cane walls of the house and it revealed dim, wavering outlines of things with black shadows rather than the things themselves.

The woman of the house was a huge, fat, brown-skinned cartoon of a creature with a simple, sleeveless, red-and-white polka dot slip that came to her knees. Her natural voice would have filled an auditorium, and she thoroughly enjoyed using it to give orders to her husband and children, thus demonstrating that she was boss. Every once in a while she would separate herself from her undersized hammock with difficulty and waddle over to the slut to relight her cigar, or she would work her way down the three porch steps to stir up the smudges. Then she would return to rebulge her hammock that always sagged and creaked and threatened to burst, carefully sticking her feet and elbows out again in their customary awkward positions.

Next day Taniu came to say that the chief, to whose little boy I had presented the plastic airplanes, had given him permission to take me to Colombia and that a friend of his would go along. So about 4:30 P.M. when the wind came up we set sail from Anasasukun hoping to reach Porto Obaldia before dark. Very soon, however, the wind became contrary and blew severely in our faces. We removed the sails and took to the paddles, still believing that we could make our goal by ten o'clock, but the sea whipped up into choppy waves, with whitecaps here and there, and great swells developed that we had to meet head-on in order to keep our small dugout from being capsized or dashed upon the coral reefs. We battled each swell as best we could and moved forward only by inches.

Obviously, we could not travel such a perilous ocean after nightfall, as the weak, crescent moon came up very late; and so we made for the shore when night was descending. Completely exhausted, we finally reached the protection of a small, rocky promontory that shielded us from the dangerous swells, but the night was already too black to see where we were when we beached our canoe in a tiny cove called Apeorkansukun. The Indians said that we were only half way to Porto Obaldia.

There we built a fire and ate some of our provisions. By the light of our campfire I saw that we were in a coconut grove, and that somebody had been repairing the hull of a tabulu there. Nearby on the shore there was a Negro style dugout. The two Indians climbed into the tabulu and were soon fast asleep, whereas I sat with a club by the campfire and kept it going because of wild animals from the jungle and the fact that the owner of the boats (armed with machete) might come back and stumble onto us in the dark, a possibility that I did not relish. So thus, I peered out into the darkness every time some little animal sounded off, and was startled whenever a tropical bat or moth fluttered about my fire. Once I saw a pair of shining eyes looking at me out of the darkness. Gathering up courage I approached them, gripping my club ready to strike, only to find two glowworms that had been talking to each other.

Wearily over and over again I banked more driftwood and more coconut husks on the ravenous fire, stirred it up, and with aching eyes I watched the Southern Cross, the Wolf, the Centaur, and other unfamiliar constellations snail across the sky.

About 2:00 A.M. a Negro with a wooden torch dipped in pitch came to look at his possessions, gave us permission to stay, and went on down the forest path to his hut singing to keep from being scared. Then the black clouds gathered and a terrible electric storm that had circled us returned and broke, putting out the fire and soaking all my matches. The Indians without ado shifted their positions to under the tabulu hull, and covered themselves with tarpaulin. I quickly turned the Negro's boat over above some driftwood, and under it I weathered the storm with its spectacular bolts of lightning that crashed down all about us.

We pushed off at dawn. After we had paddled some distance Taniu drew a long beer bottle from his pack, took a gulp, and spat it into the sea while making a rye face. "It's spoiled!" said Taniu, as he poured out the water and magic leaves over the edge of the dugout.

"What is it?" I asked.

"I just got married and a medicine man gave me this bottle of medicine so that my first baby would be a boy."

By ten o'clock we were in Porto Obaldia, the former Colombian prison colony, whose inhabitants are all Negroes save possibly a half dozen persons. Several weeks before, I had seen the Indian, Mario Porras, Cuna Representative to Panama, and he had written for me a letter of introduction to the Captain of the Port at Porto Obaldia. This I presented, asking permission to enter Colombia, because roving groups of "Communistic," armed bandits had made it unsafe for travelers, some of whom had been killed and robbed even during the past few days. For this reason the Colombian Consulates were refusing visas to foreigners.

The only white families in Porto Obaldia seemed to be those of the Captain of the Port and of Señor Kasub, a white Russian, the former operator of a Panama gambling joint, who now owned the only big store in town. Mito Vanderhans, the aviator, had introduced us the year before when his plane put down there; and I had counted 35 cases of whiskey and 10 of gin in his store, for he supplies the town's two saloons, in which he has a business interest.

The Captain of the Port was difficult to locate because he was on the other side of the town playing checkers with Señor Kasub.

When we got him hunted up he was very obliging but he said that we had to go to the other end of town to his office to make it official. Certainly, he would write for us a letter to the Mayor of Akanti, Colombia. Because his office typewriter would not work, he took time out to visit the very black schoolteacher. The schoolteacher's typewriter was also out of commission and we had to go back to the other side of town again to see about the only other typewriter in Porto Obaldia. It belonged to the prosperous Señor Kasub. When we approached the big store this time Señor Kasub was sitting outside the door petting a half grown chicken that was perched on his knee.

The red tape lasted so long that we wasted four hours, and this threw us even worse off schedule. We set out at 11:00 A.M. and by 2:00 P.M. we were in Akanti, a Negro town with banana plantations in the mountains which once boasted a ten-mile strip of narrow gauge railroad. We sought the Mayor, a young fellow of about twenty-one years, who was the only white man that we saw there.

Again we wasted time. We had to explain all my eight required documents of travel, and notes about each one had to be taken down. Then we were turned over to the Immigration Office where it was necessary for me to explain to the illiterate mulatto officer what his own ledger said, and in registering myself I noted that during the past two years only seven persons had entered Colombia legitimately by that port of entry!

At this point Taniu pulled a fast one. The two Indians had been discussing something between themselves for some time and I suspected trouble. Taniu said, "We are not going any farther until you pay me all the money that you promised us for the whole trip." Seeing that they had me at a disadvantage and not wanting to abandon my expedition in this hostile country, I paid him, wondering what would be their next move.

At last we got away. Again the winds were contrary and we paddled until night, coming eventually upon a Negro town of twenty houses, only twelve of which were inhabited. It was getting dark as we arrived, and we were told that we could not stay there, the residents supposing that because I was a white man I was probably a government agent looking for somebody. But when we promised to leave by dawn they allowed us to stay in one of the abandoned houses.

By this time our food and water supplies were completely exhausted and we were greatly in need. A Negro boy was sent to show us a nearby river where the inhabitants obtained drinking water, but when we got there by the light of a slut we found the mouth of the river stopped up with sand and the water stagnant. The inhabitants used that mud hole not only for drinking but also for washing clothes, bathing, and answering calls of nature. So, thirsty as we were, we paid the boy and decided to get water elsewhere next day. Back in the town we tried to buy food but nobody wanted to sell us anything, since the only man who sold any grocery supplies had locked up and was gone already two weeks, and nobody knew when he might return. For this reason, everybody wanted to guard his meagre food supply.

After half an hour of trying everywhere and pleading with everybody, we found a woman willing to sell us a pound of wild rice, but she was afraid of us and therefore refused to cook it for us. We walked around for twenty minutes more trying to locate somebody else to cook it and finally Melinda Mendez, a skinny Negress who appeared more intelligent and less fearful than the average inhabitant, agreed to prepare it.

We went to our abandoned house that had solid hinged shutters on all the windows. We untwisted the wire that held the entrance door shut and went in to wait for supper. A third of the thatched roof was missing, and through that great opening the bats flitted in and out recklessly. A number of the floor planks were missing and at our approach several rats scampered to safety down the spaces. Cockroaches were legion. In our house there were two abandoned iron bedsteads with no springs, just bare boards laid across them sidewise. The Indians wanted these boards to sleep on in order to try out the comforts of civilization, and that was agreeable to me because they were very close to the ground and to the creeping things. For my bed I chose rather a rough old wooden table because it had long legs, and I slept in my clothes using my rolled-up raincoat as a pillow.

Finally, a boy with a crude light appeared out of the blackness to tell us that supper was ready, and we followed him to Melinda Mendez's house where we ate ravenously from a rough board fastened to the side of the house. She had cooked our rice, added some salt and tiny pieces of fish, prepared some yucca roots left over from her family's supper, and brewed us some ginger root tea which she called anahivli. At least we got filled up. We paid the woman, thanked her, and went back to our abandoned house, as

I was especially afraid that we might be robbed of my valuable photographic outfit. We twisted the wire on the front door to hold it shut, but we found that the back door could neither be closed nor fastened in any manner. And so we tried to sleep.

Because every bone and muscle in my body ached, I lay awake and relived something of the history of this Negro town of Titumate, which, with similar Negro villages of Gloria and La Playa, was said to stand within the limits of what was once the largest city of white men in America. This was the site of the famous Santa Maria de la Antigua del Darién, the residence of Balboa and Anayansi. It was near here that after a most bloody slaughter the bearded white gods and their dragons drove Cemaco and his five hundred primitive warriors into the mountains. I thought of 1903 after the Panamanian Declaration of Independence when some five thousand Colombians landed at this place and tried to work their way overland to attack the Panama Canal region, only to be so decimated by malaria that they had to abandon their project.

As we pushed our dugout into the water at dawn, Melinda Mendez, who had cooked our supper the night before, came from her house nearby to wish us a safe journey; and I asked if she ever found bricks with writing on them, thinking that possibly some Santa Maria bricks might have been marked. She said, "Yes, I found one but I do not know what it says because I cannot read." She went to get the brick that she had brought from up the Titumate River.

I bought the brick, and even gloated that I might have a four-hundred-year-old memento of that famous city of early Spanish American history, although I could not decipher the markings in the semi-darkness. My Indians refused to go farther and because they had my money I could do nothing with them. So we started home. When daylight had arrived, I looked at my brick and my heart sank. It said: "Phoenix No. 1, Sayre and Fisher, Sayreville, N. J., U. S. A."

We went up the Titumate River until we found the water clear and flowing swiftly. But I was afraid of it even then, because I knew something of the horrible fevers that can be obtained by drinking from polluted tropical streams. There we filled our water jugs, and I took several pictures of the river and of the coast that once was Santa Maria. After this we moved away from shore.

The wind was contrary most of the way and we paddled constantly, making Porto Obaldia late that afternoon. There my Indians forsook me and went home to Anasasukun in their canoe, leaving me to shift for myself. First, I went to consult Señor Kasub after which I found a cane-walled thatched hut with a wooden floor where a colored woman served meals. I went in at the street door and called, "Hello!" There was a commotion in the back yard. A bejeweled Negress, her lactating brood sow, two small spotted pigs, and three motley colored hens rushed in to see who the customer was. The throng crowded through the kitchen door with grunts, squeals, and excited clucks, while the woman herself added to those agrarian sound effects with the sharp, rhythmic "clack-clack-clack" of her wooden sandals. Luckily, there was a gate that separated the customers from the family, and through the bars of this gate the razor back sow stuck her long nose and sniffed vigorously to investigate me more thoroughly. After a moment she gave a final snort of disappointment and disgust. Then she turned away. Here I obtained eggs, bacon, rice, and bollos del maiz nuevo (green corn patties).

Señor Kasub put me up over his big saloon in a bare room in which there was placed a canvas cot. My room was lighted by a smoky slut. Outside was a veranda from which I was able to observe the night life of Porto Obaldia, the public phase of which consisted mainly of drinking whiskey at the saloons, with their oil lamps and their scratchy old phonographs. In this night life the women were enthusiastic participants.

Because so many persons had been killed recently in the barnstorming planes which worked the San Blas coast, seldom did one come on down to Porto Obaldia any more. In addition, the Colombian tabulus, probably all of which belong to smugglers, avoid the Port of Entry of Porto Obaldia but cut across from Pito through the open sea above the Gulf of Darién to strike North Colombian towns that welcome their illegally imported safety matches, shoes, and other items on which there would be a high import duty.

I took Señor Kasub's advice and hired three Negroes to bring me next night to Claudio's house at Mulatuppu. We set out about 10 P.M. in an excellent boat, but the paddles were mechanical makeshifts and not efficient. They consisted of square boards nailed on the end of poles. Of course, the wind was against us from the beginning, the sea was black and choppy, and the young moon did not give much light. When we got as far as Pito we were struck by a hurricane that threatened to drown us, but we managed to get ashore and protected ourselves as best we could upon the narrow porch of the one big store of the town. But the wind and rain caught us even there. The storm continued all night with much lightning, and it was still raining in the morning when the owner came to open the door and stir up the fire. Because we were thoroughly soaked and shivering, I bought a can of cocoa and had the owner cook up a lot of it in order that we might get warm. We ate with it ship's biscuit and canned sardines which were about the only other food items we could buy.

When we were warmed and filled, we pushed out and the sky cleared off. The sun turned hot, and dried our clothing on us. The wind refused to blow and when it did, it was contrary. I noted that the big-muscled black fellow in my crew was interestingly primitive. On one hand he wore two golden rings and on the other, three. He had a very low brow, an aluminum religious medal at his neck, a heavy silver bracelet on one arm, and red enamel on his finger and toe nails.

It was 2:00 P.M. when we rounded Escosesa Point or Alidonmutlu through as choppy a sea as I have ever experienced in a small boat. There one of the Negroes broke his paddle. A second became deathly seasick and was not of much use the rest of the day.

It was quiet behind protection of the Sassarti Islands, and there was hardly a ripple on the glassy surface of the sea as we slowly worked our way with the three inefficient paddles that were left. We barely crawled along now because the Negroes were tired and I had given out. When the paddle broke I was exhausted, and it was a good excuse for me to give up my paddle because I was not as used to this manner of voyaging as the Negroes were.

When we came to Akla and Koetup, two of the Negroes lay down and slept, while the big black fellow with the red finger nails and the heavy silver bracelet stirred the water feebly with his paddle. The sun went down before we reached Kupa and Tuwala. Then the two Negroes who had slept stirred their paddles in a rather perfunctory fashion for an hour. Then all three of them lay down and went to sleep for the night.

We were within sight of Mulatuppu where I could mark the flickering of kwallus here and there in the huts and over to the right I could recognize the bright kerosene pressure lamp in Claudio's house. I identified it not only because of its brightness but also because its light is white instead of yellow. To the left of Mulatuppu I could see the lights of the sentinels who stayed on the scaffolding all night at the fish wier and watched for a school of tarpon. I could hear the night fishermen calling merrily to each other as they paddled their dugouts out to sea. It was tantalizing, but there was nothing to do except wait for the dawn as I did not want an argument, especially with the muscular black primitive. So I lay down also even though I could not sleep. We got to Mulatuppu next day by eight-thirty.

Chapter VIII

◇　◇　◇　◇　◇　◇

BIBLE WOMEN OF SAN BLAS

ANNA COOPE

San Jose, Narkana, Feb 2, 1913

Dear Lady,

I sent my 3 Indian to Bring you up to San Blas Coas to My Country. My people like to see you. Dear lady you By A.B.C. Book Engles and Bring your Piano up with you. No more for present.

Mr. Charles J. Robinson

This simple invitation in English from an Indian Chief at Narkana marks a new era in the history of the Cuna people. The late Miss Anna Coope, to whom the letter was addressed, had tried to enter San Blas with her Bible for a number of years, and here was the opportunity of her lifetime.

If one were to describe Miss Coope realistically it probably would be with such words as small, plain, and fanatical, but it is often given to just such persons to accomplish the impossible, as it was to Saul of Tarsus.

I never met Miss Coope, but I have talked with numerous persons in the Canal Zone and on the San Blas Coast who knew her intimately, and none of them mentioned the words used above to describe her. In every case they spoke of her great faith, her religious devotion, her enthusiasm for Christian Missions, her dogged determination in carrying through her plans, and her grand accomplishments. These are the traits of her character that will go down in the history of San Blas.

Even though I never spoke with Miss Coope, she has talked to me through a large stack of rambling old letters that I have

149

studied. They were written to her friend Mrs. Jeffrey. Several of the letters are in my possession and I have had certain passages copied from the series. Through these faded messages, Miss Coope can tell of the stormy times through which she lived more vividly than I can imagine them, and I shall date the excerpts wherever the date is known in order to establish the chronology of events.

Miss Coope was a person of firm convictions and she held very definite views about religious matters, in which she was a fundamentalist.

March 9th. . . . You ask what people who do not believe in living without sin do with certain passages? I say they deny them and make God a liar, nothing else, no other answer. Oh yes, the Church of England or Episcopal always wail they have left undone. . . , etc. There are sincere souls in Episcopal Church as in Rome or China, or India, blinded by creeds and they are to be pitied, believing they are right. Poor, deluded souls, sad indeed to think of it. . . .

August 12, 1914. . . . I see that all sects have a tinge of truth, more or less, so I can be a Methodist, Baptist, Congregationalist, Church of England, Presbyterian, Romanist so far as they take the Bible and no more. The Romanist believes that Christ died for our sins, so do I. They believe in hell fire, so do I. But as they cover up the blood by Holy Water, rag dolls and indulgences on scraps of paper, I cannot go further. I am almost as bad against Methodist, with their Mason preachers who are almost as un-scriptural as the Popes, priests and nuns of the Romish Church.

She believed that as a result of her fervent prayers she had been healed of a cancer on her tongue.

Miss Coope was born in England and her religious education was varied, to say the least. She attended the Episcopal Sunday school, although her mother was a Catholic. Her father had no use for religion.

At the age of twenty she came to the United States with her father and mother, finding employment as a weaver of damask table cloths at the Turkey Red Dye Works of Bellefont, Rhode Island. Here she came under the influence of the Nazarene Church. She became interested in missions and distributed tracts through the West Indies in 1897.

After her mother's death in 1900 she stayed with her father until his death in 1906. After that she served as a Bible Woman to the Indians of San Isidro up the Orinoco. A major epidemic ended this native town and sent her back to Panama where she tried to obtain entry to the San Blas coast in 1909.

Several excerpts tell the story.

Sept. 27, 1909. . . . I had written a brother in Colon to find out if there are any Caribe Indians near there and he says that 60 miles up the river there is a village of caribs where a man (foreigner) is not allowed to stay after 6 P.M., that some priests went there and the natives beat them and tore up their pictures and chased them out. Now you will find out that the white man, whether English or Spanish traders, have abused those poor Indians for that is the way they did in Venezuela, and these Indians have turned.

Nov. 2, 1909. . . . The Chiefs say they will let a woman (white) come in their village but not a man, for he introduces a drink that makes them lose their senses, tells them their religion is false, robs them of their women and virtue. Now I'm encouraged to enter more than ever.

By the latter part of November, 1909, Miss Coope was on her way to San Blas. Her destination was the island of Mono.

November 22, 1909. . . . I'm among the Spaniards en route to the Indians of the San Blas tribe. I've met a few here. There is a trading station here run by an American named Wilcox, who resides in Cristobal, and what do you think he said when I asked him to let me go on his vessel? He said, no, it would spoil his trade to take me, for all the traders up the coast who hear of it would refuse to trade with him. What do you think he trades in largely? Rum!

At Mono her stay did not last long, and she was thrown out violently. John Davis, the Indian Chief who invited her, said: "Oh, white lady, I am sorry but you cannot stay here. The padre has told these two men that you are a bad woman and we must not let you stay. You have a bad book." But let Miss Coope describe it further.

Dec. 28, 1909. . . . Where shall I begin? Here I am back again in Cristobal after an absence of 5 weeks in search of Indians, weary, worn out and sick. But I'm still praising God for the privilege. The traders along the San Blas coast got huffy with me for going to the San Blas Indians. Yes, I've been [there] and have been treated badly too — arrested by the Police, brought before Chiefs and Governors (Indians), pushed off the land and hustled into a canoe, but not before I'd given them a testimony of the power of Jesus to save and gave them John 3:16-17 and other scriptures. . . . To travel Spanish rule is something awful and I never had anything like it as this trip. Roman Catholic priests opposed me and stirred up both Spaniards and Indians to put me out of the Indian villages that I visited, and as the poor benighted people cannot read or write, I could not scatter tracts and Bibles, but gave them the Word of God by mouth. I also spoke to the Priest* who was the greatest devil of all, and (at Narkana) he gave rifles to the Indians to kill me, but God preserved me. I'm not afraid nor discouraged and shall still try to get to the poor, neglected Indians. . . . I did not get anything to eat for three days as the boxes with my food were down on the bottom of the boat, so I only drank water, but God preserved me and I gave them the Word of our God.

Back in Cristobal, Canal Zone, Miss Coope described the Mono drama further, and what befell the aged Brother Penney who accompanied her.

Cristobal, C. Z. Feb. 2, 1910. There is one scene indelibly impressed on my mind. In the Indian village where we were roughly handled by wild, infuriated Indians stirred up by the priests, as we were leaving, in fact, I'd been hustled back to the launch, Bro. Penney knelt down on the beach and prayed with hands uplifted. His hoary hairs which were a crown of glory because found in the way of righteousness, were not respected by those poor benighted Indians. They grabbed his wrist and dragged him off his knees to the boat; but I believe that prayer will be answered, and souls from that place will be saved. He had said he would rejoice if he was martyred for Jesus and consider it the highest honor.

Immediately, Miss Coope started goading the Panamanian officials, each time throwing in sharp barbs and giving them a telling twist. She left no stone unturned to get back to the San Blas coast.

April 26, 1910. Thursday I called on the Secretary of State and he told me the San Blas Indians were under the Panamanian Govt. But the Government could not authorize them to let me come in their village as all religious power was given to the R. C. Bishop and as the Roman Catholic religion was the religion of Panama, the Bishop and Priests were doing all they could for the San Blas Indians and would not want me up there. I said, "Then the R. C. Church still rules the Government?" "In religious matters, yes," said Dr. Valdez, then I gave him my reason for going, that I would carry the Bible to them who had been in darkness all these years, "and now the Americans had come and started to reach them, you get up and claim them as yours. Why didn't you do that before?"

Because Catholicism was the state religion of Panama there was confusion between the acts of the government and those of the State Church whose Bishop was a paid government official,

*Padre Gasso.

charged with managing the religious affairs of the nation, and undoubtedly quite hostile to Protestant religious projects, as will appear in the letters of Miss Coope and others.

In the autumn of 1912, Miss Coope was still proving a thorn-in-the-flesh to the Panamanian politicians so much so that they were finally telling her to go to San Blas, just to get rid of her. But they refused to give her written permission as that would involve them in religious and political unpleasantness.

October 28, 1912 [Panama]. The President talked a while to the men and then came to me and said, "What do you wish?" He addressed me in Spanish and sat beside me. I told him that I wanted the privilege to go into the San Blas coasts and start missionary work among the Indians. He said, "You can go where you like. It is free." I said, "Yes, Mr. President, but I would like a letter from you authorizing me to go and anyone to let me enter their coasts." "Oh, but you can go wherever you choose without a letter from me." I said, "Mr. President, three years ago I went up to the San Blas Indians' islands on the Atlantic Coast and the Roman Catholic priest incited the Indians to drive me out, gave them the guns and orders to kill me; and an Indian Chief asked me if I had a letter of authority to come there, so I wish you would have the kindness to give me a letter." He said, "Well, I am busy now, but you write me a letter stating all particulars and what you want and I will see later."

Many Indians did not want those curses of civilization, reading and writing, to come into San Blas whether by Priest or by Bible Woman, and so we find Miss Coope recording the reaction of Supreme Chief Sam Colman, resident at Ailigandi.

October, 1912. I have talked to the Indian Chief, Sam Coleman (Ikwakintipippi), who offered me his boys three years ago. He smiled and shook hands with the *white* lady, but said, "No, we do not want to learn to read or write."

Thus, when early in February, 1913, Miss Coope received the letter from Chief Charlie Robinson quoted above, asking her to come to Narkana, she took it as an answer to four long years of prayer and constant effort. Immediately she started making plans to go to Narkana and told everybody about it in the Canal Zone.

October 7, 1913. A Catholic merchant said to me, "But Miss, the Indians will treat you badly if you go up there to teach them anything. We have a good Father up there and they are stoning him and treating him badly. Lady, don't go." And then I spoke to him of Jesus and His love and keeping power.

By October, Miss Coope had arrived and was describing her stay in Narkana with great ecstasy.

October 9, 1913 [San Blas Coast]. In my galvanized mansion — with the delightful Blue-green sea lapping at the foundations of my Big House, the Biggest House on the San Blas Coast. Red! Red! Red!

Once there, she started her school on the basis of the three R's and the Bible. All her teaching was in English. The Indians, remembering four hundred years of treachery and exploitation that they suffered at the hands of the Spaniards, preferred English to Spanish. At once a host of boys flocked into her school, naked and unnamed.

Indians from other towns objected to her being on their coast, and tried to do something about it.

November 1. . . . The wild mountain Indians came down early this morning to shoot me! and burn up the house. I was sleeping peacefully and knew not that the Indians were here. My own brave Indians were fighting or keeping them at bay for my sake. The wild Indians have found out the Chief is away and they have gone to bring more tonight, while 20 of my soldiers have gone to bring the Chief home. They passed here a while ago with the flag flying on the mast. That is only put up on the Chief's boat and means a fight. Well, I'm not the least afraid.

One of Miss Coope's first enemies at Narkana was alcohol, and although she was no poet she tried the poetic approach to solving this problem for her school boys.

[No date]. . . . I heard that one of my boys about 12 years old was out of school today (Friday) drunk. When the other boys told me I cried and said, "My poor boy, poor Dick, is it true? And Andrew, Lonnie and several said, "Yes, Miss Coope, Dick is drunk."
July 24th. . . . Amador was seven years old today and I composed some poetry for him!! The Chief was pleased and he helped him to learn it by sitting down by his side and explaining in Indian what it meant. Here they are:

> My name is Amador Robinson,
> I am seven years old today.
> I will only drink pure water
> And learn my lesson each day.
>
> I will not drink any liquor,
> The Bible says it is bad.

> My father is Chief of Narkana
> And I am his eldest lad.
>
> Now boys and girls of Narkana,
> Will you not say with me
> That pure water is good for the Indians
> And the very best drink for me!

When he said "for me" he put his hand on his breast and then drank the water. . . . The Chief did look pleased. Then I had the other Chief's son say a Temperance piece. He and *my best boy Lonnie* had learned it the day before and I promised them each a Scriptural card if they said it without a mistake and they did. . . . Well, I had Joe, Lonnie and George Jeffrey recite the Temperance piece with the glass of water. It brought the house down, for we had a good many strangers. Then Lonnie recited the 23rd Psalm perfectly, and while he was reciting it I had Joe hold my Bible to follow him and see if he made a mistake.

A year after landing, Miss Coope had John Barleycorn on the run, or at least she thought she had, and her popularity with the Indians had become contagious.

Early in 1914. . . . Last year, there were eight rum shops; this year only one, praise God. The Chief's brother has given it up. While he had a load in today, yet he was advising some of the young men from the other island to come to Night School and Sunday School. He said, "Mother, my mother, she talk to me for my good. Tell you good things too, you come." Then another man spoke up, "Yes, Miss Coope our mother." Ha-Ha! first time I heard them say that I said, "Oh no, not mother." they said, "Yes, you good to us, our mother."

It is evident throughout her letters that Lonnie Powers is her favorite pupil. She loves him as she would a son, and she is constantly writing about him. She said that he was the brightest among the three hundred Indian boys that she taught. Early in 1915 Miss Coope describes Lonnie's family.

February, 1915. . . . Lonnie's mother has seven children living. Her eldest boy has been in Panama city 5 years, so she has 6 children in the home, each one I have named, also named her Rachel. Her 3 boys — Lonnie, John, Paul, and the girls — Louise, Dorothea, Doris. . . . Lonnie and John are so much like that a few days ago as I saw John standing in the canoe I called Lonnie. . . . The elder brother is called Claudio, a Roman name surely. . . .
May 26, 1915. . . . I told Mr. Price of Mr. Wilcox bringing loads of

rum, deluging these poor Indians and taking their good coconuts for
rum. He said I should tell the President. The President did not
come ashore next morning as he was in such a terrible hurry to get
away, a fidgety Spaniard. I've met him before and he said, "All schools
in the Republic of Panama must be taught Spanish." "As far as I
am concerned, it makes no difference which language they want to
learn. I will teach either one or both. But my sole object is to give
them God's Word and teach them the way of salvation thru Jesus
only." He said, "Mr. Robinson has been speaking highly of you and
the progress of the children." He told the Chief he would build a
house on this island and send a School Master to teach Spanish. See
that? Mr. Price said, "But the Indians won't like it." Then Mr.
Price turned to me and said, "You will teach Spanish later?" I answered, "Yes, certainly if they will learn, but the young men who
have been from 2 to 7 years in Panama schools cannot read as well
in Spanish as they can in English and they do not want to continue
their Spanish, although I have suggested it to them. They are eager
for the English. . . . There was a Spanish official with him and so he
had to be careful, of course. Well, the Indians last night had a big
meeting and the Chief told them what the President said and then
the Chief resigned. He said these last six months (since he was saved
they have turned against him) you have not stood with me; things
can't go on like that. I give up. . . . It was a repetition of the time
when they put me out of Mono. But this time it was not me. They
yelled and howled, "Oh no, Robinson, Chief Robinson, Chief Robinson." Then they quieted and an elderly man who was one of the
Chief's bodyguards and looked like a North American Indian (such
a hatchet face and big nose) spoke. Of course, I couldn't tell all they
said, but he pleaded for Chief Robinson. . . . He talked in a convincing, serious manner and Chief Robinson was unanimously reappointed
Our Noble Chief. Praise God. . . . He says he does not seek to be
Chief; there is no gain in it. He gets no pay, there is nothing in the
office to make it desirable. But he seeks the good of the people only.
Now they see it and so plans were laid. The President will be told
they have decided not to accept his offer; they are satisfied with their
teacher and they don't want any foreigner to mix with them. This is
a fact. The Spaniard in any position has a string of servants and they
would have to be housed and live here. They are of the low dirty
class and would mix with their people. The Chief and the Indians
have had enough experience to know, and I could add my volume to
the villainy of the Spanish people Rum and Rome ridden. They
would bring their idols with them.

This year Miss Coope claimed the conversion of Chief Charlie
Robinson. A year later we find Miss Coope taking her "best

boy Lonnie" to the Canal Zone to have him speak, and she is trying to get him into the Mission School at Nyack, New York. But as usual, she runs into opposition from the Panamanian government and the state church.

November 29, 1915. . . . I told of God's leading, etc. I spoke and Lonnie read and sang in the Y.M.C.A. Some of the Ladies' Aid are now talking of getting him into the Carlisle Indian Boys School, Pa. But I cannot let Lonnie go there; I want him in Nyack. Lonnie has chosen this school. . . . The Bishop of R. Catholic Church in Panama City has stopped the Protestants from having the convention in the theater and President Porras helped in it.

[No date]. . . . Oh! what can we do? We are helpless, and now I am stopped again. President Porras sent a letter that Gov. had decided that the Indians must have no other religion but Catholic. And when the police got their orders to deliver the letter and stop me, they called a meeting and told the Indians if they came in my house they would be fined $5.00. Well, a few have been coming and the other day they took one man up, carried out the threat. He was in for two days and nights, then his wife borrowed 20 pesos or $10.00 to get him out to work for her and children (4 small ones). I had sent the letter of Porras to the British Minister and he must have spoken to President Porras. . . . I got a letter from Porras yesterday saying he was sorry to hear that I had sent a complaint against his policemen to the Minister of Great Britain and that they were not authorized to threaten the Indians. . . . But if these disturbances continued, he thought it would be better that I sell the property, he would buy it, and I should carry on my religious work in any part of the Republic of Panama but not among the Indians.

During the same year she is fighting to keep the school alive. She designates her enemies as Rum, Rome, and the Panamanian officials who fear, with good reason, that the Indians cannot be absorbed easily if they become Protestants and speak English.

Miss Coope had been teaching in the English language and preaching Protestant Christianity to the Indians for three years when she finally arranged for her best boy Lonnie to study at Nyack.

On February 24, 1916, Lonnie sailed for New York at 5:30 p.m. on board the steamship "Colon" in care of Rev. and Mrs. Chester, Mr. Boggs and Rev. Silas D. Daugherty, D.D., Lutheran preacher, Pa. These all promised to look out for Lonnie and I've heard from Mrs. Chester. . . .

She is thrilled with Lonnie's letters from Nyack and quotes

them voluminously. Lonnie came back to San Blas in the summer of 1919, still a very devout Christian, bringing his blessings of Christian education and developed leadership.

Unfortunately, Panamanian cruelty and Indian unrest mounted to a peak, and the year 1919 was filled with many tragedies. In 1920 came worse crises, and several Indian policemen were killed including Lonnie's elder brother, Claudio. After this the Protestant missions were closed by government officials, who suspected correctly that the sympathies of the Protestant missionaries were with the Indians rather than with the government.

April 16, 1919. . . .A beautiful morning. I have been busy with my housework and now a few minutes to rest. Looking out at my door I can see the carpenters. Twenty-eight concrete pillars are going up and there are to be thirty-six. Think of it! We are preparing for other missionaries who will come. This is to be headquarters, so now it looks fine. Two weeks today they started. The foundation work is the most difficult for we are building on the beach. Oh, the enemy has been busy. On April 1st, a truly remarkable day, three Panamanian policemen came to my house, gave me a very official letter to stop building this house. Well, you can imagine my feelings. . . . He said, "Well, if you have been telling them that all these six years, they ought to be converted." I told him some of them were. He said he was a free thinker, and I said, "So am I. Whom the Son of God makes free is free indeed, and the Bible is the only Book that gives us freedom. By reading and obeying God would send His Holy Spirit to teach us how to live a free life."

June 1919, Saturday. . . . Well, some policemen come up and arrested the Chief's brother and a young married man because Alfred, the Chief's brother, whose eldest girl came to my school, and all the girls have to take the ring out of their noses by order of the President. Well, I heartily approve of it and have done my very best to get them to do it; so has the Chief and he has set them the example by not having his two little girls' noses or ears pierced. Well the Government is doing it in such a fighty way, demanding that they do it, that of course the Indians are mad clear thru. And while they have taken out the ring from the smallest girls, the big girls would not take out the ring, not even those who had been going to the public school. Ever since this order was issued they left school. Force work will never do like love. They love us and when we talk of anything that is bad and tell them, they agree and talk and think and change, so that before Government orders, many of the babies had no noserings.

July 21, 1919. . . . God has spoken and the coming of Lonnie, Willis and Walter has done wonders for them, or influenced them wonderfully. Miss Evans has had Willis Jeffrey over to her island two nights. She says he has a preacher's gift. He held the people spell-bound and the same here. He talked in English and Indian. Also he talks so intelligently of the blood of Jesus that cleanseth from all sin, and also of the coming of the Lord, the signs of the times that indicate His soon personal coming. How I do praise God for his testimony. His father and brother are bitter against me even before he came, and now he has returned it is worse. His father and brother said I had sent him to United States to be a slave, he had come back and didn't know anything. Think of that! Lonnie tells me the teacher is surprised how much he does know in Arithmetic.

September, 1919. . . . One of the islands further up had a fight on. It seems a girl had a child by a married man the father didn't know until the child came. He was so vexed he killed the child and buried it at once. Some say he buried it alive, others that it was dead, but the word got to the Spanish Policemen and they went to investigate. The man was in bed and they, led only by one of the Indian policemen from this place, began to beat the man. Of course he fought all he could. Reports say that his arms are broken and he is bruised badly, but he stabbed the Spanish policeman, then an Indian took the policeman in a canoe saying he was going to Carti Islands, near the Governor's house. Well, the Governor, the old Dago, heard of it and sent 16 men with rifles on a gasoline launch, got all the Spanish-educated Indians that drink and carouse and smoke and are 100 per cent worse than the uneducated Indian, to go with them (about 7 from this island and 2 from the next). All had guns and they took a bottle of kerosene oil to set fire to the houses, and they did. Oh, such brutality! Lon's brother is the ringleader here. He is aspiring to be Chief and he is mean. He has been educated by Rome and drinks rum. His father can't stop him and, as he is unmarried, he is still in his father's house and is boss there. He lays around all week and Friday night he takes Lon and John [the next brother] to their island, makes them work all day Saturday and Sunday, brings them home in time to go to the public school. See the plot? No Sunday for Lon.

April 24th, 1920. . . . The whole village is mourning and in fear. Lonnie's brother Claudio and his chum Augustine are both lying in their homes, dead, killed by Indians. God has comforted dear Lon. He feels as I do that Claudio is now in hell, but he has lived such a bad life, was drunk last Sunday and has scorned at God's Word and vowed that soon he'd be Chief and then he'd shut up this school. . . . The Chief of Police took Lizzie's house and made it into a prison with stocks for the feet, and so the people there were more disgusted and left. Then one of the Spanish police beat their Chief. He was an old, weakly man and he never recovered. The Indians put that death to the Spaniards and they also have from the stories of their great-great-grandfathers the cruelty of the Spaniards from whom they have fled to these islands, and now their enemy has followed them! Well, some on the other side [Island of Nusatup] came back only to be beaten and put in stocks and fined $20, $40, $50 in nuts, and many went again and have not returned. Then the police went and burned one village of the run-aways, and this Claudio has been the ring-leader, infuriated to brassiness with drink. . . . At New Year's time there came another order—all school children must wear civilized dresses. . . . Jim Phillips, one of our Christian men, had trouble. The police came and told him to tell his brother's wife, who is old, to take her ring out. He said something about it was not his wife, he couldn't do that, whereupon this dead Augustine struck him on the back with his Billy stick and ordered the Panamanian police to arrest him, and he was put in the stocks Sunday night after Easter. Well, all the men of 40 years old and over, his chums and equals, vowed vengeance on the Spaniards. . . . her brother was so vexed that his old sister had taken the ring out to please the Panamanian, that he said his old sister should not return to her daughter's house. The spies heard it and the Chief of Police sent Andrew's father to bring back the old woman and the brother would not let her go, so when Mr. Ferguson (Andrew's father) came home he was imprisoned and his wife also. For two nights he sat with feet in stocks, the little children left to look out for themselves, and the baby cried so the first night (11 months old) they took it to prison with its mother. . . . Five police, three Indians and two Panamanians, went and had a (protest) meeting, everything was very quiet and they left. The Indians went to bed and in the middle of their sleep they were aroused by the Police and it is said that Claudio led them. He with pistol in hand went in the house, called a man. The man got up, and in the act of pulling up or tightening his pants around the waist (for of course they sleep in them and no shirt, and a string ties up the pants), Claudio shot him in the chest. Several in the house overpowered Claudio and got the revolver from him and shot him three times. The others beat him with sticks till he died. Then I went to Lonnie's house and they had Claudio on the floor trying to get his clothes either on or off. . . . He was so limp looking I said, "Lon, is he dead?" And Lon said, "Yes, feel his pulse." I took that soft, clammy hand and was quite sure he was dead. It seems to me I've never felt death so ghastly as now, especially because I knew the man and his life. . . . As I write the dead body of Claudio is going in the canoe to be buried. . . . Lonnie said, "He tried his best to make me a Catholic, scoffed the Bible, said the Roman Catholic church was the oldest and the priests good, learned men, etc., etc."

After this the Protestant Missions were closed by government order. Back to Panama went Miss Coope and started needling the Panamanian officials once more. She had an extremely high nuisance value. To get rid of her they finally gave in and in 1923 she went back to Narkana.

About December 27, 1922, she is in Panama, has pressured her way to the top, and is talking to the Panamanian President.

. . . He took my hand and said, "Miss Coope, you are a conqueror, you have conquered the Indians. I'm sorry you are not a Catholic. I wish you would get 20, yea 100 women like you too, but Catholics." I told him it took salvation to make women like us, who obeyed God and the Bible. He said to his secretary, "This is a woman with the Bible religion." He said to me, "It is good, and if I could I'd let you go, but the *Bishop says we must have our Catholic religion and it is best. Why do you not become Catholic?"* . . . I showed him the picture of the school in Narkana. He thought it was fine and said, "You must be rich." I told him who built it and he said, "I'll buy it off you." I said, what for? "A school." I said to myself, Never!

On February 2, 1923, she received a message from the President. The state church had been abolished.

February 2, 1923. . . . January 30, 1923—Dear Miss Coope: I have received your letter of January 27th and have taken notice of your decision to return to your missionary work in San Blas. As you know, the Government has organized Missionary work amongst the Indians with Catholic Priests and in the Spanish language because the Indians, in order to become Panamanian citizens must speak the Spanish. . . . *There is no state church in Panama so you are free to preach any faith,* but you must use the Spanish language with the Indians. This is the only restriction you may have in your work. Yours respectfully, Belisarrias Porras.

The permission granted, back to San Blas she went and started her work once more, ready to teach in Spanish rather than in English.

March 9, 1923. . . . First meeting in eleven months last night, March 8th. House packed, Jesus is victor. Enemies said, "Miss Coope can never open that school again; never. That bell shall not ring." But it did; it did. Ah! Blessed is she that believeth. . . . Last night was a victory. When the secretary told me I went to Chief Robinson. He wept for joy. The people ran out to meet me, gave me fruit and vegetables and fish, said "Miss Coope our great friend, not afraid of Policemen, not afraid of President, God is with her."

But the injustices of the Panamanian policemen stationed on the islands continued, as the Panamanian government tried to force civilized customs immediately upon the Indians. They passed edicts against noserings (age-old tribal symbol), Indian costumes, and the corn food-drink. This latter move was tantamount to removing bread from their already deficient diet. Since the San Blas Indians had no hard stones on which to grind their grain, they did as many other tribes of Indians have done, namely, allowed the old women of the family to premasticate the maize before it was cooked. The government made no effort to supply the Indians with stones or mills, but simply forbade use of the main staple of their diet.

For several years conditions went from bad to worse until in the spring of 1925 a bloody revolution broke out at Ailigandi under Chief Sam Colman, aided and abetted by R. O. Marsh, an American explorer and adventurer. In this revolution many of the Panamanian policemen stationed on the islands and their hybrid children were killed.

Wednesday, November 5, 1:30. . . . Fight is on now. Chief boat challenge them—out goes seven men. Life-saver around one man (found out that belt was full of bullets) two men to manipulate the boat. My! You ought to have seen the men go in that canoe quickly. The wind blew the canoe and they fired the guns thick and fast until the enemy pulled the flag down. Hurrah! We have won! The soldiers came from the other side, and some Colombians had the Colombian flag and they tore it in two with a vengeance. Then all went over to rejoice with the Chiefs and their brave soldiers. Well, I have seen my first sea-fight, and mind you, it was for *me* chiefly. I prayed for my brave Indians who are fighting for the right.

Colon, Friday, March 20, 1925. . . . I am in hopes Walter will tell me what's the feeling in Washington, D. C. for he said there was quite a stir among the upper ten scientists and explorers, etc., when Marsh was there. Well, I smiled at your question, "Did Mr. Marsh write that or did you?" (The San Blas Declaration of Independence). Several said, if Marsh had not have put his name to it they would have said I wrote it, it was so much like what I had told them over and over again. But I did not write it, did not know a thing about it until I got into the city on March 1st. But not till March 2nd did I see the declaration and oh, how I praised God. Anyone with common sense and humanity couldn't help but see the over-bearing of the Panama police and Marsh had lived among them and had five brown and three whites (so-called) in his company for months, and three of them (men) could speak good English, and how could he help seeing, or not knowing facts? We cannot dictate to God but oh, daily my cry has been, "Lord, do something," and He has. I give him all the praise and glory and expect more. Where is Lonnie? On account of the wicked Company and that Indian youth, Lonnie was drafted for the fight, but U.S.A. intercepted and Lonnie is now one of the policemen at the Point, or Gov. Island. Poor Lonnie! Brother Morris, a colored Jamaican, told me the night the news was brought to us, Lonnie cried like a child. He knew judgment had come. He had said he'd never be a policeman because these officials were not doing right to his people. . . . The Panamanians do not hesitate to openly say they hate U.S. and a civil war over here seems impending, if by civil war we mean those who live next door. As the Panamanians saw the news of Panamanian Police killed by San Blas Indians, they (Pan people) beat the Indian boys and the Americans had to shelter them for a few days. That is over to a certain extent, but we know the bitterness of Panama is awful now.

May 2, 1925. . . . The latest from San Blas is that wicked Garrido, who was first Chief of Police, they have sent again with his wife as school teacher and there are eighteen police on my island, and many of the people have run away, . . . Lonnie and his father dare not return, neither the wicked Estanislau Lopez, the companion of Lon's brother and counterpart of Garrido, both vile. Chief Robinson dares not go back, for he was with the Government.

October, 1925. . . . The pastor of the Union Church (Panama Americans) received a telephone call from the governor of Colon (Roman Catholic)—told them they must stop the San Blas School. . . . He said, "We have reasons we are not going to give." But the Governor did make this confession: "We know your methods are better than ours and your morals also" . . . "But we don't want them to be like you, we want them to be like us."

December 12, 1925. . . . I inquired for Lonnie, for oh, Edith, he *is my boy,* not another I feel for as for Lonnie. He was so simple minded, so eager to learn, so obedient, and to think of him helpless in the enemy's hand! They wanted him to be a Policeman in San Blas as he came out of school. He said, "Never." . . . The mother she told me herself she hated those men and she says so now, that Lonnie, like Claudio, was ruined by them; and the first time Lonnie got drunk, forced to do it, she cried like a child, sobbed and swayed her body. "Oh, my Lonnie; my Lonnie, if he had stayed with Miss Coope he would never have been drunk." They carried him home like a log and she told me "Next time they have a festival, you must keep him. I will lock him in your house." She said it in the presence of Lonnie when he got sober and all our tears mingled together over the fall of the best boy in San Blas. Oh, how the enemy is gloating over those poor helpless Indians and Lonnie is an excellent scholar too, and could do something worthwhile if he had help. . . . I've told Lon. other Indian boys get away to U. S. by being sailors, and as all the San Blas Indians are born seamen, it would not be any hard work for him to work his passage across. I shall talk plainly to him when he comes and ask some of the Americans if they can get him on a steamer as a waiter or seaman or something.

OTHER BIBLE WOMEN

In 1919 Mrs. M. E. Purdy came to work on the nearby island of Nusatup (Mouse Island) and although she was not there as long or suffered all the tribulations that Miss Coope did, I may be doing her an injustice by not devoting more space to her efforts. It is not my intention to neglect her in this account, but I have been able to find out less about her and her experiences.

I have located two of Mrs. Purdy's letters (one now in my possession) and they reflect many of the same difficulties that Miss Coope encountered.

Mrs. Purdy's outstanding student was the son of Oloiklipippilele the Medicine Man. She named this boy Peter Miller and sent him to North Carolina to study. But let her tell something of her experiences.

September 19, 1922. . . . I have sent one of my boys with Sis. Coope to Greensborough Bible Institute, to fit himself out for the mission field among his own people. The Panamanians have been wild at me since he went, and have done about everything in their power to bring him back. I have been called into court several times and threatened with prison many times. Even a judge was brought here from Colon to look up the case. A complaint was entered against me. I was accused of sending a minor to the States without the consent or knowledge of the parents. (I had their consent but for fear of prison they denied any knowledge of his whereabouts and accused me before the chief of police saying, "She is to blame.") The chief of police, who is a Panamanian, told him he would be put in jail five months for giving his consent, so he denied the whole thing. I could see it was for fear of prison, so I did not tell that they gave their consent, but said I was guilty. . . . I told him the parents asked me to send the boy but did not want it known. He said, "They deny any knowledge of his going." I said yes, I knew that, but they did it because they were afraid the Chief of Police (Garrido) would put them into jail if he knew they had given their consent. He looked kind of wise at the secretary and smiled, then thanked me and dismissed the case. However, Garrido tried to get the Government to bring him back. Later he came to me and asked me to send for him. I said, "Not before he is finished school there." They had him booked to send to Panama to a Catholic Institute in less than a month from the time I sent him. . . . The Panamanian officials urged on by the Padre are carrying out his orders. A policeman is stationed on every side of my house to watch if any one comes on meeting nights, and if any one does come, the parents are ordered to take them out, or go to prison. That is Rome for you. However, some of the boys come in the darkness; they do not want to give up. You see, they have been saved, and would all come, but they are compelled to go to Mass every morning at 6:30 and again in the evening to vespers, driven to it by the policemen who round them up for every service. The Indians are not against us. All want to come but are kept back by about seven Indian policemen who are paid by the Government and urged on by the priest to obey orders. If it were not for the presence of the Invisible One I would be miserable. But we know that "All things work together for good to those that love the Lord."

As a result of Peter Miller being sent to the States, Oloikli-pippilele was banished from Nusatup and lived at Playon Chico for three years. In the meantime the Catholic Priests sent several boys to the United States to study, and so the town finally invited Peter Miller's father back home because now to send a boy away to study was considered all right.

Mrs. Purdy's second letter mentioned Peter in North Carolina, and the difficulties she encountered from the police because of her having sent him.

February 28, 1923. . . . You asked if anything more had been done about Peter, the boy at Greensborough. No, nothing except that the Chief of Police (after he found the judge did not condemn me) isolated me as far as possible from everybody, yet living among them. He threatened the Indians with prison if they were seen speaking to me, and told them if he caught anyone doing anything such as bringing wood, water or fuel, they should be immediately imprisoned. Yet they did it. At midnight they brought me wood and water, fish and eggs. And the women stole in and stayed nights with me when I had the fever and many times wept. The Bible boys also came in the darkness to pray-meetings.

Annie Evans came to help Mrs. Purdy. I have one of her letters telling about the confiscation of their mission house for a prison. Miss Evans died after a short term of service at Nusatup. Miss Coope describes her burial.

September 1919. . . . I said, "How do you feel?" She said, "I feel bad" and dropped down again. I bathed her head with some Florida water or Cologne she had. She dozed off. At 10:30 she gave such a groan, I asked her "What is it? Want some water? Heart hurting you? Head pain?" Not a word. I prayed over her and kept saying, "Oh Jesus, help me now. Oh Father, heal her now for Jesus' sake. Jesus, Jesus, Precious Jesus." But no recognition. . . . We had a coffin, the first one here. Chief Robinson superintended it. The first Christian funeral. We sang "Abide with Me," "Rock of Ages." We went out of the house and into eleven canoes singing, "In the Sweet Bye and Bye." The people on the two islands lined the beach. Never was such a funeral. We left the house at 10:30 A.M. and got back about 2:30. Eight of my big Christian boys rowed the large canoe that the coffin lay in. I sat at the head. Two gravediggers, fathers of some of my girls, rowed also, then ten canoes followed. . . . Dug the grave six feet with soup plate and wash bowl and an iron prong rodlike to loosen the dirt. She is buried in the Chief's family lot. Chief Lewis of the Island she labored on. And thus her grave will be a testimony. I have ordered a head board to be made by the Boss Carpenter, painted white with green letters:

ANNIE B. P. EVANS
WENT TO BE WITH JESUS
AUGUST 31, 1919
AGE 49
A MISSIONARY WITH THE BIBLE
THE WORD OF GOD

Ostensibly because the sympathies of Miss Coope and Mrs. Purdy were with the Indians in the Revolution of 1925, their missions and schools were closed permanently by the Panamanian government. Priests soon returned to Narkana, and it became the Catholic center in San Blas.

CUNA INDIAN GIRL OF SAN BLAS ISLANDS
(Photo by R. S. Gregg)

A MOON-CHILD

HULLING RICE

MOON-CHILD DAUGHTER AND MOTHER

BUILDING THE COUNCIL HALL

MEETING IN THE COUNCIL HALL

PREPARING THE EVENING MEAL

FRANCISCO OF MORTI SINGS THE COCOABEAN CHANT

IDOLS AND NAKKRUSES FOR DRIVING AWAY DEVILS

UAN, THE CEMETERY OF AILIGANDI

SAIKLA IKWANIKTIPIPPI'S PICTURE OF HEAVEN

THE EARTHMOTHER GIVING BIRTH TO THE FIRST SNAKES

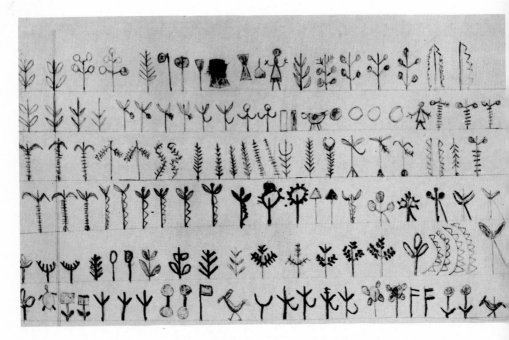

PART OF THE FORMULA FOR CURING SNAKEBITE
(From the Medicine Book of Manipekinappi)

CUNA INDIAN MEDICINES

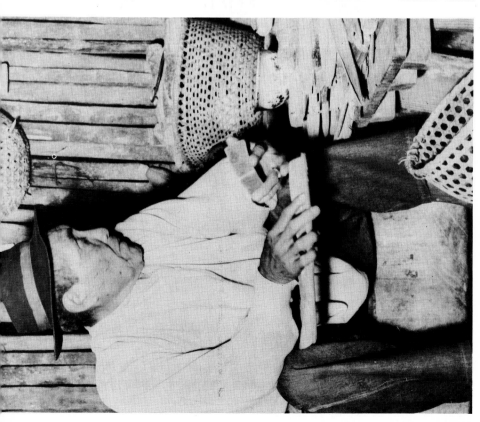

UPIKINYA, THE DEAN OF AILIGANDI MEDICINE MEN

PRACTICING DANCES FOR THE INNA FEAST

BURYING BONES TO FEED THE PLACENTA DRAGON OF THE KANTULE

A DIVINER WITH KINDRED SPIRIT IDOL AND HIS WIFE AND BABY

KANTULES AND IET WOMAN AT THE INNA FEAST

MOON-CHILD CARRIES SEA WATER FOR A FRIEND'S PUBERTY CEREMONY

MANITIKINAPPI, THE INNASOPET OF AILIGANDI,
EXHIBITS HIS BREW OF THE WATER OF LIFE

ALCIBIADES IGLESIAS AND HIS WIFE, MARVEL

GIRLS SINGING AT THE SOUTHERN BAPTIST MISSION AT AILIGANDI

Chapter IX

◇　◇　◇　◇　◇

CHRISTIANITY AND EDUCATION

THE CATHOLICS IN SAN BLAS

SOON AFTER the United States opened the Panama Canal, the pressure of civilization began to be felt along the western end of the San Blas coast. Indian trails led to Panama City and numerous Indians had been to town. A few of them could speak some English; more had a limited vocabulary in Spanish. And where here and there an Indian might be interested in Christianity and Western Civilization, hundreds of others were against it.

Had not the Spaniards with their civilization and Christian religion all but annihilated their tribe, cutting them down from about 750,000 to 10,000? Had not the double-dealing white man with his Christ extinguished numerous North American tribes, and had they not brutally driven most of the remnant west of the Mississippi? Think of the Cherokees and the Iroquois nation! Those stories had all filtered down to the Cunas. And has the white Christian ever been known to keep his word to an Indian people? Where are the many treaties that were signed? These were questions that bothered the Cunas. And besides, no Indian has ever been made a drunkard by a seasonal inna, but the use of constantly available Christian liquor changes the Indian to a slave. The standards of morality among the Cunas are high, but those of Panamanians? . . . And how about extra marital relationships? They considered these questions.

The Indians reasoned that they were living as God wanted them to live, whereas the Christians were not. To the Christians Esu Kristo had been sent; but had not God in the Sun, the Great

167

Father, sent eight cultural heroes in the quality of Archangels down to earth on Golden Sun Discs to teach the Cuna people how he wanted them to live? Had they not lived as these heavenly messengers had taught them?

Even as late as 1951 a chief said to me seriously: "If we Cuna people take on Christianity and become civilized will we have to raise an army and send it out over the world to kill people, as civilized, Christian nations do?"

When the Republic of Panama was established it was only natural, in view of Spanish tradition, that Catholicism was decreed the state religion, and the Catholic Bishop of Panama was placed on the federal payroll. This gave a Catholic impetus to the belated Christianizing of the Indians of San Blas. In 1907 Padre Gasso arrived at Narkana, and his great influence in opening up San Blas to Christianity is a matter of record. The Catholic center is on the adjacent islands of Yantup and Nusatup which are connected by a wooden bridge. In 1951 Tupili and Tikantiki permitted the erection of Catholic churches. Today the Priests of the Catholic center at Narkana (Yantup) and Corazon de Jesus (Nusatup) include Padres Jesus, Mauro, Marcos, and Col.

Madre Otilia is director of the school. The other nuns are Madres Pia, Buenaventura, Demetria, Venicia, Clementina, Sorteris, and Petra. Most of the devoted sisters resident there are mainly concerned with the Catholic schools; and several Padres are interested in maintenance, language study, and evangelism, aside from the routine affairs of the local churches.

As a result of the Catholic efforts, many of the people of Narkana are Catholics, and their religious work has spread to Rio Azukar and Playon Chico. They have done away with noserings to a great extent at Narkana. Most of them wear western dresses instead of native costumes. There is no inna feast, and the women keep their hair long. Many of them speak Spanish and a goodly proportion of them think of themselves as Panamanians rather than as Indians. However, the Narkanese still live in thatched huts and many old people and even some of the young folks still follow a number of traditional customs.

The Catholic efforts in San Blas have been recounted completely by Padre Gasso in his letters to the Journal *Las Misiones Catolicas* between 1910 and 1914. Further accounts of the Catholic missions in San Blas are given by Padre Manuel Puig in his book *Los Indios Cunas de San Blas,* published by El Independiente, Colon.

LONNIE POWERS

Masikwakikinye was a famous medicine man in Narkana at the turn of the century. He had an eight-ring akwa nusa (stone mouse) that performed medical miracles, a fine garden of medicinal herbs, an extensive collection of uchu mimmikana (mediccine idols), in addition to many magic sticks and stones. He knew many powerful medicine chants. Cleverness ran in his family and Masikwakikinye's advice was highly respected at the town council of his island. He was keen enough to foresee that the old Indian ways would pass, and that civilization would eventually come to San Blas; so he would be one to welcome it. He coveted education for his children, and when the opportunity came he sent his eldest son, Claudio, to study in Panama. As we have recounted previously, this son came under Catholic influence.

His second son showed such outstanding mental ability that Masikwakikinye was worried about him. His brain must be growing too rapidly and must be pressing against the inside of his skull! So he used to bustle this son out of his hammock at midnight and put him under a perforated calabash filled with cold water in which were medicine leaves and nakkruses. Thus, he treated him for his kurkin poni (around-the-head disease). He carefully collected the thirty-five varieties of cocoa beans, burned them in his incense pot, and sang a chant over the medicine: "May the God Physician [Tiolele] make this medicine have the effect upon the patient for which it is intended." In fact, this naked little brown boy with his necklace of wild pigs' teeth and his golden earrings had all the promise of becoming a true nele, a great spiritual leader of the old traditional type in San Blas. He had an amniotic membrane veil at birth! Already the boy was prophesying clairvoyantly about who was going to die and what was going to happen.

But even this promise of religious leadership in the tribe did not keep father Masikwakikinye from desiring for him a western education and so he had a powerful medicine man "bless his son toward the north" with a ceremony and an efficacious medicine chant. This would insure that someday he would go to the United States to study. And because his little boy had a slight stammer in his speech, Masikwakikinye made him stand up each morning and stick out his tongue before leaving the house. Onto the boy's tongue the father would place charcoal from certain medicine plants in order to correct this defect.

When Miss Coope arrived in Narkana, Masikwakikinye and his family made her welcome, and all the children except the elder son, Claudio, became her pupils. She gave names to all the children (save Claudio) who, according to San Blas tradition, had no names. Many of her letters reflect her friendship for this family, and her deep affection for the very promising, second-born lad to whom she frequently refers as *"my best boy, Lonnie."*

We have noted that in 1916, Lonnie was sent to New York to study. When Miss Coope brought to Masikwakikinye and his wife the photograph of their absent son, they broke down. Miss Coope said in a letter:

Friday night . . . I've just been over to Lonnie's house to give his father and mother one of his photos and they would not touch it, said he was dead, and the mother would not look at it at all while I was there. The father did, and his lip trembled, so I gave it to the elder brother, Claudio. He was glad to have it. He has just made a frame for his picture that was taken 5 years ago when he went to Panama City and he does look nice. So he said, "I will make a frame for Lonnie."

Some of Miss Coope's personal interpretations of the Bible were instilled into Lonnie, and these put him into some embarrassing situations at Nyack until he became adjusted and learned that there were other views as well. Lonnie said:

They put me in the 7th grade but that was too hard for me. I am now doing 3rd and 4th grade work. I get good marks in arithmetic and geography, English Reader and Spelling and Hygiene. I guess I will beat all the boys because they play a lot, but I pray to God to help me to learn quickly. I am happy all day. Tell the boys to pray to Jesus to help them to study. He will. And tell them not to be ashamed. When I come back to San Blas I will tell every man and woman about Jesus. One day on the table I see some meat. I asked the boy next to me what is that meat. The boy said "pig." I said, "I do not like that meat it is not good for us to eat, it is unclean." . . . We had read in Leviticus on the unclean animals and I had commented against the pig, you may be sure, because God says it is unclean, and I had the stinking proof of it under my nose and eyes every day for months. The children seemed rotten, to use that word, scabby heads, running sores, why, I've seen the matter drip from jawbones and the lobe of the ear onto their hands while writing. I used often to wash their ears and neck with disinfectant in water and talked to the chief so against it—every house had a pig-pen in one corner and a pack of filthy dogs and cats—that the chief has banished every dog and cat and pig.

In 1919 Lonnie returned to San Blas and took up where he left off, continuing his study of the Bible and secular books and being helpful to Miss Coope at a time when clashes between the government and the Indians became inevitable. When Miss Coope was banished from the island to Panama, Lonnie kept in contact with her from Narkana. When she returned to Narkana in 1923 there were Lonnie and all her old friends, including Chief Charlie Robinson.

Since Lonnie and his father were liberals, and on the side of civilization, though against treachery and armed conflict, Lonnie was pressured into the Panamanian police force just before the revolution of 1925. At night with his father and several other Indians he eluded the revolutionists, fled to Panama, and reported the massacre to the government. For this act both he and his father were exiled by the Indians to Panama for a number of years.

For his loyalty during the Revolution he was promised by the Panamarian government a scholarship to study in the United States. But when the showdown came, the scholarship went to the son of a Panamanian official, and the promising Lonnie Powers mysteriously disappeared.

ALCIBIADES IGLESIAS

To the Cunas the wonders of Nu Yak (New York City) are next to the delights of Heaven, and because they are good sailors, many of the Indians signed up for the sea and upon shore leave congregated about Times Square. At one period, I am told, there were more than one hundred Cuna sailors making New York their home.

It was not surprising, then, when in 1932 a bright young Cuna, who was taking a course in electrical engineering, walked into the old City Mission at the corner of Hoyt and Warren streets in the Red Hook section of Brooklyn, and said, "My name is Alcibiades Iglesias." He was interested in carrying Protestant Christianity back to his people because there had been no Prot-

estant missionaries in San Blas after Miss Coope and Mrs. Purdy
were banished from the islands in 1925. Because this young man
handled the English language well and was a devout Christian,
he was a frequent speaker at the City Mission, which was directed
by Miss Elizabeth Foth.

⟩ At that time Miss Marvel Ilya, whose desire was to reopen
the Protestant missions in San Blas, was an assistant at the City
Mission. She knew the story of Miss Coope from A to Z because
Miss Foth and Miss Coope were very close friends. The Panamanian government would not permit any Protestant missionaries to enter San Blas, but here was an outstanding young San
Blas Cuna who also wanted to take Protestant Christianity to
San Blas. Between Marvel and Alcibiades there was unanimity
of purpose. Propinquity and Cupid did the rest.

As an Indian, Alcibiades had the right to open any kind of
"private school" he pleased; and as his wife, Marvel could not
be stopped from entering San Blas because, by marrying Alcibiades, she automatically became a Panamanian citizen.

To make a long story short, in 1933 Alcibiades and Marvel,
with support from friendly individuals in the Canal Zone and
in the United States, set sail for Ailigandi to open a "faith enter-
prise" that they called the San Blas Mission. The honeymooners
sailed down the beautiful San Blas coast to Narkana, and out to
greet them rushed Masikwakikinye, the medicine man who had
befriended Miss Coope, the same medicine man who long ago
had a famous nele "bless toward the north" his naked little son
with his golden earrings and his necklace of mountain pigs' teeth.
With him were his family and friends, many of whom laughed
and wept and called the happy bridegroom "Lonnie." So now
the secret is out. Alcibiades Iglesias was Miss Coope's *"best boy,
Lonnie Powers."*

But why the change? Back in 1925, while in exile, he worked
for his government, and at that time the Panamanian government in a fit of nationalism, forced him to take this Spanish
name! And now Miss Coope's boy, in the flower of manhood,
was again bringing back from the North the manifold blessings
of Christianity and of civilization to share them with his people.
The girl by his side was the greatest blessing of all because she
was destined to become the supreme religious driving force on
the whole San Blas coast; without her inspiration, encouragement,
organization, and ability to carry through, the whole venture
might have failed.

When Lonnie and Marvel obtained permission from the Indians to open a private Christian school at Ailigandi, it was not without special conditions. Chief Sam Colman and the town council decided that not only did Lonnie have too much "foreign influence" but he also had a foreign wife; and if they should have children there would be the problem of mixed bloods, which was horrible to think about since they had usually been killed by the Cunas in the past.

In the compromise that resulted, Lonnie was not allowed to construct a house or a school on Ailigandi because of the evil of his foreign influence, but he would be permitted to build land for himself (at the side of the island). So with a canoe he gathered chunks of coral and covered them with sand to make a place for their house and their school.

Their first house was built of boards from Panama and had a thatched roof, but it lasted only three years. The voracious tropical termites saw to that. It soon became evident that the cheapest and most durable buildings in the long run would be built of cement blocks constructed from the limitless sand of the sea shore. So Lonnie obtained an iron form and cement from Panama and went to work again. He began making cement blocks, and as soon as they were hard Marvel started plastering them together to form the walls of their new house, while he continued making blocks.

The Indians watched closely the process of block making and saw in it something very unholy. Only a few blocks had been made when Lonnie was hailed before the town council for practicing Black Magic. They had seen Lonnie take sand and powder and water, mix them together with a shovel, and tamp them into an iron box. They had seen him make a few magic passes over the top with a trowel, and the next day it was not sand and powder and water any more, but a stone. "Nobody," they declared, "can change sand and powder and water to a rock unless Nia tummati [the Big Devil] does it for him."

So Lonnie had to defend himself before the town council by explaining the general chemistry of cement. He told them that it works not by diabolical intervention but by well known natural laws understood by many people in civilized countries. He told the Indians that there are millions of tons of rock made with this kind of cement that form the locks of the Panama Canal, and that many civilized countries, including the Republic of Panama, make cement. Some of the Indians who had worked in Panama could witness to the truth of the statement about the canal and the manufacture of cement.

When it came to a vote, Lonnie was acquitted of the charges of being in league with the Devil and was permitted to continue his house building. However, some of the more superstitious Indians of Ailigandi never stepped upon the questionable property for ten years, for fear that the majority might have been mistaken.

The town council had extracted a promise from Lonnie that if he were allowed to open a school, he would never educate any girls and he would not advocate removing their noserings, or the changing of their dresses and customs. For a number of years education was only for the some ninety boys that swarmed in, naked and unnamed. But one year Christina, granddaughter of Chief Sam Colman, wanted an education and did so much about it that the chief himself had to change the agreement and ask the school to educate her. And since a single girl could not sit in classes alone with so many boys she must have a companion. For this reason her friend, Fulvia, must have an education, too. The ice once broken, a few girls have attended Escuela Colman ever since, and most of them wear their molas, beads and noserings every day.

After a time the fear of Lonnie and his wife wore off. Marvel wrote:

The chief who had been opposed to our entering that island two years before, stood up in the midst of his people and said, "We are no longer afraid of Lonnie—anything that he says we will do." Lonnie responded, "We have not come to take away your noserings and Indian customs, but we wish that we could be the means of changing every one of your hearts."

One mountain Indian walked ten miles through the jungles to visit us. Upon glancing in the mirror, he became so frightened when he saw his face for the first time that he walked back and forth in front of the mirror taking his shirt off and putting it back on again.

On a Monday morning we blew a conch for a school bell and ninety naked boys matriculated. Unable to think of the strange names of so many boys on the spur of the moment, we took out our address file and began naming them after our friends in the States, but we soon found out that finding names was not our only trouble for neither the students nor the teachers could remember the individual's name. Adhesive tape would have served well, had we had some, since we could hardly pin a tag on their skin. We solved the problem by entrusting each boy with a paper recording his name. So happy were the boys to have real names instead of nicknames, such as Fatty, Skinny, Blacky, etc., that they followed us everywhere asking their names until they finally learned them.

School well on the way, we organized a Sunday school for boys only, the chief having given us to understand that we were to do nothing in any way to teach their girls.

By the time the second Christmas rolled around, the boys were able to sing carols and to recite some Christmas pieces. At the close of a short program, we surprised them by presenting each one with three yards of colorful rayon for shirts—purple, green, red, orange, yellow, and blue—their first Christmas presents. Early Christmas morning the happy boys asked if they might have a parade in the afternoon. Later, they appeared all dressed up in their bright shirts which from a distance resembled colored lights on a Christmas tree. The older students had spent all Christmas morning making their shirts while the younger ones urged their fathers to sew theirs. (Here the men make their own and their sons' clothes).

Peter Miller, Mrs. Purdy's best student, studied at the Greensboro Bible School in North Carolina, and the Beulah Park Bible School in eastern Pennsylvania. In 1933 Peter Miller graduated from high school. He then took two years of Bible training at the Chicago Evangelistic Institute and came home to Narkana (Nusatup) bringing his blessing of an education from the North. The Panamanian officials still frowned upon the Protestant missionaries in San Blas, and it appeared as though even the Ailigandi work would be stopped. Peter Miller was forbidden by the government to do any religious work. For five years he stayed at Narkana under that edict, but living a devoted Christian life and praying for an opportunity to serve.

In October 1938 he went to Ailigandi and took a chance by working for Escuela Colman. What would be the government reaction? A few days later he was summoned to appear before the governor in his office in Porvenir, a distance of seventy miles. It was with fear and trembling that Lonnie and Peter went by canoe to answer the summons, but as a result of that long trip Peter was given permission to work at Ailigandi, far away from the Catholic effort. Peter has a distinct musical talent and a facility with words that has made him invaluable not only as a music teacher and a translator of religious songs, but also in the preparation of a New Testament translation.

Today the San Blas Mission has expanded, with schools at Ailigandi, Ustuppo, and Mulatuppu. And there would be mission schools on other islands, were funds available. Not only do these schools carry on religious and educational programs, but through the years they have sent students "toward the North" to study further because the "North" has been the main source of their blessing. Recently the Home Mission Board of the Southern Baptist Convention has taken over direction and support of the San Blas Mission.

THE WOMAN NELE

The Mulatuppu School and Sunday School had been going on for six months. The town had split badly on the education issue; and the conservatives, who were against the horrors of education in all of its forms, kept to themselves and their leaders would not speak to the progressive leaders or to Claudio or his wife, who were entirely "too foreign." Nor would the conservative chief speak to me when I greeted him on the streets with a cheery "Na!"

Peter Miller and Atilio had been to Chicago (as a reward for many years of service) taking refresher courses in a mission school. While studying in the States, they had produced several phonograph records of religious songs and testimonials in the Cuna language which became highly popular all along the coast. We played these at Koetup and on several other islands, and four or five times a day visitors from all along the coast came to Claudio's house on Mulatuppu to have them played.

Among those who came was Ome Nele, the woman physician from Morti, who was as much a clairvoyant and religious leader as she was a medicine woman. She had come down to minister to the sick and to sing and advise on the ways of God. In fact, she was such an important person that she was the house guest of Olopiaite, the famous inna chanter of Mulatuppu.

Ome Nele listened with a scowl on her face. She listened carefully to each side of the records, and when it was over she left without saying a word to us. She went all over town and complained about the records saying angrily, "This is not the way God wants to be worshipped! This is not the way our spiritual ones who came down from Heaven on golden discs have taught us."

. Then she came to church and listened. She sat among the

women who were nursing their babies on the front row. I watched her eyes from where I sat. There was fire in them, and she was definitely not there to worship. The downstairs room was jammed long before time for the service to begin. There were four or five songs by the congregation, accompanied by Margaret on the little pump organ. Then Claudio and I sang a duet. After this Jaime spoke to the youngsters and Claudio preached. Several more revival songs (translated by Peter Miller) were sung and the audience was dismissed with a benediction. The crowd left and with it the Woman Nele, more convinced than ever that Claudio and Margaret were doing more harm than good.

She went back to the townspeople and advised: "Claudio and Margaret are heretics. They should be put off the island, and both their school and church should be stopped at once. God will punish Mulatuppu for tolerating them. They do not teach about God the way he wants us to believe." This was very dangerous for the mission because the Woman Nele had many followers.

Olopiaite had a grandson of fifteen who at the time had an infection on the back of his hand that did not respond to magic or the bark and roots treatment of his grandfather or the Woman Nele. His whole arm was swollen horribly and hurt him constantly. Shooting pains came in the swollen glands in his armpit. His hand was colored the deadly blue and yellow of gangrene. As a last resort Olopiaite, realizing that it was a poni tummati (disease unto death) and that he could not save the boy, sent for Claudio.

We went over to see him and decided that drastic measures were necessary. We filled him full of sulfa and penicillin and soaked his hand in a hot, saturated Epsom salts solution twice daily for several weeks. Each time we left the patient we wound his hand up in a bandage filled with ichthyol.

The Woman Nele saw what was happening, and she knew we were not being paid in any way for our ministrations—that we were doing it "Tios pinsaet" (thinking on God). Our performing of medical miracles in the name of God appealed to her. The pain in the boy's arm disappeared, and the arm returned to normal size. The hand took on its customary color.

As we went to visit the boy for the last time, the Woman Nele of Morti was present talking to Olopiaite and we were apprehensive. She was all packed up and ready to ascend the mountain to her home before dawn the next day. She said "Goodbye" to us both and then turned to Claudio. "Claudio, won't you please come up to Morti and tell my people about God—and bring your records with you!"

Opening the New Sunday School

Milton had answered the conch shell blasts daily for eight years and had received his basic education in Frank Wilbur's Escuela Nele Kantule at Ustuppo. Then he had gone to Guatamala for high school and missionary training.

When Escuela Nele Kantule had been established seventeen years before, the town had split over the education issue, as is usually the case when a school is established in a Cuna town; and the conservatives, who could see nothing but harm in becoming educated, moved to one side of the island called Okop Sukun. They drew a line in the sand between Ustuppo and Okop Sukun and said that educated Indians must never cross that line. My friend, ancient and conservative Chief Yaiaku, with his wrinkled brown face and his shoulder length hair, saw that this edict was obeyed.

Shortly after Yaiaku had been gathered to his fathers, Milton returned to Ustuppo. He went to see the new chief of Okop Sukun. "How about letting me open a Sunday school in Okop Sukun?"

"I think our people are now ready for a Sunday school," said the new chief. "You may come next Sunday morning!"

This opening service was conducted much as at Achutuppu, with gospel songs, a simple sermon about the love of Christ for all mankind, including Indians, and the distribution of colorful, second hand Christmas cards. From where I sat on a rough-hewn log seat, I estimated that three hundred and fifty participants were in the Sunmakket Neka at that opening Sunday school service or else peeping through the wall canes. Thus, another wedge of Christian civilization was inserted into the Cuna tribe.

Mission to Koetup

Claudio, Ignacio, Jaime, and I went from Mulatuppu down to Koetup (Caledonia) by dugout canoe one Sunday afternoon to play the Cuna language records of gospel songs and testimonials that Peter and Atilio had made in the United States. To pass the time on the trip Ignacio the Chanter against Sadness sang the cocoa bean chant and the others translated it for me in a mixture of Spanish and English, while I took the translation down on paper.

Eventually, we sailed into the long, narrow Koetup harbor, and Jaime deftly wrapped the sails about the mast and laid them in the canoe. Ignacio thrust the canoe pole into the soft harbor bottom and tethered it. We rolled up our pants legs and waded ashore in our bare feet. Scarcely had we touched the dry sand when a group of curious women and children gathered about us. Several were quite hostile.

"What are you doing here?" one said angrily. "Who invited you to come here? Nobody! Who wants you here? Nobody! Like as not you have come here to try to start a school!" Several others echoed her sentiments. So we carried our records and portable phonograph back to the dugout.

Jaime had just placed the mast upright within its socket and Ignacio had pulled up the canoe pole, when several naked boys appeared on the shore and asked what we had in the box. We told them that the box spoke and sang in their language; and since no box ever spoke the Cuna Indian dialect before, they wanted to hear it. When Claudio wound up the phonograph and it started singing and preaching in the boat to those on the shore I was reminded of a sermon in Galilee. Some of the women became interested when they heard the box speaking their own tongue and one invited us to come to her house for shelter from the blazing tropical sun.

Several days later a man came up to Mulatuppu from Koetup to ask us to come back the following Sunday and bring the box. He explained that the men of the town had been working on the mainland upon a community project when we came the first time and that the chief had scolded the women who had been so rude to us. So we returned to Koetup. In the town hall I saw many large wooden images of men, animals, and birds that are used in their exorcising and inna ceremonies.

We went to the house of Olomikelikinya, medicine man in Koetup, to play the records. While there I saw an enormous medicine collection of magic skulls, sticks, and stones. I noticed that a lean-to table had been built half the length of the hut upon which reposed many uchu mimmi idols. By noting a representative space and counting the number of idols in it, and then by multiplying, I estimated that he had a total of 300 uchu mimmikana in his collection, and so I thought that maybe I could purchase one as a sample. Gathering together my best Cuna I said, "An uchu mimmi kwensak pakoe." (I would like to buy an uchu mimmi).

"No, I cannot sell you a single one of those uchu mimmikana," replied Olomikelikinya. "If I should let you have one, that little fellow would say to me very sadly, 'Why did you sell me?' and then because of remorse I would have to die!"

In Their Own Tongue

Peter Miller stood at the blackboard and copied the phonetics where all could see. It was the first verse of the first chapter of Romans. The Book of Mark had just been translated, and was being typed up to be sent to the American Bible Society. Of course, I could offer no assistance except in the matter of interpretation, but I wanted to be there anyway. I wanted to get something of the thrill that comes with putting the Bible, with all that it has meant to the world religiously and culturally, into a native tongue.

I looked about me in the small classroom at Escuela Colman: I counted sixteen of us present. There were Lonnie and Marvel, Peter and Clementina, Claudio and Margaret, Atilio and Alicia, Jaime, Leonardo, Napoleon, Fulvia, and Christina. Chief Ikwaniktipippi was there and so was Williams, the peg-legged Cuna sailor, who had lost a limb in Africa.

Those trained in English followed the English text. Those who knew Spanish studied that version. All made suggestions when they saw fit. It was painstaking work because the Cuna language has a limited vocabulary with but fourteen sounds, and though all thoughts may be expressed, it is often by means of long, explicative circumlocutions. Was the Cuna construction correct grammatically, and did it mean exactly to everybody what we wanted it to mean? Or what was the original meaning in the Bible?

I remember that we struck one difficult passage and Lonnie said: "I'm not quite sure of the meaning of that word in the original. I'd better go back to the house and get my Greek dictionary." Lonnie's dictionary of New Testament Greek settled the matter for us. It had never dawned upon me that an American Indian could also be a Greek scholar.

Then there was the frequent problem of literal translation,

difficulties which nobody could foresee. For example, we are told that Judas betrayed Christ with a kiss. The Cuna Indians had never heard of kissing and to use that word would have necessitated a chapter of explanation upon the strange custom of osculation practiced among Near Eastern and European peoples. Obviously, such a chapter could not be included; so in the Cuna translation Judas betrays Jesus by smelling his face, and even this leaves some misgivings in the mind of the Indians as to just exactly what Judas was up to.

And so they worked night after night and I listened. I tried to learn something of the language and the spirit of those who daily labor for the love of God and their fellow man. Sometimes only two or three paragraphs would be all that could be counted as complete for an evening's work, for it must be grammatically correct and it must get across the message accurately.

We all realized that no Indian could pick up the New Testament translation into Cuna phonetics that we were producing and read it without previous education, because the Cunas never had a written language. There must be courses to teach them to read. Margaret and Peter and Claudio worked on this task in the mornings. Margaret had studied four summers and had taught phonetics among the Mazateco Indians of Mexico between summers. Peter was an expert on Cuna and English, and Claudio needed to familiarize himself with Cuna once more, after his six years of study in Oklahoma. In the evenings we had night classes in the church auditorium where Lonnie taught the fourteen Cuna sounds, the Roman letters that we let stand for those sounds, and finally how to learn them. During this six-week course we averaged about fifty persons in regular nightly attendance.

And here was where I could shine. Although I did not always know the meaning of the words, I could usually get the pronunciation. Half a dozen men and women would flock about me before the class was called to order so that I could give them a briefing on what the sheet of paper said that evening.

One day I remarked to Marvel: "You know, those mimeographed lessons that we are giving in the night class are the beginning of a Primer. Why don't we put them together?"

"We have thought of that, but not only have we not had extra money for the project, but we have had nobody to draw the pictures. And a Primer must have pictures!"

"Well, I'm not much of an artist, but I have always been able to make illustrations for my scientific researches. I'll try it."

And so I took over the task of making illustrations for the Primer — first sketched at Marvel's kitchen table on the backs of old mimeographed sheets. The type was set up by hand at Georgia State College for Women, one of the students helping me. Lectures on the Cuna Indians here and there in the States paid for the offset printing. And thus, as a teacher, I could rejoice that I had at least had a hand in producing the first school book in the Cuna language.

The Primer is a grand success and the children quickly learn to read it. At the Department of Education in Panama an official said it was better than the primer used to teach Spanish in the public schools of the Republic. But there is too great a step between the Primer and the language of the Book of Mark, which has since come from the press of the American Bible Society. We decided that an intermediate Reader was needed. Hence for three years Lonnie and I have been collecting Cuna Indian stories from which to choose materials for this Reader. Indeed, the selection for the Reader itself was no small matter because the Indian is rugged and earthy, and many frank details of his stories could hardly be recounted in polite society any more than could the general run of traveling salesman jokes in enlightened countries. I deemed it wise that the contents of the Reader should be stories of the Cuna Tribe, because one of the chief Indian objections to civilization is that it tries to deprive the Indian of his cultural heritage — and we must show the Indian that the writing of civilization can preserve a memory of his cultural past rather than destroy it.

As a result of the efforts of a number of people, we have the beginnings of a phonetic library in the Cuna tongue. The Book of Mark has been published by the American Bible Society, and a new edition of Bible Songs, mostly the effort of Peter Miller, has come from a press in Panama. In addition we have our Primer, and the finished Reader has also been published.

OTELIA REMOVES HER NOSERING

"How glad I am that I am Saikla Nipakinya's oldest grandchild," said seven-year-old Otelia of Mulatuppu, "because Grandpa wants me to go to school!"

Otelia had been contemplating the joys of education that lay before her as she watched Juan and other Indians construct on the Big Ischi Achu Devil's end of the island a cement block structure, the upstairs of which was to be a home for Claudio and his family. Downstairs was to be one big room for Claudio's school, Sunday school, and church. She had watched its progress for several months and now as it neared completion she could hardly wait. All she could talk about or think about or dream about was "Escuela, Escuela, Escuela!"

Otelia had seen pictures of American schools in the books that Claudio had brought with him from Bacone Junior College in Oklahoma and "Claudio had been educated in America!" So if Claudio was to be the director of the school to which she went, then she would really get an *American education,* and Otelia wanted so badly to be an American girl with an American education. She would learn to read, write, count, and find out about many wonderful things, and she imagined she would become a teacher like Claudio's wife — his American wife. And she would learn to play the little portable pump organ, too!

The more Otelia dreamed of her education the more impossible she appeared to herself when she saw her reflection in the river and the quiet sea. "American girls certainly do not have their arms and legs tightly bound with long strings of beads to keep them skinny!" So she left off her arkan mattar wini (arm beads) and her naik mattar wini (leg beads) as frequently as possible.

"American girls do not have appliqued molas like mine. They have simple dresses — I have an idea!" So she went to her mother. "Mother, when Claudio's school opens am I to get an American education?"

"Yes, my dear, we are going to give you an American education."

"But don't you realize, mother, that an American education does not go with an Indian mola? To get an American education I must have an American dress."

"I think your argument is good, my child, but we'll ask Grandfather; he has been in America several times, and, in fact, lived there for a while when he was a boy."

So the saikla was consulted. "Indeed, I believe the child is right!" said Nipakinya, who was crazy about America, in spite of his having been shanghaied as a boy to work on an Alabama farm. He still loved to dress in an old American infantry blouse whenever possible.

So mother and Otelia carried basket after basket of coconuts to the Indian coöperative store and bought American cloth for the new American dress. Then they went to Margaret, the missionary's wife. In an American magazine she found many pictures of dresses and finally they selected one. Margaret made a pattern from a newspaper, helped Otelia's mother cut it out, and showed her how to sew it together. Several days later Otelia marched up and down the Mulatuppu streets proudly exhibiting a real, honest-to-goodness American dress.

This act wrought havoc in the town. Five little girls of other families were also to get an American education; so when they saw Otelia's American dress and heard her argument, they put the pressure on their own families as only children can do. And they did it so successfully that six little girls appeared at Claudio's school on its opening day wearing American dresses.

When she was all dressed and polished for school on the opening day, Otelia sprung her final question. "Mother, did you ever see a girl getting an American education while wearing a big, round, golden nosering in the middle of her face? It certainly does not look right with my new dress!"

"It has never been done on our island before," said Saikla Nipakinya, "but I suppose that everything has to be done a first time."

Word of Otelia's daring to remove her ulasu or tribal nosering swept the town in a matter of minutes, and five other families said a decided "No!" because that was going entirely too far.

ATILIO AT TUPAK

Five boys from the Colman School at Ailigandi stepped out of their canoe at the Island of Tupak and waded ashore. It was becoming dark; so they hastened to the home of a friend. Next morning, bright and early, they went to the house of the chief and knocked at his door, thinking that when he learned that they had come to talk about Christianity he would probably throw them off the island.

"What do you want?" called the chief from inside.

"I have a written message for you," replied Atilio in a bold voice.

"But who sends me a written message?"

"The written message I have brought you is from God! Shall I bring it in?"

"By all means," answered the chief.

"God's message for you is written in this Book," said Atilio, presenting the chief with a new Spanish language Bible, "and I have come to explain that message to you."

This new, bold approach of the vigorous, young Atilio impressed the chief very much. Nobody ever spoke to him of Christianity in that manner before.

"Not only shall I listen to God's message that you have brought me," said the chief, "but I want the rest of the men of our town to hear it, too. Tonight you shall deliver your message to all of us at the council hall."

The powerful sermon that young Atilio preached that night has never been forgotten along the coast of San Blas. Now, years later, occasionally one still hears it mentioned because his audacity (reminding one of Saint Peter) impressed the Indians all up and down the coast. For a number of years the people of Tupak have been asking Lonnie to send somebody to open Christian worship and a Christian school on their island.

PETER, JAMES, AND JOHN

Peter Miller, Indian musician, linguist, and faithful Christian missionary, escorted me to the Mandinga harbor area where a number of Cuna islands lie at the Colon end of the Comarca of San Blas. We found the Governor's launch at the burned Mandinga pier and in it we rode to San Blas Point. Nobody met us at the wharf, but we had only been ashore at San Blas Point about ten minutes when down the hill with thundering, backfiring, and breakneck speed came an old, red, heavy-duty truck without a hood. As we jumped aside to save our lives, it screeched its brakes in a sudden stop. Out jumped a vivacious, medium-sized white man with disheveled gray hair, who pumped our hands and shouted: "Welcome to Hilltop Mission in the name of the Lord Jesus Christ! Praise the Lord!"

After a few words of greeting (I had written ahead that we were coming), we climbed into the red truck which tore up the hill again, snorting and backfiring in a violent fashion, with Peter and me holding tightly to the rigging and the American, John Mason, hugging the steering wheel like a demon. He held the gas lever down to the floor boards all the way. It was a wild ride, but it landed us on top of the hill in no time.

John is one of the most unusual fellows that I have ever met, and it is mighty refreshing to meet an unusual fellow once in a while. He had charge of the Pan American Airways signal station on the hilltop and lived in the large barracks and radio shop building that was still kept in good condition ever since it belonged to the United States Army in World War II. The whole station had been repaired, repainted, and considerably remodeled by the ingenious John Mason, an individual who can do just about everything. And he had stamped it vividly with his extrovert personality and his radically fundamentalist brand of Protestant Christianity.

For example, on the huge gas tank outside the Hilltop Mission, for such he called his quarters, John had painted in enormous letters the words "Jesus Saves!" He was great on carving, and in the corner of the Mission stood an immense Indian canoe paddle that he had made, stained in dark oak with attractive, incised letters painted white on the handle. One side said: "Jesus Saves!" The other: "Jesus Preserves!"

For visiting islands on Sunday afternoons he had two naval officer's uniforms, one trimmed in silver and one in gold. Instead of an anchor on his cap he had a metal cross with a wreath about it.

Working for John Mason was James Davis, an Indian with a fair education who had been lost to drink for years. John had put him on his feet again and through Christian influence had given him the strength and determination to pass up the habit and to preach the gospel on his home island of Naluneka.

About the house John would suddenly burst into a snatch of some gospel hymn with his strong baritone voice, or shout "Praise the Lord!" and "Why has the Lord been so good to me!" His speech was that of a Southern revivalist everywhere interspersed with Biblical quotations followed by chapter and verse. Sometimes he might say: "I think you will find as it says in Leviticus 24:17," and leave you hanging high and dry wondering what in the world it said in Leviticus 24:17.

Peter had something of that same evangelistic training as a boy at the mission school near Greensboro, North Carolina, and he could keep up with John to some extent; but I was completely lost.

I showed John the fifty copies of the Cuna Primer that we had brought along and explained the translation work on the Bible that was going on in Ailigandi, telling him that we must put the Cuna dialect into phonetics and teach the Indians to read the

Primer before we could expect them to tackle the Book of Mark that had just been translated.

We had along copies of the gospel song records that Peter Miller and Atilio Rivera had made in America and we showed them to John Mason. "Let's see how they sound," said John. He sent James to the shop for a piece of apparatus, then to a storeroom for another, then somewhere else for a third. He got out screwdrivers, pliers, soldering set, and what not, and in an hour he had made a phonograph attachment that would play into the loud speaker he had rigged up previously. Viewing the finished apparatus and still holding a screwdriver in his hand, he remarked with a grin: "One doesn't have to be crazy to be a radio bug, but it helps!"

He twisted the buttons. "Now that is beamed for those islands out there seven and a half miles away."

John played the record. Then he twisted the buttons once more and started all over again. "That is catching them at four miles. Now let us see what happens down there at a mile and a half."

The loudspeaker blared out the words and music of "Esu Kristo Anmar Ai" (What a Friend We Have in Jesus).

Three dugouts were crossing from the mainland to the islands laden with plantains and coconuts. They were silhouetted against the bright water and we could see them distinctly. What happened I shall never forget. When the voices from Heaven fell upon the ears of those San Blas Cuna Indians, singing of Christ and his love in their own language, every canoe paddle stopped and remained motionless and every head was bowed until the song had finished.

A well thumbed Bible was brought to the supper table and family worship was carried through, ending with a long and fervent prayer by John. I recall that, among many other things, he prayed God to "control the bugs [sandflies] on the hill so that they will not bite the visitors." And then, practical Christian that he was, and willing to do what he could to help answer his own prayer, he sprayed all around in our sleeping quarters with something that he said was the most powerful insecticide the United States Army had yet adopted.

John had given the boards from a condemned building to James and from them a little church had been constructed on Naluneka, the back end of which was being used for a school which I visited. There they organized Christian services.

I shall ever be grateful to this unusual man not only for his daring and orthodox spirit but also for the practical assistance that he gave to my scientific researches. He lent me his transportation in the form of a Navy J-Boat with James to captain it, and in it we weathered a hurricane that beached several large tabulus or coconut boats. With John's help I visited nearly all the islands not only of the Mandinga area but all the way down to Narkana. And with Peter and James as friends and interpreters the Indians everywhere made me welcome.

This visit to Hilltop Mission, with its implicit faith, its apostolic attitudes, and its scriptural quotations is a cherished memory.

Chapter X

◇ ◇ ◇ ◇ ◇

SCIENTIFIC RESULTS

The Archeology of A Medicine Basket

"AMERICAN come up mountain, we use shotguns!" said Francisco in Cuna dialect quoting the minority report of what had happened at the council meeting in his home town of Morti. Ignacio the Chanter against Sadness, Claudio, and I were ready to climb the jungled Cordillera of San Blas in the morning, and it was lucky that we received this word because fifteen years before five foreigners did try it and only two came back. Morti was also where members of the "Virago" survey party were killed with shotguns. The dissenting Indians stated specifically that they did not want Claudio, with his foreign education.

I told Francisco to inform his people that my only reason for wanting to visit the inhabitants of Morti was to make friends with them and to learn about their way of life, as I had done in the towns along the coast. Of course, just to emphasize my good will, I added that I had a white nylon shirt and a red briar pipe for the chief.

Claudio said that his great-grandparents had lived in Morti. He wanted to visit for sentimental reasons, and he was bringing metaquinin to distribute to the people because so many were dying of malaria in the mountain towns.

The adverse decision of the Morti minority was very disappointing to me because I wanted to do a bit of archeological work at several cemetery sites in the mountains and now I could only inquire about those places. However, I believed that the medicine men who combed the mountains for bark, leaves, and herbs could tell me something if they would. Accordingly, I began question-

ing the inatules wherever I went; and, if they were friendly, I
asked to see their medicine collections.

Because the ancient Caribe-Cunas of the mountains were a
primitive people, they had few articles and tools. And since the
gray coral of the shore and islands was too soft for use and because
flint was apparently not available, they depended almost entirely
upon wood as a material for making things. Indeed, they might
be said to have had and to have still a wooden culture. But in a
moist climate such as is found along the Caribbean Coast of Lower
Panama, wood and even bones decay very rapidly, and hence all
I could expect to find from these old sites would be made of hard
stone such as mountain granite. So I became particularly interested in the magic stone corner of the medicine basket.

The most powerful of all the Cuna medicine stones, so the disease chanters told me, is the akwa nusa, or stone mouse. It is a
waterworn crystalline stone, topaz in color. It possesses a powerful and beneficent spirit, particularly useful, when accompanied
by the appropriate medicine chant, for being sent as far as the
eighth layer under our earth to retrieve the spirit of the sick person who lies in his hammock, racked by disease. This is so because
diseases are caused by one of countless devils snatching and running off home down through the earth with the spirit of the
sick one.

Pablo said he was going to give me a large and highly potent
akwa nusa that his deceased father, Manikwakikinya, had found
in the middle of eight concentric circles of little stones that were
sitting there reverently worshipping it. Pablo's father had been
an important medicine man of Narkana, but even he did not
dare to touch the amber-colored eight-ring akwa nusa until after
he had burned before it his pot of cocoa bean incense and had
sung to it the purifying cocoa bean chant. But alas, when Pablo
went to get it, the akwa nusa had disappeared. He took the full
blame, however, because he said that he had forgotten to put
it in warm water twice a year, to warm it up; and "if it is not
so cared for, you will come to the medicine basket one day and
find it gone."

Oloiklipippilele sold me an akwa kwile, a disc-shaped piece of
granite that he had found up the river near Narkana. He had
seen "something in the water jumping, jumping, jumping." When
he approached it he found it to be an akwa kwile or jumping
stone. This special kind of stone is powerful medicine in the

field of obstetrics because it makes both mother and baby jump violently during parturition and thus assists the process. The next stone I examined was the dark akwa wala or fossilized heart wood of trees that grew in the mountains before the Great Flood which destroyed the earth. It is good for promoting sexual development in boys and for curing anemia in the general population. At Mulatuppu a medicine man brought a napsa machi (son of the earth) to show me. It turned out to be a seven-inch section of a fossilized leaf similar to banana, from the Turbo River in Colombia beyond the Atrato. Fossilized stems with buds on them (also called napsa machi) were said to come from the Carti region and these also had medical importance.

The quest for artifacts had begun to look a bit hopeless when Manipekinappi, a medicine man of Mulatuppu, brought me a polished hand axe of granite. Upon my inquiring what it was, he told me that it was a mala akkan or sky axe. "They come down from the sky on the tip of a bolt of lightning and you find them at certain places in the mountains along the rivers. You may stick them into the ground outside your hut during a storm and they will prevent lightning from striking it." Now I was on the trail at last.

"Just where do you find the mala akkans?" I inquired of Upikinya of Ailigandi.

"Up the Okop Tiwar [Coconut River] at a place in the forest that we call Naka."

"And do you find many of these mala akkans?"

"Aye, we find many where the water washes away the clay surface of the earth."

"What else do you find at Naka?"

"Some very fine granite mortar stones upon which we grind our rice come from there, and curiously enough, the round pestle stone is always found sitting on top of the mortar. I found that one over there at Naka," said Upikinya, indicating a fine granite mortar and pestle standing by the bright cooking fire of his hut.

"And do you find little, broken pieces of red pottery at Naka?"

"Yes, of very poor workmanship and decorated by pressing them with the tip of a stick rather than by painting them."

"What else?"

"Nothing!"

"But did you not find any of these at Naka?" I asked, drawing a well-chipped flint arrowhead from my pocket. I was anxious to know about that because the traditional Cuna arrows are tipped with five sharp barbs of black palm and nobody to whom I had shown the flint knew a name for it or had even guessed its purpose. Upikinya fingered the arrowhead thoughtfully for a moment. "It is a mala akkan pippikwa [little sky axe] or a mala machi [son of the sky] or marko, and it is found at Naka. I had one but I cannot locate it, and Sosipippi the Medicine Man has one."

Peter Miller, my erstwhile interpreter, and I went to see Sosipippi in his thatched hut, but in vain. His mala machi could not be found and the trail came to a disappointing dead end.

Several hours later Sosipippi came to the missionary's house with a fossil shark's tooth, such as the Indians said had been found from time to time at Naka, and which they thought to be the same thing as my arrowhead. It appears that sharks' teeth may have been used as arrow tips at one time.

I asked questions about everything else I could think of and finally learned that once when the river overflowed and washed away much clay from its banks, a woman had found at Naka a number of pieces of hard red coral with branches, having a hole drilled through each piece. She strung them on a thread and wore them as a necklace, but when I hunted up the woman in order to see them, they had been sold.

This experience impressed several facts upon me. First of all, it reminded me that millions of early archeological sites must have disappeared the world over because they represented wooden cultures such as that of the early Cunas, contained soft pottery, or employed natural objects such as sharks' teeth. Again, it showed me how such sites may be completely exploited and the objects carried away by later peoples for the same purposes (mortar and pestle) or for other purposes (sky axe, shark's tooth). And finally, I was amazed to learn that only one of the medicine men with whom I talked recognized Naka as the site of a previous civilization, although such eloquent archeological evidences were speaking from the Cuna medicine baskets.

FINDING THE LOST MUSIC

Few people realize the great rapidity with which the ancient, primitive culture of San Blas is disappearing. Gone are the nose-rings and earrings of men, the body painting, painted loincloth, ceremonial mete jar of the haircutting ceremony, gold working, pottery, weaving, the honor head-band. Even the memory of customs or cultural objects themselves have disappeared.

There are several reasons for this. One is that the articles of ceremony or culture and the knowledge of ceremonies are often the possession of specialists who made these traditional articles and learned the complicated ceremonies under the direction of an individual teacher. Thus, as an apprentice, the kantule chanter makes his own elaborate reed-and-feather hat. Thus, the expert on reed pipes makes his own instruments. They are not owned by others and when a man dies all his possessions are buried with him. If one link only in this personal chain of social inheritance is broken, the cultural object, the ceremony, or the special music disappears forever. There are no public manufacturers of such cultural objects, or public teachers of ceremonies. There is no adequate writing or illustration to preserve their description. Another reason is that many young men of the tribe frequently work a number of years in the Canal Zone, and when they return home to marry they have shed the old tribal customs and bring in foreign folkways from Panama.

Nowhere is this loss of the strangely beautiful native productions more evident than in the realm of music. On some of the islands jazz, played on harmonica and guitar, has replaced almost completely the entrancing and exotic tones of the armadillo skull, the fourteen reeds, the eagle wing-bone, the jaguar skull, the kantule's great kammu reed, and other reeds of lesser size, such as swalla and kokke, each instrument having a special technique and special music. On most of the larger islands somebody has an old phonograph and a collection of pathetically scratchy, honky-tonk records.

The kantule's large kammu reed and nasis rattle are still used at the "coming-out party of the debutante," but most of the kantules do not know how to blow the pelican wing-bone flutes (korki kali), of which they wear a collection of some forty about the neck. Nor do the modern kantules understand how to play the tetenono (armadillo skull), which is the sacred symbol of their office. When the kantule dies his tetenono is saved to show that there was once a kantule in the family.

The best preserved instrument is the kammu purwi, or fourteen reeds, which the civilized world knows as Pan's pipes. They come in two groups of seven each, called male and female pipes, and are played by two men in duet. Even the kammu purwi is

missing from some of the islands. Only a single set is available
at Ailigandi, one of the largest Cuna towns. There are two sets
at Mulatuppu. Many of the traditional kammu purwi pieces are
forgotten. However, I was able to record several beautiful kammu
purwi pieces played by my personal friend, Olotiptikinya, third
chief of Ailigandi, and his associate.

Only one achunono or jaguar skull is said to exist any more.
It is reported to be in the primitive town of Napikanti. It consists of a reed pierced with holes and fixed into the foremen
magnum opening of a jaguar skull that serves as a resonance box.
When the owner of this instrument dies the achunono will be
buried with him and its music will be gone forever.

There was once a reed instrument, the tollo, with four holes
and a voice softened by inserting a feather into its construction.
The tollo came in male and female pairs. It no longer exists.

At Ailigandi I saw a tetenono owned by a kamsuet (kantule's
assistant), but nobody in town knew how to blow it. At the
council hall in Ustuppo, I said I wanted to hear somebody blow
the tetenono. The chief ordered that some tetenonos be brought,
and four were found. Two men said they thought they knew
how to blow them, but they failed. Then there came forward a
man who revealed that his father had been a kantule. He remembered how to hold the instrument but he had little luck in producing tones. At last, perceiving how to hold it, and having
realized from their efforts that it makes only three tones, I took
the tetenono and blew the three tones so clearly that there was
a roar of approving voices in the dimly lighted hall. But alas,
although I could produce the tones, I knew none of the lost music
of the tetenono that once resounded so merrily at every inna
feast.

At Mulatuppu my anxiety about the lost music of the tetenono
was somewhat relieved because there I found that Richard, whose
father had been a kantule, could still produce one piece, which
I promptly took down on a tape recorder. Later Richard sold
me the same tetenono, but warned me that if I played it un-
worthily, that is, without having learned the sacred chant about
its origin and without having studied to be a kantule, upon my
death the armadillos would dig up my grave and desecrate my
bones. That was the warning his father had given him.

Olopiaite, my kantule friend of Mulatuppu, played for me on
his sacred kammu the Introduction to the inna feast. That music

is beautiful and majestic, and I was glad I caught it, but when I suggested that he sing a few measures of the kantule's chant that follows the introduction, he reverently declined on the ethical grounds that it was too sacred to be recorded. Kantule Olopiaite performed several pieces on the korkikala, or pelican wing-bone, music that the other kantules had forgotten. Then he pulled out of his pocket a sulepakkala, or eagle-wing bone, decorated with cross-hatched black scratches and dots and four strands of blue beads. Since I had heard that this instrument no longer existed I was delighted to hear its voice. It is thicker than the korkikala and therefore has firmer tone quality.

Later Richard turned up again with a perfect eagle-bone flute, which, by an accident that could not be duplicated in a million years, was accurately tuned to the key of C when compared with a plastic flute owned by Peter Miller's son. Many eagle-bone flutes are bored before a good one is made having tones that blend. Richard played on this perfect instrument a sacred song of the eagle that is singing to God in the afternoon. It is a chant that strengthens the eagle so that he may catch his food and be full, a song of praise because God has been so good to him. It is a piece that used to be played during the inna feast at four o'clock when the eagle is supposed to sing.

Peter Miller, the chief native musician of San Blas, who teaches piano, trumpet, trombone, clarinet, and voice at Escuela Colman (Ailigandi) and at Escuela Nipakinya (Mulatuppu), helped me locate the old Cuna instruments and interpreted for me. He was astounded to see and hear about primitive types of instruments which he never dreamed could have existed during his some fifty years of life.

But of all the strange and remarkable musical instruments of the past that I was able to see and record from the most primitive San Blas islands, none was more astounding than the tinku ukka, or large tortoise shell. It is best if it is from a female animal because of sex-differences in shell structure. I had always wondered why the Cunas never had the tom-tom like other tribes, but in the tinku ukka I found the answer. At Mulatuppu I located old Oloyopekinya, who said he was the last person interested in this once very popular instrument. It was used in ancient days for loudly beating time at dances of the inna feast.

Oloyopekinya sat down on a low seat and placed his instrument under his arm. The front lip of the nether shell had been daubed with muttu, a black hardening resin from the mountains. The old man stroked the lower lip of the shell, but nothing happened. Oloyopekinya explained that the tinku ukka had to be warmed up. He went to the fire and held the shell above it for several minutes. Then he returned to his seat and stroked the shell once more. I was skeptical. However, as old Oloyopekinya stroked and stroked, a small amount of resin adhering to the palm of his hand produced friction with the muttu on the lip of the shell and the whole carapace began to vibrate. It began to sing. Louder and louder and still louder the tones came! More beautiful and more resonant they grew. They were superior to the voice of any tom-tom.

As I sat and listened in Oloyopekinya's simple cane-and-thatch hut I could imagine the superb function of the tinku ukka tortoise shell as a time caller in those wild, primitive, nightly dances of the Cuna inna feast in centuries gone by.

What Moon-Children Look Like

When I got all my observations together I could describe the moon-children in detail. Measurements of height and weight show that the moon-children are slightly shorter and lighter than are normal Cuna Indians. Head shape of moon-children appears to be brachycephalic in a higher percentage than normal, but this has not been proved. The facial angle tends to be depressed. Hands are often small and soft.

The skin in general lacks all pigment and is horribly blistered by short exposures to sunshine, to which it also responds by producing scattered blotches of pigment as in true albinos. The skin may develop benign or malignant tumorous growths in some cases. The skin becomes much wrinkled by ten years of age, especially on the back of the neck, and this condition increases with age. From the age of about one and a half years, the skin may be covered with severe sores because of infection of wounds, abrasions, and insect bites. The skin is very dry. The lips are enlarged and protruding.

Head hair at birth is usually white, changing to a rich golden in youth, and then to a light brown or even reddish brown in middle life. We have hair samples for study, and some comparisons have been made. It would appear that the diameter of the hair of the moon-child is smaller than that of normal Indians. It blows about more freely in the breeze. Although normal

Cunas are very smooth skinned, the moon-children bear straight, white hair (lanugo) on their bodies which on the forearms and lower limbs may measure from one fourth of an inch to one inch in length by the age of nine years. This amazing hair was found on the appendages of all specimens examined closely.

The eyes tend to be of the oriental type in which the eyelids are invisible when the eye is open, whereas this kind of eye is fairly rare among normal Cunas. Part of this tendency may be due to maintaining tense muscles about the eyes in an attempt to shut out more light. The area about the eyes often appears swollen or enlarged. In general, the eye color is a rich blue, a much deeper blue than seen in recognized albinos of the white race, with some black about the periphery and a yellow or buff band developing around the pupil at the age of six or seven years. One baby girl with reddish hair showed a violet tinge to the eye color, and several had brown eyes. Moon-child eyes are weak and lateral nystagmus was present at all intensities of light under which they were examined—even down to the dim twilight of the Cuna hut (.8 to 1.6 foot candles).

We have been unable to determine basal metabolisms, but the indications are that metabolic rates of moon-children are reduced. Hands are often cold and clammy. Some specific gravities have been taken on urine samples and these are very low. Ultraviolet spectrum analysis of urine samples from boys show some substance, possibly a steroid esterone, to be reduced in quantity, or missing entirely. The moon-children do not appear to have an incidence of lung infection above normal, but they constantly carry colds of the nose, head, and throat. Readings taken with a manual dynomometer show that moon-children are reduced in strength in both males and females. They have a slow gait and slow movements. The physical directors of four schools say that moon-children lack endurance in physical contests. Because this lack of endurance is common knowledge, the town does not call upon them for heavy physical labor in community projects, and the home demands of them only the lightest of duties. Moon-children are slow in developing sexually. Their voices tend to be soft; this is particularly noticeable in adult males. The mentality of moon-children appears to be normal, and no less than fourteen of them have competed in formal school classes. The chiefs of two large Cuna towns, Ailigandi and Ustuppo, as well as other residents, tell us that moon-children tend to be stubborn and hot-tempered. Most of them seldom smile, and when they do it is usually a feeble smile. They definitely lack expression in the face.

Thus, the moon-child represents not merely a pigment variation, but rather a pleiotropic syndrome affecting morphology, physiology, and psychosomatic behavior, just as I had found to be the case with certain pigment variations in fish, doves, rats, mink, and other vertebrates.

Two persons have tried previously to solve the problem of moon-child heredity. John Baer went to San Blas in 1924 but shortly after his arrival he developed a tropical fever (malaria or spotted disease of the mountains) and died. Reginald Harris accompanied Richard O. Marsh to San Blas in 1925 and his efforts were quickly terminated by the outbreak of the Cuna Revolution. Not long after his return to the United States he died of pneumonia.

Harris saw in San Blas people of a series of shades from almost colorless moon-children on up to dark brown Indians, and to him the variations appeared like the manifestation of a single gene plus a number of modifying factors. Yet his data were too meager for drawing definite conclusions, and I had heard Harris discuss his findings just after his return to the States. As a matter of fact, the Indians pointed out to Harris the grades of color which they recognized, just as they pointed them out to me, but he viewed them as a continuous series, rather than as distinct steps. My four summers of effort have yielded data sufficient to prove beyond all doubt that the Indians were correct in their recognizing distinct steps of reduced pigmentation, and sufficient also to provide a genetic analysis for each type. However, my analysis is much more simple and differs considerably from the idea that Harris entertained.

The Indians pointed out to me the four grades of pigmentation: brown, light brown, blue eyed blond, and moon-child. The blue-eyed blond type is found only on certain islands, whereas the other types are present in most Cuna towns. For this reason I decided that blue-eyed blond must be an entity having nothing to do with the moon-child condition. In fact, its resemblance to the European blond type made me suspect European admixture. And credence was lent to my theory because the old Cuna men said two Englishmen and a Frenchman had been shipwrecked long ago on this coast and adopted into their tribe; their children were not killed. If this form were found in families not producing moon-children then its genetic independence was assured. Most of these persons were unfriendly and it was my third year before I was able to get definite evidence, but at last I obtained the pedigree of a family lacking the moon-child variation but segregating the blue-eyed blond in significant numbers. Thus, we must consider the blue-eyed blond as a separate entity not concerned with our moon-child problem, and probably of European origin.

How Many Moon-Children

I have related how difficult it has been to collect accurate data on the moon-children and how necessary it is to visit all the towns in order to be absolutely sure of the facts. For instance, I went to the town of Mansukun and inquired about the adjacent town of Napikanti only a mile distant. "There never have been any moon-children in Napikanti," said the chief and town leaders of Mansukun.

Then Claudio, Jaime, and I visited Napikanti. We were welcomed with food-drinks, according to custom, in the Sunmakket Neka, and half a dozen women and girls were serving. Among them was a moon-child girl of sixteen years, who handed me a cup of chocolate food-drink. "Is this Sipu girl a native of Napikanti?" I asked.

"Yes," said the chief. "She was born and raised here."

I knew that previously several persons had tried to estimate the number of moon-children in San Blas. The most recent estimate was 98. I realized a number of sources of inaccuracy in their work and so I decided to collect name (in cases where they had a name), age, sex, island of birth, and present island of residence. After two years I had records on 152 living moon-children, many of whom I had photographed and nearly all of whom I had seen.

But this does not include *all* the moon-children! Even today it appears highly probable that moon-children are done away with quietly at birth and buried in the sand of the family hut. Nobody but the midwives see the child and they will not give away the secret. Any inquiry will be answered by the simple statement: "The baby died, and one must never speak about the dead!" As a matter of fact, a prominent official of Mulatuppu is said openly to have killed his moon-child baby several years ago.

In 1954 I noticed five albino boys at Achutuppu, but no albino girls of corresponding age. When I pressed the chief about the fact that there should have been some girls, he did not want to talk about the matter. Later I got him to admit that there were also three girls born, "but they died." The chief was afraid that the Panamanian government would start investigating infanticide, which is still fairly common.

The exact size of the Cuna population is unknown. The 1940 census gave 20,822. But this record was subject to great inaccuracies. When census takers came, many people ran and hid. Often families were reported smaller than they actually were because the informant feared that taxes would be levied on the family per capita. The villages of the mountains would not permit census takers to come to them. Many Cuna men were working and living in Panama, and these were not credited to the tribe but were called Panamanians in the census.

I witnessed the difficulties that the 1950 census takers were having when I met them at Ailigandi. Their problems were the same as those of 1940. One factor had changed—many more Cuna men were working in Panama in 1950 than worked there in 1940. Alcibiades and I tried to estimate the number of migrants. We rode through the streets of Panama City and Colon in a rickety chiva and counted Cuna Indian men walking on the streets. In Panama they averaged about ten per city block. As a result of these observations we must say that the 1950 census is not accurate. The census reported 17,234. To these we must add about 1,000 for the mountain villages and almost 2,000 for Panama City and Colon. Thus, the incidence of moon-children in the tribe is about 1.75%, although it will probably not be determined with accuracy for many years to come.

INHERITANCE

The moon-child variation cannot be sex-linked because if so all the sons of moon-child women must be moon-children. Harris found no cases in which moon-children had become parents, but I discovered that the moon-child women Elvira Bolivar, Marianita, Tikinya's granddaughter, Sipu (Narraskantuppippikwa), Mikel's mother, Adolfo's wife, Sipu Clara Lopez, Margarite Perry, Riasuka, and Sipu Carti had given birth to a total of fourteen boys—all pigmented!

If the moon-child variation is due to a single pair of semi-recessive genes, then the offspring of brown-skin parents should show the Mendelian ratio of three brown to one moon-child, and these two types of children ought to be equally distributed among boys and girls. My pedigrees showed 223 children: 74 brown boys, 41 moon-child boys, 63 brown girls, 45 moon-child girls, and 3 normal children of sex unknown. If the moon-child characteristic is simple, recessive, and Mendelian, we should expect at least 70.5 moon-children, whereas 114 were found. A statistical adjustment to account for the Hardy-Weinberg law makes the correspondence between theory and fact much closer: expected, 95; found, 103.

But all the children of moon-children must carry one gene for moon-child and one for brown (unless the consort also carried a moon-child gene). So we examined their children for shade of pigmentation. Moon-children Kenny Brown, Sipur Clara Lopez, Sipu Filomena Farrell, Elvira, Marianita, Margarita, Sipu Gonzales, Bolivar, and Sipu Carti had children as follows: one normally pigmented boy, five light brown boys, and four light brown girls. The pigmented parents of moon-children must also contain one gene for normal pigmentation and one for moon-child. Of these there are four that are classified as normally pigmented males, five light brown males, and eight light females. Thus, we must conclude that when a male is hybrid for the moon-child variation, he may or may not be lighter than normal, but when a female is hybrid for the moon-child variation she is almost invariably light brown.

I obtained the pedigree of one family containing blue-eyed blonds. This family consisted of one brown boy, one blue-eyed blond boy, and three blue-eyed blond girls. One of these blue-eyed blond sisters married a brown Indian and had two light daughters. One of these married a normally pigmented man and had brown children and some that were blond with blue eyes. The other sister married a normally pigmented Indian and had four blue-eyed blond children; one boy and three girls. Thus, as we suspected, the blond gene is inherited independently of the moon-child condition.

TINES ISMIT: THE SCIENTIFIC PUZZLE

Demosthenes Smith was a lovable, little moon-child rascal one year old when I first met him. Nobody in Ailigandi could pronounce the name "Demosthenes" and nobody could do any better with "Smith," so they said Tines Ismit, and everybody knew that Tines Ismit meant "Demosthenes Smith."

The mother of Tines Ismit made him wear clothes during the daytime, and tried to keep him in the house when the bright sunshine would hurt his jittery eyes (nystagmus). But one day when his mother's back was turned, little Demosthenes took off to investigate the world for himself, and he spent about twenty minutes naked in the sunshine before he was captured. I believe that the child might have died as a result of this exposure to sunlight were it not for the fact that I had a good supply of unguentine along with which I treated him lavishly for a week and a half.

However, Tines had a skin that somehow looked slightly different from that of other moon-children and as he grew older it appeared more normal. It was less dry, and instead of blistering every time he got into the sunshine it developed a tiny bit of sallow tan. He did not have long hair (lanugo) on his arms and legs as typical moon-children ordinarily possess. Definitely, Tines was something unique, and for three years I tried to figure him out.

If Tines Ismit's genetic constitution contained one gene for normal pigmentation and one for the moon-child variation, he would have been noticeably lighter than a normal brown Indian, but he would have black hair and black eyes. So that solution was ruled out. If he had two genes for European blond, he would possess a good tendency to tan. He would have green or hazel eyes and they would not be jittery. If he had two genes for moon-child, then he should have exhibited all the moon-child characteristics such as jittery eyes and inability to tan. Having weighed carefully all these possibilities, I could only conclude that Tines Ismit probably inherited from one side of the house a moon-child gene and from the other side a blond gene. My trail stopped when I inquired about the family of the mother of Tines. "Nobody knows about her family because she is from another island," they said. However, the true reason was the stigma of the illegitimacy of her child.

"But what island?"

"Achutuppu."

"Achutuppu!" I repeated excitedly. The trail was getting hot again.

There were some blonds on Achutuppu who traced their ancestry to one of the three shipwrecked European sailors who were adopted into the tribe more than a century ago and whose children were not killed according to custom. Inbreeding had brought the blond characteristic to the surface in recent generations. I had seen some of them but they were very timid and unfriendly, and I had not been able to examine them at all. On Ailigandi I knew Freddy Morris, who was a blond of this sort and I had gone over him carefully. Could it be possible that the mother of Tines Ismit came from a family that carried the blond gene? If so, she would have one gene for normal brown pigment, and one for blond. I wanted to take a canoe and go to Achutuppu at once, since it was socially impossible to ask Tines' mother about her relatives.

"But there is an unrelated man in Ailigandi who was born in Achutuppu," said Alcibiades. "He knows the mother's family, and I am sure he will give you the information."

In fifteen minutes I had the pedigree complete, and sure enough, Tines' grandfather and grandmother on his mother's side were both blonds with blue eyes, and therefore his mother must carry one gene for blond. Her brother is a blond and he has two blond daughters in addition to a moon-child son. Thus, it is highly probable that my interpretation of Tines Ismits' genetic constitution is correct: namely, that he carries one gene for blond and one for moon-child.

Antiquity of the Moon-Child Variation

Several descriptions of the moon-children were made during the seventeenth century when Spanish colonial efforts in Panama were crumbling before the hordes of pirates that murdered, robbed, plundered, burned cities to the ground, and made trade next to impossible. The littoral region of San Blas occupied by the Cuna tribe today was the famous Pirate Coast where buccaneers often hid their vessels among the many uninhabited islands and waited for Spanish merchantmen to bring gold of the Incas up the Pacific side to Panama. From there the gold was carried across the Isthmus by the Las Cruces Trail to the Caribbean port of Porto Bello for shipment to Spain.

In 1687, after looting the Spanish gold mines on the southern side of the Isthmus, a band of more than a hundred buccaneers, mainly English, crossed the Isthmus from south to north through

Caribe-Cuna territory to the Pirate Coast. Six of these men
wrote accounts of their adventures: William Dampier, Basil Ringrose, Lionel Wafer, William Ambrosia Cowley, Bartholomew
Sharp, and John Cox. The narratives of the first three named
authors were published and became well known. Both Ringrose
and Wafer mentioned the albinos (moon-children), and Wafer
gave the most accurate and detailed account of these variants that
has been published to date. It is quite possible that Dampier
knew about the moon-children but did not include their description in his book because for him crossing the Isthmus was merely
an incident within "A New Voyage Round the World," whereas
Ringrose and Wafer dealt with American adventures only.

It may be, as Sir Albert Gray suggests, that Dampier was interested in geography, winds, tides, plants and animals, and in
keeping his journal posted up. Possibly this author omitted reference to the moon-children purposely in deference to his com-
rade, for he writes: "I might have given a further account of
several things relating to this country: the Inland Parts of which
are so little known to Europeans. But I shall leave this province
to Mr. Wafer, who made a longer abode in it than any man that
I know, and is now preparing a particular description of this
country for the press."

It appears that an untrained observer might readily overlook
an occasional moon-child in Spanish or buccaneering days because it was then customary for the Indians to paint their bodies
in such a fashion that even Wafer himself was disguised and taken
by his fellow-pirates for an Indian. Dampier says: "Mr. Wafer
wore a clout about him and was painted like an Indian: and he
was some time aboard before I knew him." Wafer recalls his
colorful decoration by saying that he was so "ador'd" by the Indians that they tattooed him "in yellow, red, and blue, very bright
and lovely."

Again, in crossing the Isthmus at a rate of five miles per day,
with its jungles, mountains, and tropical storms, the buccaneer
band to which Dampier, Wafer, and Ringrose belonged camped
in the forest, and probably only a few of their leaders got into
Indian villages at all. They were most concerned with procuring
food, supplies, and guides, and the suspicious Indians were not
anxious for visitors; so that it seems probable that their dealings
were mostly made with adult Indian males who came to their
camps. Ringrose in 1681 observed "several women fairer than
the fairest European with hairs like the finest flax."

The question has been raised as to why Spanish explorers such as Balboa, Espinosa, and Pedrarias did not report moon-children if they existed in the early contact period. The historian, Raynal, 1772, does represent Balboa as finding moon-children at Darien, but whether or not this is based on references or on conjecture is not clear.

Having found at Darien, where riches abounded more than elsewhere, a small number of Spaniards (who were attracted alone and established themselves), he put himself at their head with the project of forming a solid colony. The country offered to him at once little white men of which one finds the species of Africa and among several islands of Asia. They are covered with a down of striking whiteness. They do not have any hair at all. They have a red complexion. They do not see well except at night. They are feeble, and their instinct appears more undeveloped than that of other men. These savages occur in small numbers; but on the coast is found another species, strong enough and hardy enough to dare to defend their liberty. Balboa succeeded in dispersing, in overcoming, or in capturing them, and he established his nation on their territory.

One has merely to read the account of Peter Martyr d'Anghera to realize that after Balboa the Spanish colonists of Darien waged incessant war for the extermination of those Caribs that they could not enslave, treating them with the greatest of cruelty, slashing them to pieces, burning their towns, seizing their food supplies, and occasionally carrying away their girls. The slaves, both men and women, according to Spanish records, were worked to death in the gold mines on the southern side of the isthmus.

It would appear, then, that seldom did the Spaniard enter a Carib village under peaceful conditions or with the inhabitants present, for those had usually fled for safety into the jungled mountains. And because the moon-children were too weak for battle, they would have fled with the other villagers.

In addition, it is possible that few moon-children existed in the region immediately surrounding the Darien colony of Santa Maria de la Antigua, because few are said to exist there today. Nordenskiöld says *no* albinos are found east of the Gulf of Uraba, that is, in the region of Rio Caimanes. However, Wassen quotes Ruben Perez as having seen one albino woman in Darien in 1935. In addition, Louis Lyons, Cuna Indian captain of a coconut boat and of reliable reputation, told me that he saw two albino boys and two albino girls at Arkia in 1937. Again, there is further evidence of the moon-child gene in Arkia because Iwanipikinya was born in that town and had a moon-child daughter. However, the gene may have invaded these towns because of the migrations of 1909 and thereafter.

By 1681 moon-children were generally distributed in the mountains to the northwest of Darien, judging from Wafer's account, and so numerous were they that he estimated them as occurring with a frequency of one in two or three hundred. This high incidence could not have been built up in a short time. Again, infanticide of moon-children was undoubtedly practiced even much more extensively in former times than it is today. That is admitted openly by many of the Indians, in line with the statement of Ruben Perez to Wassen a few years ago, "The old people say that they were formerly always killed." Alcibiades Iglesias recalls that infanticide was common practice at Narkana during his youth. We have already stated that a newly appointed official of Mulatuppu killed his newborn albino baby about 1942.

Cossigny (1774) refers to stories coming from America to the effect that near Mexico there is a tribe of white Indians. These stories may have originated with the Spanish Conquistadores because Cortez saw captive albinos in Mexico City. However, in Seville, Spain, there is still a wealth of accounts of Spanish explorers that have never been combed for reference. These may someday yield descriptions of Cuna moon-children from the sixteenth century.

It is possible that moon-children were seen by Columbus in 1502 near Trinidad. Peter Martyr d'Anghera writes of the Indians in a canoe that they encountered: "These natives are on the contrary white, and have long, straight, blond hair . . . the natives of both sexes have bodies as white as ours, save those perhaps who pass their time in the sun."

Salcedo, 1649, recounting the experiences of Adrien de Santo Tomas a few years earlier, says: "In this province there are many people as white and blond as Flemings, and these are attributed to be descendants of the first chief who came down from the sky, and they never beget others like themselves, but brown ones."

The Caribe-Cunas today declare that one of their eight cultural heroes who floated down from heaven on golden discs (olopatte), Nele Sipu, the savant-seer, was a moon-child. It was he who declared that "all men are brothers." This is undoubtedly the same story referred to by Salcedo three hundred years ago.

Another story is found in the strange "declaration of Independence and Human Rights of the Tule People of San Blas and of the Darien." Nordenskiöld thinks this was written by the fantastic explorer, R. O. Marsh, in collaboration with Cuna Indians, and this was certainly the case. In this document there is an account of the mythical hero, Aobo, who lived at the beginning of time and who was white. After the Great Flood there came down through the clouds upon the sacred mountain Tarcarcuna, a white man and a white woman, a light brown man and a light brown woman, and a dark brown man and a dark brown woman, and from these the Cuna Indians now living have descended. It will be noted that this statement mentions the three principal shades of pigmentation commonly recognized by the Cunas in their tribe.

The appearance of the moon-child variation in nearly all island villages of the Cunas today suggests that the mutant gene was widely distributed in the germ plasm of the tribe before the dispersal of these groups—because until very recently there has been little intermarriage between villages, and hence each village tends to inbreed.

As a matter of fact, the mutant gene may well have been present during some very early migratory period because some of the Cunas feel that they are related to the Mayas in Guatemala, the Aztecs in Mexico, and the Navajos in the United States; and, curiously enough, Mayas, Aztecs, and Navajos have moon-children. However, I feel certain that ethnologists will object to the tenuousness of this suggestion. Frescos on the temple walls at Chichen Itza bear colorful figures of what are undoubtedly moon-children. Near Steamboat, Arizona, I examined two Navajo albinos (a male and a female) so identical with Cuna moon-children that I could have taken out of my files photos of two particular Cuna moon-children and could have readily passed them as photos of the two Navajo albinos.